**SAINSBURY'S**
REGIONAL WINE GUIDES

# ITALIAN WINES

D1326924

MAUREEN ASHLEY

SERIES EDITOR
OZ CLARKE

Published in the UK exclusively for
J Sainsbury plc, Stamford House, Stamford Street,
London SE1 9LL by Webster's Wine Price Guide Ltd,
Axe and Bottle Court, 70 Newcomen Street, London SE1 1YT

First published 1990

ISBN 1 870604 04 0

Typeset by Dorchester Typesetting Ltd, Dorchester, England
Colour separations by Scantrans (PTE) Ltd, Singapore
Printed and bound by Tien Wah Press (PTE) Ltd, Singapore

Conceived, edited and designed by Websters International Publishers

# CONTENTS

# INTRODUCTION
# OZ CLARKE

I was rather frightened of Italy at first. I mean, Latin – that's Italian, isn't it? And then my brother – he always used to be ill whenever we went out for an Italian meal. And girls ... Yes, perhaps it was that. The despair I felt at 15 or thereabouts, all pink-cheeked and shy, at how raven-haired, olive-skinned Lotharios from the distant Mediterranean were always the preferred fantasy of any of the girls I knew. So I stuck to France. Good old, safe old France. Family holidays, school outings, university vacations, too, always focused on the rush to the South from Calais.

Until I eloped. Well, not quite eloped. But my girlfriend's parents did not approve of me and so we plotted to escape for a holiday. We wanted to steal away to some place full of uncertain promise of mischief and romance. Italy. Of course, Italy. As the train pulled out, I was embarking on my first adult adventure, and Italy was waiting, far south and across the snowy Alps, to enthrall me.

It was on that trip that I first experienced the bustling fury of Italian street life, that I first realized that in Italy eating is an exuberant social activity and that cheap simple Italian wine, drunk carefree and lighthearted, can be, on the right day, in the right place, with the right friends – the most perfect wine on earth.

I was sitting in a bar on the less fashionable side of the Grand Canal in Venice. I ordered some red wine. A jug arrived, the liquid deep plum-skin purple, still spitting with the unrestrained bubbles of its youth. Raboso, the waiter called it. Heavenly. A crude splash of raw unsubtle fruit, a sourness which only served to heighten my appetite and darts of effervescence trailing down my throat as I swallowed. I'd never had wine like this in France or Spain.

And a little village south of Florence, where I stopped one warm late morning and asked for bread, and meat, and wine. I'd have to wait, the man said, and he ambled off to a shed behind his shop. He moved his bicycle out of the way, picked out a litre bottle from the pile, and squirted it full of frothing pink-red wine. A turn or two later in the country road, in a field of vines sweeping up towards the mountain top, I drank a wine so bitter-sweet, so rasping yet so ripe, brimming with the flesh of orchard fruit, yet slapped about with pips and skin and stalks, that I can recall every nuance of its flavour. Chianti. A flavour full of such seeming contradictions that it cannot work but it does.

Contradictions are at the heart of Italian wine, in particular Italian red wine. Whereas France has created models of wine styles which are carefully honed by long experience, and by long exposure to a sophisticated export market, Italy is different. Its myriad grape varieties are different, barely planted outside its own boundaries. Its wine styles have developed over the centuries for the satisfaction only of the local wine-drinking population. Consequently, Italy has a wine culture completely its own, and along with that of France, it is the most important in the world.

But it is a wild and confused brilliance. The passionate belief which results in a great Barolo, a great Chianti or a great Amarone is too often matched by a sullen torpidity determined to preserve the status quo. The quality regulations first introduced in 1963 to counter the state of chaos in Italian wine are, in some areas, reassuringly successful in raising standards, while in others they are little more than a joke.

Which is why we need a guide. Which is why a few years ago, I needed a guide. As I moved from the joys of simple Italian wine drunk on the spot in Italy to the horror of cheap Italian wine in Britain, and then on to the supposed peaks of achievement in such styles as Barolo, Barbaresco, Chianti, Brunello and others, I found myself faced with a mixture of the sublimely delicious and the ridiculously awful. But every time I felt like giving up, I felt a tug at my elbow, and there was Maureen Ashley saying – come back to the tasting table, let's try again, let's get rid of those Francophile prejudices and try to understand the heart and guts of what Italian wine is, good, bad and indifferent.

In the last decade, there has been an explosion of originality and innovation in Italian wine. And through this mayhem, Maureen picks her way, offering guidance which I have found completely invaluable in making sense of Italian wines, and I am sure that you will too.

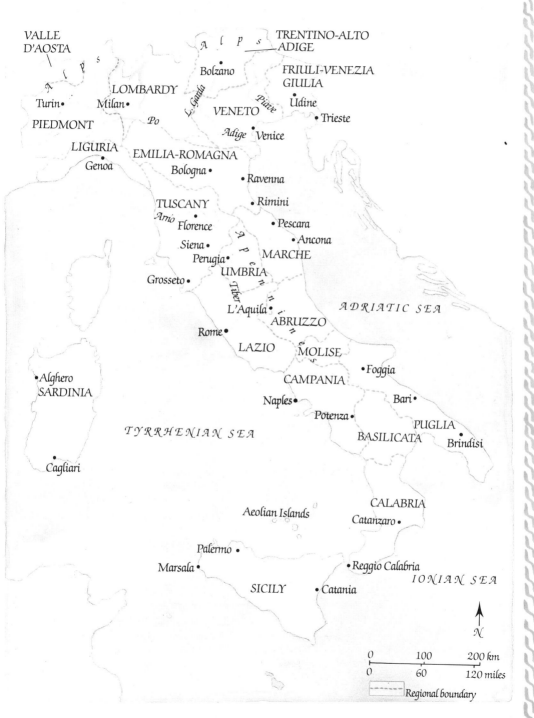

VALLE
D'AOSTA

*A l p s*

TRENTINO-ALTO
ADIGE

Bolzano •

FRIULI-VENEZIA
GIULIA

*A l p s*

LOMBARDY

*L. Garda*

*Piave*

Udine •

Turin •        Milan •

VENETO

• Trieste

PIEDMONT

*Po*

*Adige*    Venice •

LIGURIA     EMILIA-ROMAGNA

Genoa •     Bologna •

• Ravenna

TUSCANY

• Rimini

*Arno*

Florence •

• Pescara

Siena •

• Ancona

Perugia •

MARCHE

Grosseto •

UMBRIA

ADRIATIC SEA

*Tiber*

L'Aquila •

• Rome

ABRUZZO

LAZIO

MOLISE

• Foggia

CAMPANIA

• Alghero
SARDINIA

Naples •

Bari •

Potenza •

PUGLIA

TYRRHENIAN SEA

BASILICATA

Brindisi

• Cagliari

CALABRIA

Aeolian Islands

Catanzaro •

Palermo •

Marsala •

• Reggio Calabria

IONIAN SEA

SICILY

• Catania

N

| 0 | 100 | 200 km |
|---|-----|--------|
| 0 | 60 | 120 miles |

- - - - Regional boundary

# THE WINE REGIONS OF ITALY

It is almost impossible to define 'Italian wine', because the country stretches from Austria in the north almost to Africa in the south, and houses a huge number of soil types, climates, altitudes and, most varied and important of all, grape varieties; there are literally hundreds, many of them strictly localized. And even the more widespread grape varieties have developed different characteristics in different parts of the country. So there is an almost infinite number of flavours. Even more exciting, many of these grapes produce such characterful wines that they just beg to be tasted. And, unlike the most important French varieties, hardly any are planted outside Italy, so if you want a swig of Dolcetto or Ribolla, say, it has to be Italian. As the vine is grown in all Italy's 95 provinces there are no clear boundaries between one wine region and another; changes in style are gradual. The provinces lie in 20 political regions whose boundaries bear little, if any, relation to wine types. So although they are a convenient method of sub-dividing Italian wine and we may talk about Tuscan reds or Friuli whites, categorizing wine styles needs a more broad-brush approach.

In broad terms, therefore, the north-east relies for quantity on its reds and quality comes from the whites, mainly from single-varietal aromatic grapes, often of French or German origin. The north-west produces firmly-structured red wines. Long ageing and serious high quality come from the Nebbiolo grape, younger, zippier wines from Dolcetto, Barbera and others. The central Po valley is Lambrusco country. The central-west's grape is red Sangiovese, its major wine Chianti and innovation its byword. There is more Sangiovese across to the east too, which gives way to Montepulciano as you head south. Whites are as important, from the Trebbiano, Albana and Verdicchio varieties. Rome is Frascati, Frascati is Rome, and the whole south is in the process of upheaval, changing from heavy whites and stewy reds to something as yet ill-defined, but surely much better.

Italy has wines that are dry as a bone or lusciously sweet; wines that are light and dainty or great strapping monsters; wines that are the essence of subtlety or outlandishly brash. Most of them are streets better than they were even five years ago and the difference between now and 20 years ago is nothing short of revolutionary. The turnabout has been prompted by a number of developments. First came the ready availability of stainless steel and new technology which together made fermentation temperatures easily controllable. Imagine the delight as fresh, crisp charmers replaced rather dull, flat, deeply coloured white wines. So heady were the new tastes that there was a tendency to overdo it, fermenting at such low temperatures that all that was left was freshness and crispness. After a while producers began to learn which temperatures best suited their grapes to get freshness *and* personality. Winemaking schools flourished too, teaching the improved techniques. Soon many winemakers were making wines as good as they could possibly get from the grapes they had.

Then Italians went back to their vineyards. In the 1950s and 1960s an unremitting drive for quantity made them go for high-yielding grape varieties and push them to their limit. The higher the yield, though, the more dilute a wine's flavour. 'Back to the vineyards' didn't often mean replacing the high-yielders, but it did mean reducing their yields, often drastically; investigating methods of pruning and training them to optimize quality; and, when they needed replanting, using the best clones available. Vineyard experiments, though, take several years to give results and there are endless research programmes still underway.

At the same time some started to reserve grapes from particular vineyards that gave wines of special quality or character to make single-vineyard or *cru* wines, some of which have been quite brilliant. Once the mood of experimentation took hold it knew no bounds. Producers started to look at the admirable wine scene in France and the innovative, professional scene in California. They planted the universally diffused, and universally loved, Cabernet Sauvignon (red) and Chardonnay (white) grape varieties from France, everywhere. But innovation is one thing, a headlong dive into fashion another. Once Cabernet Sauvignon was all the rage, everybody, it seemed, was. planting it. Then vines all over the country were ripped out for Chardonnay. *Novello* wines are being made whether local grapes suit the style or not. And as for small, new French oak *barriques*, there is scarcely a cellar to be found without at least a couple. There are innumerable 'experimental' wines for sale – always at high prices – that

have come from first attempts with new grapes, or wine-making or ageing methods. Just because a taste is remarkable and unusual it doesn't necessarily mean that it is *good*. But that lesson remains to be learned. A further problem is the number of producers, especially in the south, who still haven't learned the basic lesson about keeping yields right *down*.

So not everything in the garden is rosy. And when we discover wine that isn't up to scratch we should say so – loud and clear. For Italy has such tremendous potential for greatness in her wines, it is criminal not to exploit that potential to its full.

▼ You can only make a good wine from good grapes. Good vineyard husbandry involves patient, labour-intensive work as here at Casorzo in Piedmont where young Barbera vine shoots are being tied to wires.

# MAKING WHITE WINES

**M**aking a white wine isn't difficult. All you need is some grapes. You press the juice from the skins and leave it. Without further prompting it starts to ferment. It fizzes, froths and gets pretty heated about the whole business. Then the bubbling slows to a trickle and eventually stops. You leave your wine for a bit, then bottle it. Making *good* white wine is a different matter. Grape juice, or must as it is usually known, is a tricky substance. It can easily fall prey to harmful bacteria which will turn it acetic (vinegary), and it may be affected by undesirable yeasts that create 'off-flavours' as well as the beneficial yeasts that turn must into wine which are present in the bloom on the grape's skin. All this happens even more readily with white musts than with red as they lack the protective substances from the skins (red wines are made from the skins as well). Finished white wine, too, can be a delicate beast, needing but a few gulps of air to oxidize, deepening in colour and going flat, dull and fruitless. And many native Italian white grape varieties give wines that are particularly prone to oxidation.

So, just how do you make *good* white wine? First you ensure you have the best quality grapes, you harvest them at the best moment (any time from August to October depending on the variety and the weather), you collect them in small containers so the grapes underneath don't get crushed and start fermenting, and you get them to the cellars pronto, without any messing. Then you press your grapes very gently to extract just the best juice. Your next task is to get rid of all the odd bits and bobs of solids still in the must, usually by leaving it for a few hours so the gunge falls to the bottom, but you have to chill it pretty well first to stop the fermentation starting before you are ready. Or, if you don't mind the loss of the odd bit of flavour you can centrifuge or filter the must.

You next bung the must in a container big enough so it's no more than two-thirds full and doesn't overflow when bubbling at full pelt and fermentaton begins. There are so many natural yeasts in the must, swept off the grape skins

during pressing, there is rarely a need to add more – unless you have eliminated most of them by filtering, centrifuging, or over-chilling, or you prefer using a specific yeast culture.

The most vital stage of the whole procedure is controlling the temperature of the fermentation. The chemistry of the transformation of grape juice into wine is complicated, and creates all sorts of by-products, depending on temperature, which make the flavour. If it is too high you lose all the nice fruity tastes, and a lot else besides, and you get fat, flabby, baked-tasting wine, even more prone to getting oxidized or vinegary than usual. If the temperature is too cool, you get a perfectly crisp, clean wine which may be as refreshingly pleasant as you could wish, yet totally characterless. The skill is in understanding the best range of temperatures for the grape varieties you are handling, and in adapting them to the vagaries of each vintage without losing the style you want to achieve – not easy! Stainless steel is one of the best substances for fermentation because it is inert, easy to keep clean and there are simple ways to control the wine's temperature inside.

After the fermentation there may be a second transformation, spontaneous or induced, of the appley malic acid naturally in wine to the softer lactic acid, called malolactic fermentation. But as fruity acidity makes wine lively, the malolactic is usually prevented unless there is likely to be too much acidity.

All this takes a matter of mere weeks. White wine may be on sale by the Christmas of the year of harvest. It will have been racked off the lees of dead yeast cells and other solid matter that always forms. It will also probably have been fined to get rid of any matter too minute to see but which may cause a haze later, kept quite cold for a short time to precipitate out temperature-sensitive acids and filtered to make sure the wine is completely stable and clear.

The Italians like their whites indecently young. But producers know that, if they can resist the pleas for the new vintage and can keep it in vat, cool and undisturbed, for several months more, it will improve considerably. A small, but increasing amount of white wine is matured in *barriques*, small (225-litre) barrels of new French oak. This gives a sensuous oaky overlay to wines from some grapes (such as Chardonnay) and blasts others to smithereens, leaving nothing but an oaky taste. Only experience shows which varieties can take *barrique*-ageing and for how long.

With the best will in the world, the only way (so far) to be sure a white wine won't oxidize in bottle is to add a little sulphur dioxide. But all over Italy producers are finding ways of adding less and less and the day is fast approaching when they may be able to eliminate it entirely.

SWEET/PASSITO There are various ways of making wine sweet. You can stop the fermentation before it has finished, while there is still some sweetness left in the must, or you can add grape must or concentrated grape must (not sugar) to the finished wine. But the most common method in Italy, *passito*, is both one of the most natural and most traditional methods of making wine sweet. After picking, the grapes are laid on mats or in shallow trays, or the bunches hung from rafters. They begin to dry out, losing water. All the other constituents, especially the sugars, are retained and concentrated. By the time the grapes are crushed they are so sweet that even after fermentation to a fair alcoholic degree some sweetness is left. The drying can vary from two weeks outdoors in the burning sun in Pantelleria to four or five months indoors in Trentino. Vin (or Vino) Santo is a particular type of *passito* wine, aged for years in tiny barrels, typical of Tuscany, Umbria and Trentino.

SPARKLING Have you noticed how sparkling wine has tiny bubbles that keep on appearing, while fizzy drinks have huge bubbles that disappear quite fast? The way to make wine sparkling is not to pump carbon dioxide gas into it, as if it were a fizzy drink. The most classic way (called *metodo classico*) is to put finished wine into bottles, with a carefully calculated amount of sugar and yeast, and cork them. The yeast ferments and the carbon dioxide bubbles are trapped in the bottle. You then wait a while for the bubbles to get well dissolved and a yeasty, sparkling wine taste to develop. Simple really. But then you have to get the dead yeast cells out again, which is not so simple. You have somehow to coax the cells down on to the neck of the bottle and, faster than light, whip out the

▲ It takes skill and patience over several weeks to shift the yeast sediment steadily down into the neck of a bottle. This method, seen here at Fontanafredda in Piedmont, is used to make the most classic type of sparkling wine.

cork and the sludgy stuff, top up the volume lost and recork the wine – without losing the bubbles. It is easier if the neck of the bottle is chilled so the sludge becomes a frozen pellet but *metodo classico* is still slow, labour-intensive and therefore costly.

An easier method, preferable too for wines like Prosecco which need to have the same taste whether sparkling or still, is to add the yeast and sugar to wine in an *autoclave* (pressure-resistant tank) and when the pressure is sufficient and the wine is ready, filter it, under pressure, into bottle.

Asti Spumante has a special method. There aren't two fermentations as for normal sparkling wine. When the first fermentation is part-way through, the wine (without anything added) is put in an *autoclave*. The fermentation continues but the bubbles created are trapped as its fizz. When the pressure is right the wine is bottled but there is still some natural sweetness left, ensuring Asti is light, sweet and grapy.

FORTIFIED To make a *liquoroso* (fortified) wine, such as Marsala, all you have to do is strengthen, or fortify, it by adding spirit. This must be of grape origin and, for Marsala and most Italian fortified wines, is added to the finished wine.

# MAKING RED AND ROSÉ WINES

White wines come from white grapes, red wines from black grapes, right? Wrong. Red wines have to come from black grapes but white wines can come from either colour grape, because if you split open a grape and look at it you will see that the pulp (which makes white wines) is nearly always greenish white. What makes a red wine red is keeping the grape juice (or must) in contact with the dark grape skins.

Just as with white wines, much of the potential quality of red wines is determined by the time the grapes reach the cellar door. It is probably even more important for reds that vineyard husbandry should be first rate, that yields are kept well in check, and that the harvest is at the right time (usually from September to November). After all, every bit of the grape contributes to the wine. The bunches should be put in small containers and rushed to the cellar without delay to prevent fermentation starting too soon.

Once at the cellar the grapes will usually be

de-stalked. This is not essential, as stalks can be of use to add tannin to a wine. But as tannin – vital to help wines age, but mouth-puckeringly drying if in excess – is one thing most Italian reds certainly do not lack, the stalks will be whizzed away. Then the grapes are crushed mechanically. Nothing else has to be added or taken away and fermentation soon starts.

More or less quickly, depending on the grape variety, the depth of colour of the skins and the temperature, the must will pick up the colour from the skins, and tannins and other substances too, necessary for the structure, ageing potential and taste of the wine. So it is important to keep the liquid in contact with the skins even though they float to the top of the vat where they lodge and form a concentrated cap. There are various methods of breaking this up, the most common of which is *rimontaggio*: pumping the juice over the skins once or twice a day. Other methods include 'punching down' the cap with sticks, or fixing a horizontal grid inside the vat below the wine level which prevents the skins rising above it. The embryonic wine may stay with its skins for only two or three days (as in many north-eastern or southern reds) or it may stay for four weeks (traditional Barolo) but five to 10 days is a reasonable average. It is then racked off the skins and, if it hasn't already finished, the fermentation continues. The skins may be

▼ The traditional, large *botti* for ageing Barolo make a different style of wine from the fashionable, small *barriques* of new French oak.

pressed, more or less fiercely, to extract the last of the colour and tannin, and some or all of this harsher, deeper press wine may be added back into the main mass of racked wine, depending on what style the winemaker wants to achieve.

Just as for whites, controlling fermentation temperatures is important, but there is a little more leeway in the range of 'best' temperatures to aim for. They will also be several degrees warmer than for whites because you need enough warmth to extract the right elements from the skins – and enough of them. Too cool, and the wine will be a gaunt, hollow beast. Let the fermentation really rip, though, and a nasty, baked, acetic (vinegary) monster will result.

Apart from *novello*, made from early picked grapes and deliberately intended to be young and fruity, ready to drink in November, most red wine has to age, even if it is only for a few months, prior to bottling. Some wines will be kept for two years or more and some may be kept in bottle for a while too, before we can get our hands on them. The containers used for ageing a wine can make quite a difference to its taste and the winemaker has to decide what will be best for what he wants to achieve. He may choose inert containers such as stainless steel or vitreous-lined cement. He may prefer almost-inert wooden containers such as large, old *botti* or *fusti* (barrels), whose inner walls have become encrusted with a crystalline deposit from the young wine they have stored. Or he may scrape the inner walls of the *botti* or *fusti*, exposing a fresh layer of wood surface to give a little oak character to the wine. The wine might also be aged for up to a year or more in pricy *barriques*, small, 225-litre, new or almost-new barrels of French oak. These cede masses of oakiness. *Barriques* became all the rage but results were mixed – some great, some disastrous, yet no-one seemed deterred. There is scarcely a producer who hasn't made at least one 'experimental' wine aged in *barriques* and scarcely a grape variety that hasn't been tried in them. A few grapes (Cabernet Sauvignon, Barbera, Sangiovese, for example) seem really well adapted for the treatment, some are disastrous. Like all crazes, this one seems to have passed its peak and with luck, the future should see this admirably useful container settling only where it does most good.

It is worth remembering that the winemaker will not always have an absolutely free choice as to how long and in which type of container he ages his wine. Numerous DOCs specify minimum ageing requirements for wines and sometimes specify a minimum period in wood too. It is just not sufficient to bung the wine in one container or another and forget about it. It will need racking from time to time to leave all solid matter behind, yielding a clear wine. Many wines will also have to be fined, to get rid of any sediment that remains in suspension and some will be filtered for absolute security. But filtering can strip a wine of some of its taste, so the top wines normally escape this final pre-bottling hurdle.

Once in bottle the wine continues to develop and change. Fine wines, destined for long ageing, will with time change colour, lose their tannin and develop a sediment.

ROSÉ Pink wines get their colour from just a brief flirtation between the grape juice and the black grape skins. They may spend a few hours together but in many cases merely crushing the grapes and letting the juice run out causes it to pick up enough colour. While the juice and skins are together they are handled as red wine, as soon as they are separated the wine is handled as white. Colour may vary from palest pink to light red. It is purely a matter of tradition in each area, or what the winemaker chooses. The length of time needed to extract the colour depends on the grape varieties used and the fermentation temperature.

PASSITO Sweet red wines are less common than white but are made by the same *passito* process, with grapes being left to dry out until they produce a rich, sticky, concentrated juice which does not ferment to dryness. There are also non-sweet red *passito* wines (Recioto della Valpolicella Amarone is the most common), with grapes dried in the same way but the fermentation continuing until there is no sweetness left.

FORTIFIED Fortified or *liquoroso* red wines are made simply by adding grape spirit in the same way as for white wines. Red fortified wines are not seen all that often in Italy but come in various styles, dry or sweet, *passito* or not.

# CLASSIFICATIONS

When you try to impose on a country a classification system devised for somewhere else it is bound not to work too well. When the country is Italy, whose inhabitants pay scant regard to rules and regulations, chaos is likely to result. So it is a compliment to Italy's wine classification system to say that it is only *nearly* chaotic. Italy had no choice but to develop some sort of system. As one of the original six members of the EC, it had to follow EC laws. And the EC had split wines into 'quality wine' and 'table wine' and had come up with a complicated series of rules for each type, following the systems devised by the French for their wines.

What Italy conceived for 'quality wine' was a system called DOC – *Denominazione di Origine Controllata* (controlled designation of origin). It did all the right things: defined the area of production for each wine, stipulated which grapes could be used and their maximum yield, laid down the minimum alcohol content and the minimum ageing required, and so on. DOCs had to be requested by the local producers. The criteria for any particular DOC had to be based on 'local tradition and practice'. Note those words. If local practices were shoddy and traditional wines pretty dismal (as many were in 1963 when the DOC law appeared) that is what got enshrined. After all, the EC definition of 'quality wine' does not say this 'quality' has to be high. The inclusion of the term also eliminated, at a stroke, the chance for exciting, innovative wines to become DOC.

Requests for DOC started to flood in and dozens were awarded. The number is now well past 200, and new ones are still appearing regularly. Some DOCs are well-known names, like Soave, others are unbelievably obscure. Some cover tiny areas or only two or three producers, others are huge, covering vast tracts of land. The quality may be anything from excellent to dire. DOC guarantees only that the wine is of a certain type and comes from a certain area; no more. Yet DOC, much as observers of the Italian scene and many producers berate it, is still apparently in demand.

On the quality front there remained one ray of hope: a higher category called DOCG, the G indicating *e Garantita* or guaranteed. DOCG wine was meant to be the top category. Only the finest wines would be elevated to this super-bracket and would have more stringent controls placed upon them including going before a tasting panel before being awarded DOCG. Despite the snag that entire DOC areas had to become DOCG, not just the best wines within them, all went well at first. Then Albana di Romagna, an uninteresting (often worse) white wine was elevated, mainly as a result of political wheeling and dealing, without even tightening its slack production criteria. Faith in DOCG was shaken and producers of other uninspiring wines started to reckon, quite logically, that they could get DOCG too. Sadly DOCG looks set to follow DOC as no more than an indicator of any reasonably decent wine.

While all this was going on, the Italian wine scene was being revolutionized almost beyond belief. There were new grapes, new vinification and ageing techniques, and many new wines, often of brilliant quality. The DOC straitjacket couldn't accommodate them, so all that was left was *Vino da Tavola* or VdT – the EC 'table wine' category. *Vino da Tavola*, theoretically at least, was meant to represent the simple, everyday quaffing level of wine. But this is Italy, so why shouldn't things be turned upside down? Why not register some of the best wines as 'basic' VdT? And that is what has happened, with the name super-*vini da tavola* (for example, Ronco di Mompiano and Vintage Tunina) unofficially coined to describe them. Tuscany has been the centre of this movement, so much so that such wines there are called super-Tuscans instead.

Straightforward *vino da tavola* is still only the basic glugger the rules were set up for. To emphasize its ordinariness it can't declare any particular place of origin, nor grape varieties, nor even a vintage. There is also meant to be a more elevated *vino da tavola* category, called *Vino Tipico*, where all these factors can be disclosed. However, the first version emerged only in 1989 after ten years in drafting – to a very mixed reception. In the meantime *vino da tavola con indicazione geografica* emerged to bridge the gap and this is where the super-*vini da tavola* slot in. The actual 'geographic

▲ Labels showing a selection of Italian wines. (Top row, from left to right) Barolo, a DOCG wine, and Soave and Verdicchio dei Castelli di Jesi, both DOC wines. (Above, from left to right) Flaccianello, a super-Tuscan, Notarpanaro, a *vino da tavola con indicazione geografica*, and Preludio, a super-*vino da tavola*.

indication' has, like DOC, to be requested by producers, who were not slow in coming forward though without, of course, any consistency of approach. There are hundreds approved and the list changes every year. Some cover regions, some provinces, some communes, others just a vineyard which happens to have a locality name.

The message is clear: the classification really doesn't matter, the wine does.

CONSORZIO Various wine areas in Italy have a *consorzio*, an association to provide control on the wines' quality and also to provide promotion and marketing assistance. Membership is voluntary but usually nearly all producers join a *consorzio* if it exists. Standards vary widely. Some seem to do little more than print the small neck stickers which go on approved bottles of members' wines. Others have strict standards of quality and wine-testing procedures, provide a valuable information service, and are tireless protagonists for their area's

wines. The best known and most influential is the Gallo Nero (Black Cockerel) *consorzio* of Chianti Classico.

VIDE is a group of around 30 small to medium-sized estates from all over Italy dedicated to the highest quality. VIDE on a bottle neck or label brings great credit because, although members' dues are based on the full amount of wine produced by an estate, a particular wine may not get VIDE status every year. It depends on how it performs in the strict tasting and analytical tests. This avoids estates benefiting in perpetuity from a single batch of good wines that gained them entry or borderline wines being approved just to raise loot.

PREDICATO A group of Tuscan producers has devised a 'rival' classification system, called Predicato, for some new-wave wines from central Tuscany, putting firm constraints on yield, vineyard altitude and so on. There are four different Predicatos (di Biturica for Cabernet/Sangiovese blends, di Cardisco for mainly Sangiovese, del Muschio for Chardonnay, del Selvante for Sauvignon). Its few adherents have ambitions of it gaining official recognition and maybe spreading throughout Italy. But everyone else is completely indifferent.

13

# A–Z OF WINES, GRAPES AND WINE REGIONS

The lists on the following pages cover most of the major and not-so-major Italian wines, as well as some of the quirkier ones you are likely to come across. There are also entries on Italy's regions and the main grape varieties.

The wine entries all follow the same format, the left-hand column containing the name of the wine, its classification, the region and the grape varieties (up to a maximum of four), usually in order of importance (see below for a sample explained in more detail). The grape varieties are divided into red, rosé and white. For DOCs with single-variety wines all the permitted grape varieties are listed in the left-hand column. The right-hand column gives the wine description with, where appropriate, recommended producers, vintages and when to drink.

If you cannot find the wine you want in the A–Z, it may mean that it is listed under a different name. In such cases consult the Index where alternative forms of wine names may be found.

The most important wine regions of Italy (Alto Adige, Chianti, Emilia-Romagna, Friuli-Venezia Giulia, Piedmont, Sicily, Tuscany, Veneto) are each given a whole spread to themselves with maps and lists of wines and grapes found in the region. The names in these lists can be found in their appropriate place in the A–Z.

---

The wine name and its classification. This wine is classified as Denominazione di Origine Controllata or DOC, the most widespread term for quality wine in Italy.

**FALERNO DEL MASSICO DOC**

CAMPANIA

The region of Italy where the wine is made. Campania centres on the bustling, chaotic city of Naples.

♥ ♥ Aglianico, Primitivo, Piedirosso

The grape varieties listed in order of importance up to four named varieties. For DOCs that cover single-variety wines, such as Alto Adige or Aquileia, all the varieties permitted under the DOC legislation are listed.

The symbols stand for red ♥, rosé ♥ and white ♥ wines.

♥ Falanghina

---

The name of the region.

**ABRUZZO**

SOUTHERN ITALY

The area of Italy.

These wines are listed elsewhere in the A–Z in their appropriate place.

*Wine entries:* Montepulciano d'Abruzzo, Trebbiano d'Abruzzo

---

◄ A tranquil scene in the hills of Tuscany in late autumn.

## ABRUZZO
SOUTHERN ITALY

*Wine entries:*
Montepulciano d'Abruzzo,
Trebbiano d'Abruzzo

It's a moot point where central Italy becomes the south. It seems always to begin a little further south than where the person you are talking to comes from. But for me, when chugging down the Adriatic side of the boot, the little thrill of excitement that always signals my arrival in that splendid part of Italy northerners love to hate, hits me just after I arrive in Abruzzo. It is gloriously beautiful, not all that well known and would probably be even more obscure if its name had not been included in its two major wines: Trebbiano d'Abruzzo and Montepulciano d'Abruzzo, both DOC.

Those who moan you can't produce good wines in the south because it is too hot forget Italy's saving grace − its mountainous backbone. In Abruzzo the Apennines are higher than anywhere else. There is little flat land in the region and in many of the scattered hill and mountain villages the inhabitants have ultra-local dialects. They even need to resort to Italian to communicate with folk in just the next village. Wine-making practices here sometimes verge on the eccentric too. Most production, though, is in the hands of the co-operatives and some of them, like the exemplary Tollo and Casal Thaulero (now privatized) could teach a few of the individual producers a thing or two.

The major grapes grown in Abruzzo are white Trebbiano and the superb red Montepulciano, some of which is made into a rosé or lightish red called Cerasuolo. There is also a little Sangiovese (not DOC) and bits and bobs of Merlot, Barbera, Dolcetto, Malbec, Riesling, Traminer, Tocai, and the three Pinots (Bianco, Grigio and Nero). Too much is currently planted on the high-yielding *tendone* system. But nowhere is perfect.

## AGLIANICO

Among the dozen or so black grapes clamouring for admiration in the south of Italy, there really is no competition for top billing. Aglianico has a head start as it is wholly responsible for the two most distinguished and potentially great southern reds, Taurasi (from Campania) and Aglianico del Vulture (from Basilicata), and has a good stake in a third with high-quality potential, Falerno (from Campania). It produces rich, earthy, chocolaty wines of intense colour, high tannin, firm acidity and concentrated flavour, all of which promote long ageing. It also has the ability to create a wine of complexity without the need to blend in other varieties, and it is ideally suited to the length of growing season and the microclimate of its homelands. So you can see why Aglianico is well ahead of its rivals. Grown mainly in Campania and Basilicata, there are also some plantings in Molise.

## AGLIANICO DEL VULTURE DOC
BASILICATA

🍷 Aglianico

Vulture is an extinct volcano 1326 metres (4350 feet) high, in the north of Basilicata, the instep of Italy. Thank goodness it is extinct; its wine is far too exciting to lose. The vineyards for the wine, Basilicata's only DOC, are on the east-facing (coolish) slopes, from 200 metres (656 feet) to about half way up. Aglianico del Vulture's renown is based exclusively on one producer: Fratelli D'Angelo, whose name is almost synonymous with the DOC. They command the best grapes from their suppliers and are even confident enough to invest in expensive *barriques* for an oak-aged Aglianico called Canneto.

But the general standard of Aglianico del Vulture is improving fast and other producers such as Paternoster and Sasso are beginning to get a look in. Good Aglianico del Vulture is a big, intense, earthy wine that, with time, softens and develops complexity, especially if it is from a specially favoured vintage like 1985 or '81. From these and other good years it will be at Riserva level, with at least five years' ageing. A rare sparkling version exists too.

## ALBANA DI ROMAGNA DOCG
ROMAGNA

♀ Albana

Albana di Romagna, produced over a large area between Bologna and Rimini, became DOCG, the top classification for Italian wine, with the 1987 vintage. It's such an innocent little statement that it is hard to credit its profound significance. It meant that any hopes that the Italian bureaucrats might acquire enough common sense to act in the best interests of their burgeoning quality wine industry were once more assigned to the bin. For Albana is, let us be kind, not the most exciting of white wines. Let us not be so kind; it is of extremely variable quality, often dull as ditchwater, sometimes appallingly bad, and just occasionally rather nice. Oh, and it can be either dry, *amabile*, sweet, sparkling or *passito* too. Anywhere else in the world the plan would have been laughed out of court, but bureaucracy, political scheming and self-aggrandizement won the day. And they haven't even tightened up the slack production rules – which DOCG ought to do. Still, when it is made well, it is a very attractive, if unobtrusive, nutty, creamy, crisp wine for drinking young. I only wish a few more estates would follow Fattoria Paradiso's lead and try at least to do the best they can with it.

## ALCAMO DOC
SICILY

♀ Catarratto, Damaschino, Grecanico, Trebbiano Toscano

Take the road west from Palermo and round the bite-shaped Gulf of Castellammare, and the names of the towns continually remind you that this is Mafia territory, where offending no-one and taking care of your kneecaps is of utmost importance. Turn inland past Alcamo and you drive for miles along a twisty road, through such tight hills you can rarely see more than a few hundred yards in any direction. Excellent bandit country, in fact. But every single slope of every hill is dark green with vines.

There are few DOCs in Sicily, most producers preferring to make *vini da tavola* so they can choose whichever grapes they prefer. Alcamo is DOC but the producers do not make a great play of it. The label of the lively, crisp, appley and almondy white Rapitalà, for example, far and away Alcamo's best estate, looks the same as for their red and rose, which are *vini da tavola*.

But if you expect all Alcamo to be as interesting and refreshing as Rapitalà, you are going to be disappointed. The Catarratto grape is ideal for western Sicilian whites if, and it's a big if, its yield is kept down. Those who exploit its prolific productivity then add neutrality with over-cropped Trebbiano, turn out wine that isn't worth the bottle it comes in. Drink young.

## ALEATICO

The Aleatico grape is odd: it is so Moscato-like in aroma, style and longevity that some reckon it is a Moscato mutation, but is so deeply coloured that others reckon it can't be. Wines made from it are dark red, usually richly sweet, tasting of wild strawberries, redcurrants and other berried fruits. They are alcoholic, rounded and absolutely delicious but hard to track down.

In Lazio the grape makes the obscure DOC Aleatico di Gradoli, produced only to the north-west of Lake Bolsena on the Tuscan border. There are odd outcrops in neighbouring Tuscany, from where it has even gravitated to Elba where it is venerated, and Umbria too. No more than 450 hectolitres of Aleatico di Gradoli are made but what there is may be rather delicate, with as little as 9·5 per cent alcohol, or robust, strong and longer lasting, with 15 per cent or more. Either way it is sweet. Production is left to the tender mercies of the local co-op.

In Puglia it is also DOC, Aleatico di Puglia and Salice Salentino. Sweet here too, it is best with three years' ageing (compulsory for Riserva) and is sometimes fortified. Either of them, with a wickedly indulgent pastry perhaps, would make the perfect end to a meal.

# ALTO ADIGE

Until 1918 the province of Alto Adige, or Südtirol as it is called by the German-speaking majority, belonged to Austria and even today, more than 70 years on, about half the population reacts strongly against any Italianization of their lifestyle or language. So why doesn't this stunningly beautiful district cede from the Italian Republic? Because they are doing very nicely, thank you, care of the Italian state. They have secured the status of autonomous province and have acquired massive grants from central government to perpetuate their bi-lingual education system and other aspects of their culture. They also have, in Italy, a large and eager market for their abundant agricultural products, particularly apples.

Oh those apples! The bane of a wine lover's life, as much prime vineyard land has been uprooted in recent years for the more profitable apple crop, particularly close to the river valley. The Adige river (Etsch in German) and its tributary the Isarco (Eisacktal) flow through the province, meeting just south of the city of Bolzano, its capital. The vineyard area forms a Y-shape around the confluence of these rivers.

Their valleys are narrow and the hills rise steeply on either side, giving winemakers an unprecedented opportunity to grow a wide variety of grape types. As many as 15 is not uncommon. Reds, such as Lagrein, Schiava and Cabernet, grow lowest down. French varieties, such as Pinot Grigio, Chardonnay, Pinot Bianco, Sauvignon, are planted a little higher and Germanic grapes such as Riesling and Sylvaner are found on the highest slopes. All are grown on pergolas. The view of rushing river at the bottom of the valley, then the deep green of the vines covering the hills like a velvet cloth, followed higher by the wooded slopes which are topped by the bare crags of the mountains, often snow-capped and pink-tinged by evening, is a magnificent sight.

The vine-growers of Alto Adige have much to be thankful for. The sub-alpine climate may be pretty cold in winter and always cool by night, but by day in summer the temperature climbs rapidly, so much so that Bolzano is often the hottest provincial capital of Italy. This gives plenty of stimulus to the grapes to ripen fully, while the cold nights ensure slow ripening.

There is a huge market in Austria, Switzerland and Germany for the light, barely red wine from the Schiava grape and this is the backbone of Alto Adige's wine industry. But it is on the white wines that the reputation of the area hangs. Even though yields are often too high, resulting in a dilution of the wines' taste – and producers are sometimes tempted to stretch the generous DOC limits further than they should – the combination of climate, altitude and slope allows a wonderfully pure expression of varietal character in Alto Adige wines. This means if you want to know what Sylvaner or Pinot Bianco, say, should really taste of, Alto Adige is the place to find out.

MERANESE DI COLLINA

A L T O    A D I G E

Bressanone•

VALLE ISARCO

Merano

SANTA MADDALENA

Isarco

Adige

Bolzano

LAGO DI CALDARO

COLLI DI BOLZANO

TERLANO

TRENTINO

Red wines
White wines
Alto Adige DOC
Regional boundary

0    10 km
0    10 miles

N

ALTO ADIGE - SÜDTIROLER
*Rhein Riesling*
RIESLING RENANO
DENOMINAZIONE DI ORIGINE CONTROLLATA
Abfüller Imbottigliatore:
FR. KUPELWIESER!
SALURN · SALORNO (BZ) · ITALIA
0.75ℓe    Qualitätswein b.A.    13% Vol.
Nr. Reg. 46/82

ALTO ADIGE
DENOMINAZIONE DI ORIGINE CONTROLLATA - V.Q.P.R.D.
PINOT GRIGIO
1987
COLTERENZIO
Prodotto ed imbottigliato all'origine dalla
CANTINA PRODUTTORI COLTERENZIO
CORNAIANO (BZ)
750 ml e    ITALIA    12% vol.

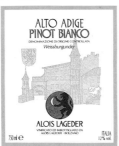

▲ Schloss Lebenberg with a panorama of the Adige valley behind. Alto Adige, almost in Austria, is a dream of a wine zone, with carpets of pergola-trained vines covering the steep hillsides.

| WINE ENTRIES | GRAPE ENTRIES |
| --- | --- |
| Alto Adige | Cabernet Franc |
| Chardonnay dell'Alto Adige | Cabernet Sauvignon |
| Feldmarschall | Chardonnay |
| Goldmuskateller | Lagrein |
| Lago di Caldaro | Malvasia |
| Lagrein Dunkel | Merlot |
| Lagrein Kretzer | Moscato |
| Moscato Rosa | Pinot Bianco |
| Santa Maddalena | Pinot Grigio |
| Terlano | Pinot Nero |
| Valdadige | Riesling Italico |
|  | Riesling Renano |
|  | Sauvignon |
|  | Schiava |
|  | Traminer |

## ALTO ADIGE DOC
ALTO ADIGE

🍷 Cabernet Franc, Cabernet Sauvignon, Lagrein, Malvasia (Malvasier), Merlot, Pinot Nero (Blauburgunder), Schiava (Vernatsch)

🍷 Lagrein, Moscato Rosa (Rosenmuskateller)

🍷 Chardonnay, Moscato Giallo (Goldmuskateller), Müller-Thurgau, Pinot Bianco (Weissburgunder), Pinot Grigio (Ruländer), Riesling Italico (Welschriesling), Riesling Renano (Rheinriesling), Sauvignon, Sylvaner, Traminer Aromatico (Gewürztraminer)

Up in Alto Adige, the part of Italy that is almost in Austria and has official Italian/German bilingualism, from the border with Trentino north to past Merano and Bolzano, the vines grow on the steep slopes of the mountains that tumble down to the Adige river and its tributary, the Isarco, and sometimes on the narrow valley floor too.

Of the 17 grape varieties that make up the DOC, all being used to make single-varietal wines, some have their origins in Germany, some in France, a few in Italy. Many producers have a goodly number of them planted (or buy the grapes) and so need an above average command of wine-making techniques to handle them all properly. Not only that but, for example, they might well make two versions of Chardonnay and Pinot Grigio, ageing one in *barrique*.

Although Chardonnay is seen more and more, it is Pinot Bianco (which it much resembles) that really hits its delicate but penetrating, creamy, salty apogee in Alto Adige, while Germanic grapes, like the steely, floral Riesling, the rounder, grapier Müller-Thurgau, or the leaner Sylvaner, grown on the highest slopes, can be piercingly clean and pure-tasting. Moscato Giallo is delicately musky-grapy and sweetish (though made dry – and therefore not DOC – it is more intense and can be brilliant). All are usually drunk young, although from the best producers they will improve after two or three years and sometimes much longer.

Schiava is the predominant red, light-coloured and strawberry-yogurt-and-bacon-flavoured, while Lagrein is Alto Adige's best red. It can make a light strawberries and plums rosé, or an assertive bilberries and chocolate dark red, that is good at two to three years but will age too. There is also some very good sparkling wine made from Chardonnay and Pinots Bianco, Grigio and Nero. The best, using the *metodo classico*, is Vivaldi. Lageder and Tiefenbrunner stand out among the producers. Giorgio Grai (particularly), Hofstätter, Laimburg, Niedermayr, Walch, and the co-operatives of Colterenzio, Muri-Gries, St Michael-Eppan and Terlano are also good.

## ANGHELU RUJU
SARDINIA

🍷 Cannonau

Anghelu Ruju is a luscious *passito* wine, made from red Cannonau grapes which have been dried on cane mats for about 20 days. In that time they become concentrated enough to develop a hefty 18 per cent of alcohol with plenty of sweetness spare to give to the wine. Five years' ageing in large oak barrels produces a deep amber, nutty, toffee-like tooth-attackingly sweet dessert wine that has droves of admirers. It is made by Sella & Mosca, a large estate based at Alghero, in north-west Sardinia.

## AQUILEIA DOC
FRIULI-VENEZIA GIULIA

🍷 Cabernet Franc, Cabernet Sauvignon, Merlot, Refosco

🍷 Merlot

🍷 Chardonnay, Pinot Bianco, Pinot Grigio, Riesling Renano, Sauvignon, Tocai, Traminer Aromatico, Verduzzo

Aquileia is one of several blanket DOCs of Friuli in north-east Italy that cover numerous single-varietal DOCs. Apart from 13 separate DOCs, there is also an Aquileia Rosato for a blend of mainly Merlot with Cabernet Franc, Cabernet Sauvignon and Refosco. The region stretches inland northwards in a tall, narrow strip from the Gulf of Trieste with vineyards on a mere 620 hectares (1530 acres) of flattish coastal land, well drained by two rivers. Aquileia produces about 25,000 hectolitres, two-thirds of it red, predominantly Cabernet in one of its three forms (either Cabernet Sauvignon or Franc or a blend of the two) and Merlot.

There is a soft spot in the heart of many Friulians for Aquileia's soft, fragrant, delicate, youthful whites, and cheerful, fruity reds which are usually best within three to four years of the vintage. Watch out for the superb 1988s! Most of the wine is made by the reliable Cantina Sociale Cooperativa del Friuli Orientale, but Ca' Bolani, Giacomelli and Valle have some decent bottles, too.

## ARNEIS

Arneis can be an excellent white grape variety, subtly intricate, releasing a fascinating array of perfumes – apples, pears, nuts and liquorice – and revealing hidden depths of complexity of flavour. But surely there is little point in a grape being rescued from near extinction, growers investing in planting it and a great bally-hoo being made about how marvellous it is, if its wines can be just as uninteresting as those from any better established 'quality' grape. So let's make it very clear that it is the *potential* of Arneis that is fantastic. Its wine *will* excite but only when made by dedicated growers. The grape originated, it is believed, in the Roero hills on the left bank of the river Tanaro, north of Alba, in Piedmont and its cultivation is still mainly concentrated there, the wine being sold as Roero Arneis DOC. There is wide variation in wine style depending on the winemaker and the year, from light, delicate and ephemeral to (occasionally) rich, full and powerful.

## ASPRINO
**Vino da tavola**
BASILICATA, CAMPANIA

♀ Asprinio

The antidote for those who say wine gives them a headache? Or the way both to get a hangover and avoid it at the same time? Sadly it is neither. Asprino is a diminutive of *aspro*, which means sharp in Italian. Fancy a glass of Sharpish? Most Asprino (just in case you were wondering, aspirin in Italian is *aspirina*) comes from the province of Caserta in Campania, around Naples, whither it zooms quick as a flash to cool the fevered brows of Neapolitans avoiding traffic jams, the noise and heat, or just trying to get by in their frenzied city. The rest hails from Basilicata, from the little town of Ruoti not far from the Campania border, and most of that is rushed off to Naples too. Asprino is low in alcohol, high in acidity, lemony bright in colour and light in weight, which makes it fine stuff to glug – ice cold, probably from an anonymous jug, and the younger the better – if you are hot and thirsty. You will sometimes see it called Asprinio, after the grape from which it is made.

## ASTI SPUMANTE DOC
PIEDMONT

♀ Moscato Bianco

Asti Spumante is delicious stuff. Light, fresh, effervescent, delicate, grapy – oh so grapy. It's just like crushing Muscat grapes and whisking them up like egg white until they lose their stickiness and become soft and frothy. And it is sweet – gracefully, not cloyingly sweet. It tastes so good you just can't help smiling. It is pretty low in alcohol too (between 7·5 and 9 per cent) and in these health-conscious days that's an important asset. What a marvellous ambassador for Italy it is!

It is also worth remembering that traditional Asti Spumante is produced by the most natural way ever of making sparkling wine. It is different from most other fizz which has to have two fermentations: the first to make a still, dry wine, the second, set off by added yeast and sugar, to trap the bubbles. Asti needs no such additions and has just the one fermentation. Part way through, while there is still plenty of natural grape sweetness left, the part-fermented wine is put in sealed tanks and the bubbles of fermentation are trapped. Even when the pressure has reached its optimum, there's still some sweetness around. That's why it is low in alcohol and its sweetness so light and natural.

Many of the big sparkling wine and vermouth houses of Turin make Asti Spumante as well. Who wouldn't want a share of the wine, especially when the grapes are just an hour away (to the south-east around Canelli, near the town of Asti)? Many of them, like Cinzano, Gancia, Riccadonna and Martini, are pretty reliable too. Better still are those from Arione, Bera, Duca d'Asti, Fontanafredda, Vallebelbo, and, particularly, Vignaioli di Santo Stefano. Don't keep Asti. The fresher it is the better. Buy it from somewhere where the stock shifts fast and pop the cork at the first opportunity.

## BARBARESCO DOCG
PIEDMONT

🍷 Nebbiolo

▶ Barbaresco is nearly always aged in traditional, large *botti* of up to 100 hectolitres or more capacity. They acquire a crystalline lining from deposits made by the wine. Some producers regularly clean it away so the wine gets a little oak character. Others leave it, but even they have to chip the layer away from time to time when it gets too thick.

People talk about 'Barolo and Barbaresco', never the other way round and they say 'Barolo is the king, Barbaresco the queen'. But there are advantages to being number two. You tend your Nebbiolo grapes and make your wine in comparative peace. Your wine is a little lighter than Barolo, so you have more chance of getting some elegance into a notoriously four-square style. Few growers in Barbaresco would be much inclined to change places.

Barbaresco's somewhat lighter style is due partly to its lighter soil, partly to the more gentle slopes of its hills, north-east of Alba in Italy's north-west. It also benefits from a mite less alcohol (12·5 per cent is the minimum) and a less stringent ageing requirement of just two years (four for the Riserva category) of which only one need be in wood.

Whatever the site of its grapes and however long it is aged, though, the weight of any Barbaresco will depend a great deal on who makes it: how ripe the grapes are, how much the yield is restricted, how long the grape skins stay in contact with the juice and so on. Nevertheless, the fascinating taste of the Nebbiolo grape with its flavours of violets and raspberries, prunes and chocolate, truffles and liquorice, its assertive acidity, and its firm tannin, which needs age to soften it (up to 15 years), should always be present.

You may need a second mortgage to try the wines of Gaja, but just see what Marchesi de Grésy, Roagna, Cigliuti, Bruno Giacosa, Pelissero, I Paglieri, Secondo Pasquero Elia, Giuseppe Cortese, Traversa, Glicine, Parroco di Neive, Moresco, Rizzi or the Produttori del Barbaresco co-op can do in a smashing year like 1985 or a classic like '82. Or try comparing the Barbaresco of predominantly Barolo producers Pio Cesare, Prunotto, Vietti, Cortese, Rinaldi, Scarpa, Barale, Ceretto, Mascarello or Oddero with their Barolo – they make both.

## BARBAROSSA
Vino da tavola
ROMAGNA

🍷 Barbarossa

In 1955 Mario Pezzi of the important estate Fattoria Paradiso, inland from the Rimini coastline, discovered by chance an unusual-looking vine in a plot of very old Sangiovese, due for uprooting. After tests it was pronounced a genuine natural mutation. Sugar levels were surprisingly high and the wine distinctive-tasting and good. Rich, big, plummy, pruny, tangily spicy and long-lived, it has become one of Fattoria Paradiso's specialities, and is now being avidly copied by other estates round about. Best years: 1988, '87, '86, '85, '83, '82, '80.

## BARBERA

Barbera crops up all over the place; in Lombardy, Emilia-Romagna, Puglia, Campania, Sicily and elsewhere, but its homeland, and one of the few regions where they are not ashamed to sport its name on labels, is Piedmont, particularly around Alba, Asti, Tortona and the district of Monferrato. In recent years there has been far too much Barbera around for comfort, so the heights of ingenuity have been employed to use up the surplus. This has resulted in light Barbera, white Barbera, fizzy Barbera and well-publicized brands called Rovetto, Arengo, Barbesino and Verbesco. Good straight Barbera, though, is great stuff and Italian to a T: vividly coloured, plum-skins sweet-sour, fruit-packed, with enlivening high acidity, and a bone-dry, astringent finish. With carbonic maceration or in lighter style it is at its liveliest when young; traditionally vinified with sensibly low yields, it shines when two to four years old. In Piedmont it is DOC as Barbera d'Alba, Barbera d'Asti, Barbera del Monferrato, Colli Tortonesi and Rubino di Cantavenna. In Oltrepò Pavese and Colli Piacentini, both on the Piedmontese border, Barbera is lighter, often a little *frizzante* or mixed with softer, rounder Bonarda in Gutturnio.

## BARBERA D'ALBA DOC
PIEDMONT

🍷 Barbera

Despite endless conflicting claims for 'best' Barbera zones, if, like me, you go for extract and concentration in wines and get enthused by smokiness highlighting ripe, redcurrant fruit and balancing exciting acidity, choose your Barbera from Alba. Best producers: Altare, Barale, Brovia, Castello di Neive, Pio Cesare, Clerico, Aldo Conterno, Giacomo Conterno, Gaja, Bruno Giacosa, Giuseppe Mascarello, Prunotto, Ratti, Vajra and Vietti. It ages for two to three years, especially in good vintages like 1988, '87, '86, '85.

## BARBERA D'ASTI DOC
PIEDMONT

🍷 Barbera

Usually regarded as the most typical incarnation of the grape, Barbera d'Asti acts as piggy in the middle between the weighty style of Barbera d'Alba and the more frolicsome one of Barbera del Monferrato. It is usually best drunk quite young but occasional vintages (like 1985) produce wines with staying power. The banner waver for Asti's Barbera (but in a most *atypical* style) is Giacomo Bologna with his *cru* wines La Monella, Bricco della Bigotta and the *barrique*-aged, complex Bricco dell'Uccellone. The best of the more typical producers are Bricco Mondalino, Rivetti and Scarpa.

## BARBERA DEL MONFERRATO DOC
PIEDMONT

🍷 Barbera, Freisa, Grignolino, Dolcetto

For young, lively, gulpably light, sometimes *frizzante* Barbera, the Monferrato hills, south-east of Asti, are the place to look. Avoid the Superiore style which has to be aged two years and therefore apes, not too successfully, the firmer styles of Barbera d'Asti and d'Alba, check your stomach enjoys a good bite of acidity, and search out the freshest samples you can from Gaudio, Nuova Cappelletta, Bava or Duca d'Asti.

## BARDOLINO DOC, BARDOLINO CHIARETTO DOC
VENETO

🍷 🍷 Corvina, Rondinella, Molinara and others

Bardolino is one of the three great names of the Veneto (with Soave and Valpolicella). It can be good but, sadly, it often isn't (even from the Classico zone) and that can be the fault just as much of our importers for not keeping a tight enough rein on stock throughput as of lazy wine-making. The overall standard, however, is getting better. Bardolino has a vibrant, ripe cherries and slightly bitter almonds character that is often better the younger, cheerier and less serious the wine is. In the hands of a few, sure-footed producers like Boscaini Masi (especially La Vegrona) and Guerrieri-Rizzardi who really know what they are up to, more serious, two-year-old plus Bardolino can work well. Otherwise stick to non-Superiore young wines and names such as Le Vigne di San Pietro, Gorgo and Fraterna Portalupi, or take a gamble on Arvedi d'Emilei (which can be superb or merely decent).

Even more exciting, give the Bardolino grapes just a few hours' skin contact and out pops all of their fruit but none of their harsher elements. The result is Bardolino Chiaretto, a rosé wine that has the crispness and freshness of a white, but the ripe cherry-like fruit you would only ever find on a red. 1988 was a great Chiaretto year, as you'll discover from the wine of any good Bardolino producer such as Fraterna Portalupi, Gorgo and Le Vigne di San Pietro. Masi's 'Fresco' is similar in style, but deeper in colour.

## BAROLO DOCG
PIEDMONT

🍷 Nebbiolo

Once you pick up on the glories of Nebbiolo, you fall in love with Barolo. And I mean love. This is no fleeting infatuation, but a full-scale love affair that endures the rest of your life. For tough, tannic and astringent it may be, but there is a wonderful nugget of fruit that seems to flow round the more abrasive elements to make a remarkably alluring whole. Barolo can be as exhilarating as a summer pudding of raspberries and other berried fruits. It can be as ethereal as the scent of violets. It can be earthy, truffly, smoky, deep and mysterious. It can be pruny, chocolaty, rich and seductive. Or it may be any combination of them. Mind you, it is only the great Barolos that can inspire the muse. If it is not expensive, it may well be enjoyable but it won't be revelatory. Barolo's homeland in the steep, angular Langhe hills of southern Piedmont can induce a wonderful sense of calm and peace. The tranquillity has disguised a ferment that has involved nearly all Barolo's producers at one time or another. One argument was whether it was better to make separate wines from favoured vineyard sites to capture the individuality they provided? Or was it better to make just one wine? More and more producers have taken the former view.

A more fundamental argument concerned the making of the wines. A new breed of winemakers had grown up, led by Altare, Clerico and Voerzio, who wanted more obvious fruit in their wines and adapted wine-making methods to get it. Their wines were a revelation to those who had remained unmoved by the wonders of traditional Barolo – no longer was there any need to wait patiently for the fruit to emerge from its chrysalis, it came bounding out of the glass to meet you. But was this, admittedly very attractive sort of wine, real *Barolo* asked the traditionalists like Conterno and Mascarello. But the dilemma solved itself. For 'modernist' Barolo, if made from hard-pruned vines with a very low yield, can be tough enough to satisfy the staunchest traditionalist. And 'traditionalist' Barolo, from lighter, less 'classic' years like 1983 and '84 (if selected carefully), acquires a delicious, cheerfully lively raspberry fruitiness that gets the modernists' nod of approval.

There is room in Barolo for all styles: basic and magical, *cru* and non-*cru*. There is room for vintages like 1987, '84 and '83, which are ready to drink in five years; for the brilliant 1985, '82 and '78 which need up to ten years at least. And there is certainly room for producers of the calibre of Altare, Barale, Bovio, Brovia, Cavallotto, Ceretto, Clerico, Cogno-Marcarini, Aldo Conterno, Giacomo Conterno, Cordero di Montezemolo, Fontanafredda (*crus*), Bruno Giacosa, Grasso, Bartolo Mascarello, Giuseppe Mascarello, Pio Cesare, Prunotto, Ratti, Francesco Rinaldi, Giuseppe Rinaldi, Sandrone, Lorenzo Scavino, Paolo Scavino, Sebaste, Vajra, Vietti and Roberto Voerzio.

▼ Young vines slowly being trained along Barolo's angular hills to take on their characteristic *spalliera* formation along stakes, while the wild flowers are allowed to remain to prevent the vines becoming too vigorous.

## BASILICATA
SOUTHERN ITALY

*Wine entries:* Aglianico del Vulture, Asprino

Basilicata is the instep of Italy, a smallish region sandwiched between Campania, Calabria and Puglia. Historically known as Lucania, it is Italy's poorest region and the second lowest in population. The march of progress has been slow. Even the *autostrada* didn't arrive until the beginning of the 1980s. It is hilly and mountainous and unreasonably cold in winter. On the other hand, the beaches along the Ionian (instep) and the fragment of Tyrrhenian (west) coasts are not to be sneezed at. The uplands bring welcome cool in summer, folk are friendly and it is peaceful and unspoilt.

There's not a lot of wine, either. Just 450,000 hectolitres, and less than two per cent is the sole DOC: Aglianico del Vulture. The Aglianico grape thrives in the climate, is well diffused and also makes red *vino da tavola*, rosé and sparkling wines. Other southern grapes such as Bombino Nero and Bianco, Malvasia Nera and Bianca and Moscato have their presence too and there are outcrops of Trebbiano, Verdeca, Asprinio, Sangiovese and Negroamaro, plus grapes from the north like Pinot Nero and Chardonnay. If you ever reach the Ionian coast, there's Bianco, Rosato or Rosso di Metaponto to refresh you.

## BIANCO DI CUSTOZA DOC
VENETO

♀ Trebbiano Toscano, Garganega, Tocai and others

Up until a few years ago most white wine drinkers in the bars and *trattorie* of Verona would have gone for Soave. Now it is more than likely to be Bianco di Custoza. The reason is mainly the grape mix. Even though there's less Garganega (not necessarily a good thing) and more Trebbiano (definitely a bad thing) than in Soave, the other grapes that make up the shortfall (Tocai, Cortese, Malvasia, Riesling Italico) have character and aroma and add greengage and peachy fruit, floweriness and zip. Producers such as Cavalchina, Fraterna Portalupi, Gorgo, Le Vigne di San Pietro, Tedeschi, Zenato show the form, especially when the wines are young and at their best. Increasingly producers are making sparkling Bianco di Custoza too.

## BIANCO VERGINE VALDICHIANA DOC
TUSCANY

♀ Trebbiano Toscano, Malvasia and others

If Tuscans want to make white wine with their traditional grapes they really have an uphill struggle. Trebbiano can be frankly boring and Malvasia is devilishly hard to keep fresh and perfumed. Bianco Vergine Valdichiana is a case in point. Much of the wine is yawn-worthy. But those who prune their vines hard get a soft, creamy, herby, lightly salty, highly nutty, elegant glassful. Flavour-coaxing producers: Avignonesi, La Colonica. Drink as young as possible.

## BIFERNO DOC
MOLISE

♀ ♀ Montepulciano, Trebbiano, Aglianico

♀ Trebbiano Toscano, Bombino Bianco, Malvasia Bianca

Biferno includes three separate vineyard areas, the best cover the hillsides that slope down to the Adriatic. You can roll off the vineyard and straight on to the beach. Bliss! It has made an impact because of just one estate, Di Majo Norante. Its red, Ramitello, is a remarkable earthy, pruny, tobaccoey number that can seem lean until partnered with food, when its fruit springs out of hiding. Superb at six years old, from vintages like 1986, '85, '83, it can easily last longer. Ramitello white is not DOC because Di Majo uses Falanghina. It is a fabulous mixture of candied fruit, ice-cream, lime and orange flavours.

## BOCA DOC
PIEDMONT

♀ Nebbiolo, Vespolina, Bonarda

Up towards Lake Maggiore lies Boca, with only 20 vine-growers, even fewer producers and less than about 300 hectolitres to its name. With a little age, from years such as 1988, '86, '85, '82, it should get violetty (Valloni's is most characteristic). Watch out for it, après-skiers!

## BONARDA

About 55km (35 miles) south of Milan is the Oltrepò Pavese where the red Bonarda grape makes scrumptious, gulpable, plummy, cherryish, lively, bitter-finishing wine. A hop east and we're in Emilia-Romagna and the Colli Piacentini. The modification in Bonarda's style is precisely zilch. Here, though, there's official recognition of the starry partnership between Bonarda and the more acidic Barbera in a blend of the two called Gutturnio. The grape is also known as Croatina. Confusingly, Bonarda Piemontese is a different variety.

## BRACHETTO D'ACQUI DOC
PIEDMONT

🍷 Brachetto

Just imagine this guy, whom you reckon is a pretty smart wine connoisseur, telling you that one of his favourite wines is a bit like strawberry-ade with roses. You'd think the world had turned on its head, wouldn't you? But it's not always the most revered wine that gives the most delight. Brachetto d'Acqui is one of my favourite indulgences. Light red, with a bit of fizz, it smells a bit Muscaty-grapy but rather more like sweet strawberries and tastes light, delicate and sweetish. Just imagine such a *non*-serious fun wine hailing from just a spitting distance away from Alba and its Barolo and Barbaresco – the most solemnly serious Italian wines of the lot. Best producers: Bologna, Viticoltori dell'Acquese, Scarpa.

## BRAMATERRA DOC
PIEDMONT

🍷 Nebbiolo, Croatina, Bonarda Piemontese, Vespolina

Ask the traditionalist producer Sella anything about Bramaterra and he'll whip out a huge relief map of northern Piedmont and fill you in on altitudes, soils, rainfall, drainage and winds around the vineyards of the Vercelli hills until you understand that it is *meant* to be different in character from Barolo, *meant* to be spicier and more violetty, *meant* to be lighter bodied and more elegant, but will still age well for up to ten years or more in vintages as good as 1985 and '82. Apart from Sella, Perazzi is the only other producer to keep Bramaterra's flame burning.

## BREGANZE DOC
VENETO

🍷 Cabernet Franc, Cabernet Sauvignon, Merlot, Pinot Nero

🍷 Pinot Bianco, Pinot Grigio, Tocai, Vespaiolo

Breganze's name is closely associated with that of Maculan, its major and most quality-conscious producer. Fausto Maculan's large range of Breganze wines is as impressive for its number and diversity as much as for its high level of quality. Among the best are Prato di Canzio, made from Pinot Bianco with some Tocai and Chardonnay and given a few months in *barrique*, which results in the wine needing a good two or three years for its enticing biscuity creaminess to harmonize; and two Cabernets, Palazzotto and Fratta.

The Vespaiolo grape is a speciality of Breganze. It is normally made into a dry light, fresh, appley, lemony wine. Maculan also makes a *passito*, floral and honeyed version called Torcolato that is one of Italy's outstanding sweet wines.

## BRICCO MANZONI
Vino da tavola
PIEDMONT

🍷 Nebbiolo, Barbera

Valentino Migliorini has a comfortable 20 hectares (50 acres) of vineyard on an estate called Podere Rocche dei Manzoni in Monforte d'Alba, one of the best Barolo zones. He makes a pretty mean Barolo, but what does everyone go wild about? This wine called Bricco Manzoni, where he has cut the Nebbiolo with 20 per cent of acidic Barbera and bunged the resulting brew in very un-traditional *barriques*. On the face of it, it doesn't sound a brilliant idea. But the wine is fabulous. The truffly, blackberry-like 1982 is superb. The '85 will be even starrier when mature in a few years' time.

## BRINDISI DOC
PUGLIA

🍷🍷 Negroamaro, Malvasia Nera, Montepulciano and others

For miles beforehand as you appoach Brindisi, large billboards exhort you to buy your ferry tickets HERE. Brindisi is an Adriatic port in the far south of Italy's heel and the stepping-stone to Greece just a few hours away across the Strait of Otranto. Those who assay a glass of red before they leave will encounter the Negroamaro variety. Dark, powerful, liquorice, chocolate, herby stuff with a bitter twang (Negroamaro means 'bitter black'), it needs plenty of ageing (or blending with other grapes, especially Malvasia Nera) to soften it down. It can also be a decent enough rosé. Best is Cosimo Taurino's Patriglione and Cantine Distante's is worth a try.

## BRUNELLO DI MONTALCINO DOCG
TUSCANY

🍷 Sangiovese

▶ The blue-grey, undulating 'moonscape' that heads almost to the Tuscan coast stops abruptly at the large hill of Montalcino. Sangiovese vines for Montalcino's prestigious wine are now the most important crop.

Drive through Tuscany south to Siena, and your path is accompanied by innumerable splendid vineyard vistas. Once past Siena you leave Chianti Classico behind and you see not a hint of a vine for miles. The surroundings get yellower, less green, and the atmosphere gets noticeably warmer – you feel you have crossed an invisible climate barrier. After about half an hour you notice an enormous hill on the horizon with a castle on the top. This is the town of Montalcino. After the haul to the top, go into the castle. Look one way from its ramparts and you will blink in disbelief. There is just an undulating blue-grey 'moonscape'. The other direction is just as green and vine-clad as you would expect. It then becomes clear what a unique enclave Montalcino is.

Brunello di Montalcino is often referred to as simply 'Brunello', although this is really the name of the grape, a clone of Sangiovese which got its name from the brownish hue it has when ripe. Brunello is good stuff and usually pretty expensive too, but then quality rarely comes cheaply. A certain Ferruccio Biondi-Santi is responsible. During the 1860s, believing the area to be capable of great wines, he researched his theories, planted the Brunello grape, which he reckoned to be the best Sangiovese clone and found his ideas were substantiated. That's not to say there was no wine from Montalcino before. There was, but nothing to write home about. Biondi-Santi is still the pre-eminent name and the estate's wines are still far and away the most expensive, but nowhere near the best. One advantage of starting a prestige wine from scratch is that others attracted to follow in your footsteps tend to have the same ideals. In Montalcino practically all the newcomers have dedicated themselves wholeheartedly to producing the best wine they can, in the way that only true *amateurs* can. Mind you, the counterpoise is lack of experience, making the overall picture patchy apart from the great vintages of 1988, '85, '83, '82 and '78.

Brunello di Montalcino should be a long-lived, big, rich, powerful wine, with all the firm, peppery-spicy, tea-and-cinnamon, figgy character of the grape. It has one of the longest legal minimum ageing periods, four years, which some growers feel is too long. It *is* too long – if you don't take care to look after your large oak barrels properly, or if you don't keep them well topped up with wine. But to blame the length of ageing for below-par wine, as some people do, is no more than the equivalent of a bad workman blaming his tools. Those who want to make a younger, livelier style of wine have a separate DOC, Rosso di Montalcino, to sell it under. Tenuta Caparzo, Altesino, Col d'Orcia, Il Poggione and Case Basse show what Brunello is all about. Others, good or very good, include Barbi Cerbaiona, La Chiesa di Santa Restituta, Colombaio di Montosoli, Costanti, Lisini, Il Poggiolo, San Filippo, Talenti, Villa Banfi.

## CA' DEL PAZZO
Vino da tavola
TUSCANY

🍷 Sangiovese, Cabernet Sauvignon

The name means 'House of the Madman'. Ca' del Pazzo, though, is one of the more memorable super-Tuscans. It is made on the exemplary Brunello di Montalcino estate of Tenuta Caparzo by Vittorio Fiore, who has a real talent for making the most of the Sangiovese-Cabernet blend. This one is 50–50 and aged for nine months in *barriques*. First made in 1982, '83 is super-rich and maturing harmoniously; '85, though, is joyous but too young and '88 will blow your socks off.

## CABERNET
THROUGHOUT ITALY

🍷 Cabernet Sauvignon, Cabernet Franc

More and more frequently you see red wines with the word 'Cabernet' predominant on the label. Why is this? Pretend, for a moment, you are Italian. Your red wines, which you drink practically every day and reckon are the bee's knees of viniculture, are somewhat astringent, either light and gluggable, or meaty and tannic. Fruit they may have, somewhere,

but fruity they most certainly are not. Then one day you try a velvety, voluptuous, fruit-filled Cabernet. What a revelation! The next thing you discover is that Cabernet thrives in your own vineyards. What's more, just a little of this wonder-grape can make your traditional wines richer, rounder and much, much fruitier. That, in a nutshell, is the discovery innumerable Italian producers have made in the past decade or two, and that is why there are so many Cabernet and Cabernet-blend wines from the peninsula jostling for buyer's attentions. 'Cabernet' may mean Cabernet Franc, Cabernet Sauvignon or both.

What the Italians forget is that others, particularly in the UK, don't reckon Cabernet to be such a revelation. We've been courted by it for years. Our shelves are full of Cabernet from practically every wine-making country of the world, and far from being newly astounded by its brilliance, we are beginning to get rather bored. We certainly don't see why *we* should be charged a huge premium for Italian Cabernet just because it is causing such a stir down *there*. Italians, please take heed. Occasional Cabernet is seductive; too much is a huge turn off. Of course Cabernet has tremendous potential, but so have the native varieties. And that is where your true glories lie.

## CABERNET FRANC

Cabernet Franc is brilliantly suited to the north-east of Italy, probably better than anywhere else in Europe and just as well if not better than Cabernet Sauvignon. There, in the hilly parts of Veneto, Friuli and Trentino-Alto Adige it gets plenty of sun and warmth by day, enabling it to ripen fully. The nights, though, are chilly, ensuring it doesn't get too ripe too soon. It thus develops to the full the grassy, herbaceous blackcurranty-ness it gives to its wines, lending them richer fruit than in its 'classic' areas outside Italy (Bordeaux, Loire), and a balance of lively acidity without excessive tannin. The grapes are either macerated for two or three days on the skins, for a cheery, characterful wine for drinking young, or for longer to give a longer-lasting, more classically structured red.

Cabernet Franc is scattered throughout Italy, some recently planted for the fashionable 'Bordeaux blends'. It combines with Barbera, Nebbiolo and Merlot in Lombardy's idiosyncratic blend, Franciacorta Rosso DOC. Its most surprising incarnation, however, has been in southern Puglia. Here, although theoretically far too hot for the grape, by picking early a soft fragrant version can result.

## CABERNET SAUVIGNON

The most blessed of the blessed is Cabernet Sauvignon. Wherever this fashionable much-in-demand red grape is planted, within very broad limits, it thrives and produces wine that retains the rich, plummy, spicy, blackcurrancy character that is its hallmark. Though now spreading like wildfire the length and breadth of Italy, it has long been known there, longest, it seems, in Tuscany. Whoever first brought Cabernet Sauvignon to Tuscany was either prescient, lucky or inspired, for I reckon this is where the wine hits its peak. It matures splendidly from a mouth-attacking blast of fruit. extract and tannin to an irresistible sensual opulence. It has also found its perfect marriage in Tuscany. Just a small percentage added to Sangiovese makes a heavenly blend – essentially Tuscan but universally engaging. The resulting wines are all so appealing I am almost tempted to forgive the excess of Cabernet Sauvignon plantings, changing the unique Tuscan styles for a more international flavour.

Also traditional is Cabernet Sauvignon in north-east Italy. In Friuli, east Veneto and Trentino-Alto Adige the cool nights and hot days give a pulsed rhythm to the ripening pattern which enhances the wines' grassiness and makes them much more like Cabernet Franc, with which, in any case, Cabernet Sauvignon is sometimes blended. It also plays a major role in the increasing number of French-style Cabernet-Merlot blends, some DOC, others, such as Castel San Michele, Pragiara, Foianeghe, Navesel and Ronco del Gnemiz, super-*vini da tavola*. Cabernet is increasingly staking its claim to vineyards in Piedmont, home of the great Nebbiolo grape, with successful results too. Is there no limit to its incursion into prime sites for native varieties?

## CALABRIA
SOUTHERN ITALY

*Wine entries:* Cirò, Greco di Bianco, Melissa, Squillace

▲ Calabria's high, rocky interior gets blasted to a barren beauty during the dry, bakingly-hot summers. Wherever the scrubby lands can support vines, as here at Frascineto near Pollino, they will be grown, traditionally staked low against the wind. Reflected heat gives the grapes added ripeness and so extra alcohol to the wines.

If I ever get my chance to run away and eat lotuses somewhere, I just might choose Calabria – Italy's toe – maybe even staying at the focus of sybaritic existence, the town of Sibari itself. I could hop from side to side of the region and choose from miles of deserted beaches or dive from rocks where the imposing mountainous interior meets the coast. I could roast by the sea, then climb into the never-distant hills for a bit of cool, and get blown to bits by the wind in autumn. If I fancied a change of scenery, I could nip over to Sicily, just a few minutes away across the Straits of Messina.

Eating? Simply but well on the healthy Mediterranean diet. To drink? There's no shortage of wine around, over a million hectolitres a year, but, unless I supped regularly from the occasional boutique winery, like that of Odoardi near Cosenza, I'd have to get used to strong alcoholic reds and rosés from the Gaglioppo grape and peachy-earthy whites from Greco, so strong that my first experience of actually drinking Cirò, the best known DOC, is lost in an inebriate haze. Still, there would be the consolation of the occasional sip of delicious, sweet Greco di Bianco to help down the lotuses.

## CALUSO PASSITO DOC
PIEDMONT

♀ Erbaluce

North of Turin, around the Olivetti town of Ivrea, is a strip of vineyards cultivated with the hardly earth-shattering Erbaluce grape which usually makes the dry wine Erbaluce di Caluso. But if the grapes are laid out to dry, for anything up to six months, then fermented, perforce slowly due to the concentration of sugars, and aged for at least five years, Erbaluce blossoms into a rich, sweet, citrus and cream delight called Caluso Passito which just might make the earth quiver a bit. Vittorio Boratto heads the producers. Gnavi's (wood-aged) is fatter and coarser, but deliberately so, and Bianco's is up and coming.

## CAMPANIA
SOUTHERN ITALY

*Wine entries:* Asprino, Capri, Falerno del Massico, Fiano di Avellino, Greco di Tufo, Ischia, Lacryma Christi del Vesuvio, Ravello, Solopaca, Taurasi

This is the region centred on Naples; bustling, chaotic, where the black economy is *the* economy and theft is raised to an art form. And it's the region of Sorrento, Amalfi, Ravello, Capri – 'a little piece of heaven fallen on earth' as the holiday brochures smugly quote from the Italian original. Campania is a geologically unstable region, with Pompeii and Herculaneum monuments to Vesuvius' power and memories of the 1980 earthquake immovably lodged in Campanians' minds. And it is the region of wines such as Falerno, Fiano di Avellino, Greco di Tufo, Solopaca, Taurasi and others, some of them reaching cult status, some still little known, as well as home to the overrated Lacryma Christi del Vesuvio. Its 13,595 square km (5250 square miles) cover five provinces, of which by far the smallest, Naples itself, houses over half the population of just over 5·5 million. The vine, though, is most concentrated in the province of Benevento to the north-west.

Campania's face to the world is represented by just one estate, the highly respected Mastroberardino, which has more or less sewn up production of Greco di Tufo, Fiano di Avellino and Taurasi. Every region has at least one grape that it can proudly claim is theirs. Campania boasts four: red Piedirosso and white Fiano, Coda di Volpe and Falanghina. But Greco gives the 'taste' of the region for whites and Aglianico fields the greatest reds. So ancestry isn't everything.

## CAMPO FIORIN
Vino da tavola
VENETO

♥ Corvina, Rondinella, Molinara

Campo Fiorin could call itself Valpolicella DOC but doesn't. Masi, who produce the wine, prefer to carve out a separate identity for their *ripasso* – a wine made by enriching Valpolicella with the lees of *passito* Valpolicella – by a separate name. Whatever the label does or doesn't say, Campo Fiorin is textbook *ripasso* Valpolicella: plenty of bitter cherries, spice, coffee and leather, plenty of suppleness, more richness, weight and alcohol than straight Valpolicella, but less than Amarone. Best years: 1988, '86, '85 and '83.

## CANNONAU

It is fitting that Cannonau, Sardinia's most important red grape, comes from Spain where it is called Garnacha – many aspects of the north of the island have a Spanish feel from Castilian rule. Cannonau is made in all sorts of ways. It can be dry, medium or sweet; fortified, dry or sweet; averagely alcoholic, pretty alcoholic, or self-igniting; deep purple, mid-ruby, or insipid; all stainless steel and modernity, or all wood and mellowness (or oxidation). Apart from the sweet, fortified, *passito* Anghelu Ruju, it tends to be aged, alcoholic and best avoided if made artisanally in Sardinia's hinterland, and lightish, dusty, savoury and simply quaffable when produced elsewhere by the most advanced co-operatives. Cannonau di Sardegna is DOC; Cannonau di Alghero and Cannonau del Parteolla aren't, and so, free of DOC restrictions, can be as young or as low in alcohol as their makers wish. Best producers: C.S. di Dolianova and Sella & Mosca. Drink it as soon as you buy it.

## CAPITEL SAN ROCCO
**Vino da tavola**
VENETO

Corvina, Rondinella, Molinara and others

Garganega, Durella and others

Like several producers in Valpolicella, Renzo Tedeschi makes, apart from Valpolicella and powerful Amarone, a *ripasso* Valpolicella, a sort of half-way house between the two, which he calls Capitel San Rocco. It has more of the Amarone style about it than most other *ripasso* Valpolicellas, with a bitter-sweet, coffee and cherries taste and is reliably cheering at three to eight years old. Best years: 1986, '85, '83, '81.

Tedeschi also grows white grapes, mostly Garganega, the Soave variety. But you can't make Soave in Valpolicella, however good your wine may be. So Tedeschi's white also parades as Capitel San Rocco, theoretically just a 'simple' *vino da tavola*. If only most Soave producers managed such concentration of creamy, almondy flavour! It easily doubles the 18-month life-span of most Soave too.

## CAPRI DOC
CAMPANIA

Piedirosso and others

Falanghina, Greco, Biancolella

I suppose it is nice if you are holidaying on Capri to drink your very own local DOC to refresh you and lubricate your meals. And I suppose it might be nice to bring a few bottles back to keep your memory of the holiday alive. I can't see what other benefit there would be in uncorking a bottle of Capri though. The island may be beautiful and interesting enough to write home about, but the wine certainly isn't.

## CAREMA DOC
PIEDMONT

Nebbiolo

▲ The 40 hectares (100 acres) of Carema vineyard are high, chilly, windblown and cling to steep craggy slopes on the narrowest of terraces.

We might think wine-making is a full-time occupation. Yet Carema, without doubt the best wine of north Piedmont, is produced almost entirely by the evening and weekend pottering of commuters to Ivrea and Turin. They then part with their prized grapes to the co-operative or to a private producer such as the assiduous Luigi Ferrando. It is not easy work cultivating the grapes either. Viticulture is only possible because the Dora Baltea river flows swiftly through the district and keeps the air moving, therefore bringing sun to a narrow strip when all around is cloud-covered. If you find it difficult to believe the Nebbiolo grape can be elegant without losing its intrinsic character, try Carema. If you've never yet found the oft quoted violets in Nebbiolo, try Carema. If you want to see the wine at its best try Ferrando's Black Label – only produced in the best years, like 1985, '83, '82, '78, '74, '71; his normal label is white. Or try the Cantina Produttori's (co-op's) selected reserve wine, Carema Carema.

## CARMIGNANO DOC
TUSCANY

🍷 🍷 Sangiovese, Cabernet,
Canaiolo and others

In Carmignano, west of Florence, there is tons of evidence, from wine pots found in Etruscan tombs to citations in the 1300s and endless eulogies penned during the last four centuries, that the local wine has been revered. It is a remarkable pedigree. Rules for the wine's production were formulated in 1716 and the region's boundaries stipulated. Yet it took the authorities until 1975 to recognize Carmignano as a DOC, separate from the blanket of Chianti all around, and only then because of tireless work by Conte Ugo Contini Bonacossi of Villa di Capezzana, the area's sole consistently high-quality estate. Now they are more amenable and have agreed to upgrade Carmignano to DOCG. When this happens, Barco Reale (meaning Royal Property – a Medici term), younger and livelier in style but otherwise similar, will, with luck, fill the breach by becoming DOC.

Contini Bonacossi enshrined Cabernet in the blend because he managed to convince the bureaucrats of its traditional presence in the times of the Medici. The wine is elegant, classy, restrained – just what you would expect from the most charming, self-effacing member of the aristocracy you could ever hope to meet. Some vintages from before World War Two are still going strong and 1931 is legendary. Usually, though, the wines last well up to ten years with 1983 and '85 showing the form. The DOC also covers Rosato (Capezzana's pink is called Vinruspo and a sheer delight it is too) and Vin Santo.

## CARSO DOC
FRIULI-VENEZIA GIULIA

🍷 Terrano and others

🍷 Malvasia Istriana

The Carso DOC stretches in a thin strip between Yugoslavia and the Gulf of Trieste. The red wine is principally from Refosco, grown widely all over Friuli, but of a locally isolated clone called Terrano which, confusingly, is actually the Yugoslavian term for Refosco. It's dark coloured and of reasonably good, tangy, tarry, grassy flavour, if a little harsh and with an occasional tendency to hollowness.

The DOC regulations limited the number of styles of Carso to three: Carso DOC, a red with minimum 70 per cent Terrano; Terrano del Carso, with minimum 85 per cent Terrano; and white Carso Malvasia, made from the delicate, appley Malvasia Istriana grape – which bears only a passing resemblance to the apricotty Malvasia of further south. Drink the white young, the red after three or four years – if you can find it.

## CASTEL DEL MONTE DOC
PUGLIA

🍷 Uva di Troia, Bombino Nero,
Montepulciano, Sangiovese

🍷 Bombino Nero, Uva di Troia,
Montepulciano

🍷 Pampanuto, Trebbiano, Bombino
Bianco, Palumbo

Castel del Monte is inland, in the uplands west of Bari, and the comparative coolness those hills bring is a boon. Castel del Monte Rosso can be a hearty yet fragrant glassful reminiscent of rich strawberry jam, with a bitter-dry finish, fine at around three years old, even though Puglians may prefer it older. It owes its character to Uva di Troia, 'the grape from Troy', a gutsy, high-quality variety, which, when handled properly, makes wine that improves for up to a decade or more. Bombino Nero, on the other hand, develops less alcohol, retains good acidity and yields extract and colour quickly. This makes it a natural for rosés, and Castel del Monte Rosato is a surprisingly graceful fruity wine. I find myself at a loss, though, to capture the essential quality of Pampanuto, or Pampanino as it is sometimes called, that differentiates this Bianco from any one of a number of southern whites. Vaguely earthy, minerally, appley; there are far better things to drink. New varietal wines are now appearing from Aglianico and Pinot Nero (red), Aglianico (rosé) and Chardonnay, Sauvignon, Pinot Bianco and Pinot Nero (vinified white) for the whites.

The producer Rivera has cornered the market, especially with his rosé and his red Riserva, Il Falcone. Torre Sveva and Miali are good too. Best years: 1987, '85, '84, '83.

## CASTELLER DOC
TRENTINO

🍷 Schiava, Lambrusco, Merlot

▲ It can be a sticky, messy job picking grapes, but at least the typical pergola-training system used in Trentino provides shade against the autumn sun.

The character of Casteller belongs to Schiava, with its unusual but addictive raspberry-yogurt nature. A light red which may be no more than deep pink, its minimum alcohol is stipulated at only 10·5 per cent. It is one of Trentino's everyday, drink-it-and-forget-it wines, to be drunk young; less innocuous than the district's ubiquitous Valdadige, but less distinctive than its numerous single varietals. The production zone stretches along practically the entire length of the Trentino section of the river Adige but is not allowed to stray far from the river to right or left. Most of the grapes are mopped up by the co-operatives such as the huge Càvit or La Vinicola Sociale Aldeno, which ensure reliable, but unexceptional, quality.

## CASTELLI ROMANI
LAZIO

Head out of Rome south-eastwards, parallel with the coast, and after what seems like an interminable crawl through the suburbs, the view suddenly clears and you have the choice of two three-lane highways, streaking forwards at about 15 degrees to each other. In front is a ridge of hills. The roads lead up, one to the Colli Albani and the other to the Castelli Romani. The difference between the two zones geologically or climatically is imperceptible but they are usually separately defined areas of land. The more southerly Colli Albani are DOC; the Castelli Romani aren't but since they include the zones of Frascati, Marino, Montecompatri Colonna and Zagarolo, all of which *are* DOC, local pride is well satisfied.

White Castelli Romani wines are like unclassified Frascati, soft, creamy and nutty but somewhat dilute, or, as has been so aptly put, like frascati with a small f. Reds are minerally and like sweet cooked plums, but rather coarse, not too dissimilar to Cerveteri or Velletri. They all need drinking as young as possible and you'll be lucky to see one in anything other than a jug.

## CELLARO
**Vino da tavola**
SICILY

🍷 Nerello Mascalese, Nero d'Avola

🍷 Nerello Mascalese

🍷 Catarratto, Trebbiano, Inzolia

Sicily's best rosé comes from this co-operative, the embodiment of what most 'ordinary' Sicilian production ought to be like and a surprising find in the inauspicious hamlet of Sambuca di Sicilia, located in the west of the island, above Sciacca on the south coast. Instead of settling for obscurity, like other southern co-operatives, Cellaro called in Sicily's best consultant winemaker, refrigeration equipment (so necessary in a climate where summer can last till November and the harvest occurs in very hot conditions) was installed bit by bit as the money was found, and payments to growers based on grape quality (instead of quantity and alcoholic degree) were gradually introduced. The wines improved apace. The red has strawberry fruit and balanced tannin and acidity, the rosé is delicate with strawberry flavours too, the white is soft, almondy, perfumed. Cellaro wines are not great. They are not intended to be. They are, though, good value and far more characterful than all but the best wines from privately run estates.

## CEPPARELLO
**Vino da tavola**
TUSCANY

🍷 Sangiovese

In ten years Paolo de Marchi has turned from enthusiastic young Turk of the Chianti wine scene to producer of some of the most brilliant wines of the region. He is still young, he still has Turk-like tendencies and he still experiments – but now they work. Cepparello is his super-Tuscan, mainly from 40-year-old vines on his estate, Isole e Olena. His endless tinkering had shown him the potential of Sangiovese on its own before most of his peers. It has now found its mark with extended maceration and a year or more's *barrique*-ageing. The 1983 is legendary, the '85 has immense class and power and needs laying down for longer than temptation will permit, and the '86 has vibrant, plummy fruit and exhorts 'drink me'.

## CERASUOLO DI VITTORIA
**DOC**
SICILY

🍷 Frappato, Nero d'Avola

Even though I believe it is vital that wines retain their traditional grape varieties and characters and we, the drinkers, should learn to accommodate strange or initially unattractive styles I couldn't accept Cerasuolo di Vittoria. I had tried to appreciate its finer points, but it still struck me as oxidized and dull. It is meant to age splendidly for up to 30 years. It doesn't. Yet, in Sicily it is held in esteem. Coria is the name usually recommended. But what a revelation there was in 1988. A small, cossetted estate called C.O.S., which had already caught my interest with its powerful but clean 1984 and '85 wines, produced a wine that quite took my breath away. It was a shockingly deep red-purple, unique for Cerasuolo di Vittoria, and was full of pepper, spice, rich violets and blackberry perfume, with balanced acidity and firmness. Stunning! If this sort of wine is the future of Cerasuolo di Vittoria I'm first in the queue to stock up my cellar.

The name Cerasuolo means cherry-coloured. It doesn't necessarily imply a pale red/deep rosé: cherries include morellos!

## CERVETERI DOC
LAZIO

🍷 Sangiovese, Montepulciano, Cesanese and others

🍷 Trebbiano, Malvasia

The best reason for seeking out Cerveteri is to get a handle on a typical Roman red. A crueller soul would have said, 'to see why Romans drink white all the time!' Yet the grape mix is certainly promising, with all three major varieties highly rated in their home regions: Tuscany (Sangiovese), Abruzzo (Montepulciano) and Lazio (Cesanese) respectively. And Cerveteri Rosso, from the north of Lazio, along the coast south of Civitavecchia, is not all that bad when youngish, with its soft, minerally, sweet plums taste. The white is along Frascati lines, but with more creamy flavour than some and a little less squeaky clean than most. The co-operative controls most of the production.

## CHARDONNAY

Chardonnay grows more or less anywhere, produces something more or less interesting however it is handled, and has a taste that is universally admired and appreciated. No wonder it's so fashionable. There is scarcely a high-profile, or aspirant high-profile, Italian winemaker who hasn't been knocked sideways by Californian Chardonnay and isn't keen to emulate those big, buttery, biscuity wines. So the necessary *milioni* of lire are found, the sites located, the vines planted or regrafted and *de rigueur* new oak *barriques* bought. Even prime Nebbiolo sites in Piedmont aren't immune to the invasion. We are being asked to pay as if the wines were already good, when most of them are currently technically proficient, but rather lumpen. The best so far is Caparzo's 1986 'Le Grance' from Tuscany. Avignonesi's Il Marzocco and Lageder's Portico dei Leoni are also attracting great attention. But the Italians learn fast, so each vintage brings new developments and surprises. Those producing Chardonnays without oak have been quicker to achieve character and local style. Outstanding examples include Chardonnay di Capezzana (Tuscany), Terre Rosse's 'Giovanni Vallania' (Emilia) and Preludio No 1 by Torrebianco (Puglia).

The north-east of Italy was cultivating Chardonnay long before it became fashionable. Except it wasn't distinguished from Pinot Bianco (an unrelated variety) and both were lumped together as Pinot. It need hardly be said that once Chardonnay was the name everyone wanted on their labels research to sort out what was what proceeded at a remarkably swift pace and, would you believe it, there was far more Chardonnay around than had been imagined. Which means that you don't need an overly cynical mind to suspect that some of those pleasant but uninspiring Chardonnays from Trentino, Alto Adige, Friuli and so on contain a good dollop of Pinot Bianco too. Even at their best they tend to be subtle wines, delicately floral but tight and slender. Much Chardonnay also finds its way into *metodo classico* fizz.

## CHARDONNAY DELL'ALTO ADIGE DOC
ALTO ADIGE

♀ Chardonnay

A feather in the cap of the Alto Adige producers is that they were among the first to achieve a DOC for their Chardonnay. What a shame that so much does not realize its potential. It relies on two companies, Lageder and Tiefenbrunner, to keep the flag fluttering. Alto Adige has the capability to produce Chardonnay more excitingly steely-fresh and acutely varietal than from the rest of north-east Italy. Too often, although while clean and aromatic, it is rather indistinct and more reminiscent of Pinot Bianco (which itself is rather good rather often). Over-cropping must take much of the blame.

## CHIANTI DOCG
TUSCANY

♀ Sangiovese, Canaiolo, Trebbiano Toscano and others

Chianti is an enormous region, covering much of central Tuscany, producing practically a million hectolitres of wine, most of which is thankfully divided into seven sub-districts. If a wine doesn't come from a sub-district, or if its producer so opts, it will have no more glorious title than Chianti, plain and simple. This denomination is most commonly seen on the own-label Chiantis that flourish in supermarkets and high street chains or used for the basic wines of the major brands. The advantages are twofold: the large producers can buy grapes from wherever in the region suits them for consistency of quality and style and, even if the wine does come from one of the seven sub-districts, labels are kept simple. Most wine sold as plain Chianti is red-purple, youthful, tasting of tea and not-quite-ripe plums with a twist of bitterness on the after-taste. It can start tiring after as little as 18 months, though usually lasts a good bit longer. Sangiovese takes up 75 to 90 per cent of the blend. 'Others' can include Cabernet, up to ten per cent.

# CHIANTI

C hianti is a microcosm of the change in Italy's fortunes in the past few years. It used to typify our impressions of Italian wine: cheap, acidic, rough and not to be taken seriously. The mock wicker-covered flask, which supported many a lampshade and adorned innumerable restaurant walls and ceilings, was never more aptly named a *fiasco*. The arrival of DOC in 1967 for Chianti helped eliminate the most grossly fraudulent rubbish that masqueraded under its name. But few noticed. It wasn't until the early 1980s that the message seeped through that Chianti didn't taste that bad any more. But it was still a commodity wine: 'Chianti' was like a brand name and it was stuff to be bought as cheaply as possible and to be knocked back without thought.

Meanwhile, in the Chianti vineyards in central Tuscany, there had been a massive replanting programme. The clone of Sangiovese (the major Chianti grape) that found most favour was Sangiovese di Romagna, brought in from across the Apennines, primarily because it yielded highly. More grapes meant more wine which meant more income – that was the argument. As a result there was a glut of Chianti on the market and prices were forced down to below production costs. Producers either cut corners and cheated; turned to production of other wines (the first super-Tuscans); or plodded on regardless, bending the DOC rules to improve the quality of the wine and keeping their fingers crossed for the return of better times.

Relief came from a surprising source: the legal classification system. Chianti had been trying to win the (then) coveted DOCG for some time. It was approved suddenly, in a rush, growers being told to accept the accolade now or lose the opportunity. It was 1984, the poorest vintage of the decade and not a good moment for proclaiming the merits of a new, improved Chianti. Prophecies of gloom and doom abounded. Yet the fears were groundless. In just four years Chianti was profitable, of vastly superior quality and recognized as such. What had DOCG done?

It had reduced the maximum yield, eliminated the need for large quantities of white grapes in the blend and withdrawn the right from the three best sub-districts (Chianti Classico, Colli Fiorentini and Rufina) to add a proportion of grapes or must from outside the growing region (for that, read southern Italy). It also still permitted the inclusion of up to 10 per cent other grapes (for that, read Cabernet).

These days high-calibre Chianti is abundant and the number of estates turning it out is increasing. That is not to say everything in the garden is rosy. There is still too much Sangiovese di Romagna around, testing growers' resolves to keep yields contained; the whiff of grapes from Puglia and Calabria can still be discerned from time to time; some super-Tuscans bear a startling resemblance to the same estate's Chianti (the super-Tuscan costs considerably more); not everyone selects the grapes destined for the longer-aged and image-carving *Riservas* strictly enough. Nevertheless, the turn-around in fortunes is unprecedented and the general improvement is phenomenal.

▲ A classic Chianti landscape with cypress trees and vines.

| WINE ENTRIES |
| --- |
| Chianti |
| Chianti Classico |
| Chianti Colli Aretini |
| Chianti Colli Fiorentini |
| Chianti Colli Senesi |
| Chianti Colline Pisane |
| Chianti Montalbano |
| Chianti Rufina |

| GRAPE ENTRIES |
| --- |
| Cabernet Sauvignon |
| Malvasia |
| Sangiovese |
| Trebbiano |

Regional boundary

Chianti DOCG
1. Classico
2. Colli Aretini
3. Colli Fiorentini
4. Colli Senesi
5. Colline Pisane
6. Montalbano
7. Rufina

N

0    50 km
0       50 miles

TUSCANY

39

# CHIANTI CLASSICO DOCG
TUSCANY

 Sangiovese, Canaiolo, Trebbiano Toscano and others

The Classico is Chianti's heartland, the central area between Florence and Siena that was first delineated in 1716 and whose territory was last defined, a little more extensively, in 1932. Classico growers will make much of the innate superiority of this 'classic' zone, but don't believe them too religiously. It's true most of the best Chianti comes from the Classico, but there are several non-Classico estates that can knock spots off their 'superior' cousins.

Chianti Classico is the heart of innovation. There are more 'experimental' wines here than anywhere else in Chianti. Abundant use is made of Cabernet as an 'other' variety. Super-Tuscans are rife: practically every estate has at least one high-priced *vino da tavola*. Most are straight Sangiovese, or Sangiovese-Cabernet blends, and *barrique*-ageing features heavily. In the late 1980s investigations were started into the character of the various communes of the area. For a long time producers in Radda, for example, knew that their wines had a particular character that made them different from those in Panzano or Castellina, say, but could not define or explain that character. Now, by soil analyses and tastings, the information is being pieced together but tantalizingly slowly. There is also a major plan to prepare for the turn of the century when many of the vineyards will need replanting, by propagating the best clones possible to underpin the continuing drive for better quality. Chianti is alive with new ideas and experiments.

When DOCG was established in 1984 the Classico was given special dispensation to keep the amount of the undesirable white Trebbiano and Malvasia grapes down to two to five per cent – which in effect means zero, as these levels are undetectable. Everywhere else in Chianti had to have five to ten per cent. The Classico also, along with the Rufina and Colli Fiorentini sub-districts, lost its right to add grape must from outside the zone – and quite right too. That the other districts can still get away with bunging in the odd tank-load of soup-up juice from the south shows the power of political influence over common sense.

Great years like 1988, '85 and '83 bring forth superb Classico wines and brilliant Riservas usually best around six years old. Drink others sooner. Top producers include Badia a Coltibuono, Capannelle, Castellare, Castell'in Villa, Castello dei Rampolla, Castello di Ama, Castello di Cacchiano, Castello di Querceto, Castello di San Polo in Rosso, Castello di Volpaia, Castello Vicchiomaggio, Chianti Geografico, Fattoria di Vistarenni, Fattoria di Felsina, Fontodi, Fossi, Isole e Olena, Lamole, Monsanto, Montagliari, Monte Vertine, Pagliarese, Poggio al Sole, Riecine, San Felice, Vecchie Terre di Montefili and Villa Cafaggio.

# CHIANTI COLLI FIORENTINI DOCG
TUSCANY

 Sangiovese, Canaiolo, Trebbiano Toscano and others

The 'Florentine Hills' sub-district is partly sandwiched between Florence and the northern limit of the Classico, which it also partly envelops. At its best it is indistinguishable from refined Classico, at its worst deadly boring. Both young, light quaffers and more serious, aged numbers are produced. Producers worth trying include Fattoria dell'Ugo, Fattoria Lilliano, La Querce, Pasolini dall'Onda Borghese, Uggiano. Best years: 1988, '85, '82.

# CHIANTI MONTALBANO DOCG
TUSCANY

 Sangiovese, Canaiolo, Trebbiano Toscano and others

Lying west of Florence, between Pistoia and Empoli, Chianti Montalbano would be hardly worthy of mention were it not that it is also the zone of Carmignano (slopes can belong to one denomination or the other, not both) which contains some pretty go-ahead winemakers. They produce light, easy-drinking Chiantis, which gain nothing from more than a brief ageing. Best producer: Villa di Capezzana; Fattoria di Artimino is also good. Best years: 1988, '85, '82.

## CHIANTI RUFINA DOCG
TUSCANY

🍷 Sangiovese, Canaiolo, Trebbiano Toscano and others

Rufina (pronounced 'Roo-fi-na' and not to be confused with the huge producer Ruffino who has cellars there) has sound claims to be held in high consideration; as high, or higher, dare I say, than the Classico. It is the smallest Chianti sub-district with just 12,500 hectares (30,000 acres) and lies east of Florence, centred on Pontassieve. The soils are like those of the central Classico but most vineyards are higher and the microclimate is different, giving superb style potential and higher acid levels. Hence the wines age better – a great cachet, especially on foreign markets where drinkers seem to equate longevity with quality. Vintages like 1977, '75, '68 (stupendous), '65 and even '58, if found, can still provide memorable drinking. 1984 is best avoided; '83 and '86 need a little patience; '82, '85, '88 need lots. The best producer is undoubtedly Fattoria Selvapiana, followed by Frescobaldi (Montesodi and Castello di Nipozzano wines).

## CHIANTI COLLI ARETINI DOCG, COLLI SENESI DOCG, COLLINE PISANE DOCG
TUSCANY

🍷 Sangiovese, Canaiolo, Trebbiano Toscano and others

Three Chianti sub-districts get ignominiously lumped together because, at the risk of offending lots of egos, they may be geographically separated but they are qualitatively similar. Colli Aretini is scattered in various parcels between the east of the Classico and Arezzo. Invigorating acidity is the wines' hallmark. Best producer: Villa Cilnia.

Colli Senesi is the largest sub-district, scattered extensively south of the Classico, and around Montalcino and Montepulciano. If there is a distinguishing feature it is body and alcohol. Good producers are mainly those like Avignonesi, Fattoria del Cerro and Poliziano who are also good Vino Nobile di Montepulciano or Brunello di Montalcino producers. Amorosa and Il Poggiolo are also worth a try. Colline Pisane is in the west of the region, south of Pisa and behind Livorno. Its wines are light and soft. All these Chiantis are best drunk without much age. Best years: 1988, '85, '82.

## CINQUETERRE DOC
LIGURIA

🍷 Bosco, Albarola, Vermentino

You need tenacity to track down Cinqueterre. It is a slip of a zone (in 1985 only 3300 hectolitres were produced) just west of La Spezia, on the border with Tuscany. The vines are planted on precipitous terraces along the coast, some of which can only be reached from the sea. Despite its erstwhile fame standards had slipped shamefully in recent years until the co-operative made the leap from complacency to action. It is called Riomaggiore Manarola Corniglia – just imagine asking for a bottle in a restaurant. Apart from 'normal' Cinqueterre there's the rare Sciacchetrà, a *passito* version. If you manage to get a bottle keep it safe from other inquisitive souls who might snaffle it or drink it fast.

## CIRÒ DOC
CALABRIA

🍷🍷 Gaglioppo, Trebbiano Toscano, Greco Bianco

🍷 Greco Bianco, Trebbiano Toscano

Cirò has been around since the times of Ancient Greece when it was known as Cremissa – a much prettier name – and, so the story goes, was the wine given to Olympic winners all those years ago to toast their success. To retain the tradition, the modern-day Italian Olympic team still gets Cirò rations. It is also Calabria's best known wine.

The red is the standard bearer, and the best chance to see Gaglioppo, Calabria's most important red grape, show its paces. I get the feeling that red Cirò could well be an excellent beast: structured, weighty, with concentrated fruit, spice and a touch of chocolate – if only I could find the right bottle, perhaps from the Classico zone. The rosé can be coarse and alcoholic; the colder it is, the better it tastes. The white ought to be good. But from the dull, flabby wines of yesteryear, to the too-cold fermented, crisp, pleasant but characterless wines of today, it has yet to find its way. Best known producer: Librandi.

## COLLI ALTOTIBERINI DOC
UMBRIA

♞ ♟ Sangiovese, Merlot,
Trebbiano Toscano and others

♟ Trebbiano Toscano, Malvasia and
others

The Tiber is a much longer river than you'd imagine from a trip to Rome. It rises way up north and flows right through Umbria before heading down to the Eternal City. In its upper reaches, the Alto Tiberini, there are hills, the medieval city, Città di Castello, which pulls in a few tourists, and vines. If you happen to be there try a glassful of something to help down lunch. Otherwise don't bother. The best even their fiercest champions can find to say about the wines is that because the region lies close to Chianti, Marche and Romagna, any wines made there just must be good.

## COLLI BERICI DOC
VENETO

♞ Cabernet Franc, Cabernet
Sauvignon, Merlot, Tocai Rosso

♟ Garganega, Pinot Bianco,
Sauvignon, Tocai Bianco

Colli Berici, just south of Vicenza, may have had an illuminating past, but after replanting following the arrival of the bug phylloxera which destroyed much of the vineyards, its illustrious history ground swiftly to a halt. You may get some decent wines; possibly some grassy Cabernet, some succulent, fruit-cakey Merlot or some steely Pinot Bianco – but don't count on it. The best producers, Lazzarini (of Villa del Ferro) and Conte da Schio (of Costozza) often don't even bother with DOC. In Padua the zone metamorphoses into Colli Euganei.

## COLLI BOLOGNESI DOC
EMILIA

♞ Barbera, Cabernet Sauvignon,
Merlot

♟ Pignoletto, Pinot Bianco,
Riesling Italico, Sauvignon

Most of Emilia-Romagna is unrelieved pancake so the odd outcrops of hills bring great relief. The Colli Bolognesi may not be the highest range of hills in the world, but 100 metres (330 feet) or so helps enormously, especially when the slopes are so conveniently angled. The best thing about Colli Bolognesi is the estate Terre Rosse. There are 20 hectares (50 acres) of vine, not even a splinter of oak barrel, and a wonderfully refined Cabernet Sauvignon, excellent Chardonnay and Pinot Bianco, and remarkable Sauvignon, Riesling and Malvasia.

## COLLI ORIENTALI DEL FRIULI DOC
FRIULI-VENEZIA GIULIA

♞ Cabernet Franc, Cabernet
Sauvignon, Merlot, Pinot Nero,
Refosco, Schioppettino

♞ Merlot

♟ Chardonnay, Malvasia Istriana,
Picolit, Pinot Bianco, Pinot Grigio,
Ribolla, Riesling Renano,
Sauvignon, Tocai, Traminer
Aromatico, Verduzzo

Colli Orientali is the number two wine district in Friuli in north-eastern Italy; Collio is number one. So say most of the books – and also the producers in Collio. When you come down to the facts you will find that grudges, sulks and local politics have more to do with it than the wines themselves. Colli Orientali scores Brownie points for its 'sole rights' to the delicately floral sweet Picolit and the brambly Schioppettino, also for its new zonal DOC, Ramandolo, covering prime sweet Verduzzo territory. But as far as the quality potential of the wines is concerned, there's little to choose between the two districts.

Colli Orientali's aromatic, restrained, youthful whites, especially the lemony native Ribolla, the salty Pinot Bianco and the broader nutty Pinot Grigio are made to captivate you slowly, not bowl you over at first sip; while its reds, from grassy, blackcurranty Cabernet, to redcurranty Merlot, tangy, tarry Refosco, and, increasingly successfully, Pinot Nero, are firm, ripe and rounded from three years of age (less for Merlot) to several more. 1988 is excellent, '86 and '85 good. Of the numerous good producers Abbazia di Rosazzo, Giovanni Dri, Ronchi di Cialla, Ronco del Gnemiz, Ronco di Fornaz and Volpe Pasini stand out.

## COLLI PERUGINI DOC
UMBRIA

♞ ♟ Sangiovese, Montepulciano,
Ciliegiolo and others

♟ Trebbiano Toscano, Verdicchio,
Grechetto and others

Umbria is certainly worth a trip. There are fascinating Etruscan remains, the glorious Lake Trasimeno for calm, freshwater swimming, and the town of Perugia with its urban sprawl below and its cobbled medieval town above. Perugia's edible temptations are its wine and its chocolates. There's no competition. Go for the chocs. The wines aren't bad; they will quench your thirst pleasantly enough. But Trebbiano needs intense dedication to get anything out of it, and if you've had Sangiovese elsewhere, Perugia's reds just don't bear comparison.

## COLLI PIACENTINI DOC
EMILIA

🍷 Barbera, Bonarda, Pinot Nero

🥂 Malvasia, Ortrugo, Pinot Grigio, Sauvignon

▼ Fine wine begins in the vineyard. These well-tended vines, belonging to Mario Schiopetto who makes some of Collio's greatest wines, are a perfect example.

A quirk of the regional arrangement has the boundary between Emilia and Lombardy come plumb through a prime viticultural area. The result is one district with two names: Colli Piacentini (Emilia) and Oltrepò Pavese (Lombardy), miles away (literally as well as figuratively) from the typically Emilian Lambrusco. Colli Piacentini is an umbrella DOC, covering various sub-denominations and varietal wines. The jewel is Gutturnio, a brilliant raspberry, truffly, mocha blend of Bonarda with 55 to 70 per cent Barbera. Monterosso Val d'Arda, Trebbianino Val Trebbia and Val Nure are all light spritzy whites, often *amabile*, from a mixture of aromatic grapes (Malvasia and Moscato), damped down with Trebbiano and localized by the indigenous Ortrugo. Best producer across the board: Fugazza, who usually use the Romito label for their Colli Piacentini wines.

## COLLIO DOC
FRIULI-VENEZIA GIULIA

🍷 Cabernet Franc, Merlot, Pinot Nero

🥂 Malvasia Istriana, Pinot Bianco, Pinot Grigio, Ribolla, Riesling Italico, Sauvignon, Tocai, Traminer

If you want to understand Italian white wines give yourself a week or more drinking nothing but whites from Collio. At first you may well find them all rather similar and uninspiring. Then you get accustomed to their deliberate understatement; begin to understand their subtlety and start enjoying them as excellent food partners. If, after your indoctrination period, you delve into a good rich Chardonnay from some other country, I guarantee you will find it outrageously big and brash and wonder how on earth you could ever have admired such a crude monster. Once used to the whites – all single varietals except one blend called just Collio – try the reds. They used to be nothing like as good as the whites. But quality is improving fast.

Collio is an arc of land along the Yugoslav border. The grapes are a mix of local, French and German. It's the local ones (like Ribolla) which are held in lowest esteem, unnecessarily so, while everyone loves fashionable Pinot Grigio and refined Pinot Bianco, and would love Tocai if only there were not so much of it on the plains further west. It is Collio's hill ridge which enables the growers to get much higher quality than in the plains of Grave del Friuli, and only sloping sites are entitled to the DOC. Most of the hill ridge ended up in Yugoslavia after World War Two. They say that all the best slopes were left in Italy and nobody with land right up on the unfenced confine *ever* brings grapes across. Well, they would, wouldn't they?

There is no shortage of good producers but, predictably, given the number of varietals they have to handle, not all are consistently good across their range. Of those that are, Jermann and Schiopetto set the tone. Look out also for Borgo Conventi, Caccese, Ca' Ronesca, Stelio Gallo, Gravner, Princic, Radikon, Russiz Superiore.

## COLTASSALA
**Vino da tavola**
TUSCANY

🍷 Sangiovese, Mammolo

If a concept as recent and dynamic as a super-Tuscan can have an archetype I reckon Coltassala is it. It has the necessary preponderance of Sangioveto (the smartest Sangiovese clone), the recommended year's ageing in those natty little barrels of new French oak, and every stage of its development is fussed over with mother hen-like care. Coltassala comes from a prime site (the estate of Castello di Volpaia) and it emerges spicy-rich, firm, elegant, classy and very, very Tuscan. 1982, '83 and '85 (not yet ready to drink) should give you the idea.

## CORVO
**Vino da tavola**
SICILY

🍷 Nerello Mascalese, Perricone, Nero d'Avola

🍷 Inzolia, Trebbiano, Catarratto

Clever old Corvo has got its name so well known that it is easy not to realize that this megalith of Sicilian wine-making is just the trading name of the Casa Vinicola Duca di Salaparuta, based at Casteldaccia near Palermo. Being a private company and having all the production as *vini da tavola* is incredibly convenient. It means grapes can be bought from anywhere on the island to achieve quality and consistency.

Corvo white isn't exciting, but it is fresh, with a touch of almonds. It needs drinking young. The dull, earthy stuff you get served too often in Italian restaurants is too old. The red has firm acidity and can be like steamy leather and meat stock. Quite why it is the mainstay of so many Italian restaurants defeats me. There is also a sparkling wine and a long-aged, fortified *stravecchio*.

The estate has decided, though, to nail its banners to the mast with two super-*vini da tavola*. The white, Colomba Platino meaning Platinum Dove (Corvo means crow) has a high proportion of aromatic Inzolia making it more fragrant than Corvo's ordinary white. The red is called Duca Enrico and 1984, the first vintage, appeared in 1989. It has been aged in *barriques* of course and its rather voluptuous jammy, pruny fruit is saturated with oakiness. To make you understand just how 'super' these two wines are there are super-inflated price tags to go with them.

## DOLCETTO

Apparently a whole generation of embryonic Dolcetto slurpers has steered clear of the wine, using tourist Italian to convince themselves that it is sweet. The name is certainly a diminutive of *dolce* but the sweetness is that of the grape juice, not the wine. Dolcetto, the wine, is as dry as most reds, although its vibrant gulpable quality and not over-high acidity can give a sensation of sweetness like ripe berry fruits. Dolcetto's home is south-western Piedmont, where it is grown alongside the flag-waving Nebbiolo and the prolific Barbera.

In Piedmont it proudly sports no less than seven DOCs, clustered close together in two, practically adjacent pieces of land in the south-west of the region. Dolcetto di Ovada had some stunning, firmly structured wines, all produced by Giuseppe Poggio. Since he sadly died, there are no more. Dolcetto d'Acqui is characteristically soft and light, rated most highly by the citizens of Acqui (try Viticoltori dell'Acquese); Dolcetto d'Asti is similarly light and forward, undoubtedly the most elevated, according to the growers of Asti (Brema, Carnevale); and so on. The proponents of the refined Dolcetto from the tiny enclave of Diano d'Alba even include some from outside the zone, which is encouraging (Fontanafredda's *cru* La Lepre). Next door is Dogliani, with its rich, perfumed Dolcetto (Chionetto), and the Langhe Monregalesi, which is all name and no wine. In Liguria Dolcetto calls itself Ormeasco and is grown along the western half (the Ponente). Light, fresh and bouncy in youth, the wine goes enticingly soft and rounded – if you can resist the temptation to consume it sooner. It is rarely found outside Piedmont and Liguria.

Its acidity level is one aspect that endears it to its many enthusiasts. Another is that it ripens early, three or four weeks before Nebbiolo. This reduces risks to the crop because the later in the season you get in Piedmont, the less reliable the weather. In 1988 and '87, for example, the long, dry summer eventually spluttered to a close in a torrential downpour. Dolcetto was by then safely picked, Nebbiolo was deluged.

Most Dolcetto is made to be drunk young when its flavours are at their most thrilling. The exceptions are vintages like 1985 when the wines were so unusually big and powerful that they needed at least a year or two to tone down before they were approachable. The Piedmontese condemned the vintage as untypical – others loved it. There are also various producers who always age Dolcetto to give a more mellow quality.

## DOLCETTO D'ALBA DOC
PIEDMONT

🍷 Dolcetto

Among Piedmont's seven Dolcetto DOCs, Dolcetto d'Alba stands out, not necessarily for intrinsic quality – that would be tempting the wrath of the other six – but for the number of high class producers turning out infinitely gluggable wines. This is not so surprising when you consider that although many of these producers make Barolo and/or Barbaresco and often Barbera too, it's actually Dolcetto that they drink at practically every meal. Within the area you will find the whole gamut of Dolcetto styles. Good producers are legion, among them Altare, Bovio, Brovia, Castello di Neive, Cavallotto, Cigliuti, Clerico, Cogno-Marcarini, Aldo Conterno, Giacomo Conterno, Cordero di Montezemolo, Gaja, Bruno Giacosa, Glicine, Grasso, Bartolo Mascarello, Giuseppe Mascarello, Pelissero, Prunotto, Ratti, Rinaldi, Sandrone, Scavino, Secondo Pasquero Elia, Aurelio Settimo, Vajra, Vietti, Roberto Voerzio.

## DONNAFUGATA
Vino da tavola
SICILY

🍷 Nero d'Avola, Nerello Cappuccio, Pignatello

🍷 Nerello Mascalese and others

🍷 Catarratto, Inzolia, Grecanico

Donnafugata hails from good, old vines planted 300–400 metres (1000–1300 feet) high around Santa Margherita Belice towards the south-west of the island. The ethos behind the wines is to choose the moment of harvesting to optimize the acidity and so ensure longevity. In some years, though, there isn't enough behind the acidity to make the ageing harmonious. But they are certainly superior to your normal Sicilian quaffer. The red, when on form, is a strapping beast of good structure which opens to coffee and truffles after about five years. The white is delicately almondy. There is also a rosé, a light *frizzante* white called Damaskino from the Damaschino grape, and a creamy *cru* white, Vigna di Gabri, that has had a short stay in wood.

# EMILIA-ROMAGNA

LOMBARDY     VENETO

*Po*

*Piacenza*

COLLI PIACENTINI

*Po*

*Po*

• *Ferrara*

*Parma*   *Panaro*   2

BOSCO ELICEO

*Reggio Emilia* •   1   3

*Reno*

*Modena* •   4

*Bologna* •

TREBBIANO DI ROMAGNA

COLLI DI PARMA

Red wines

White wines

Red and white wines

Regional boundary

BIANCO DI SCANDIANO

*Enza*

COLLI BOLOGNESI

*Imola* •

*Ravenna* •

*Faenza* •

*Forlì* •

ALBANA DI ROMAGNA

TREBBIANO DI ROMAGNA

*Secchia*

*Reno*

5   *Cesena* •

*Rimini* •

San Marino

1. Lambrusco Reggiano
2. Lambrusco Salamino di S. Croce
3. Lambrusco di Sorbara
4. Lambrusco Grasparossa di Castelvetro
5. Pagadebit di Romagna

TUSCANY

SANGIOVESE DI ROMAGNA

MARCHE

0   30 km
0   20 miles

▼ New plantings in Romagna. The vines extend into the horizon and the rare slope is prized by vine-growers.

| WINE ENTRIES | GRAPE ENTRIES |
|---|---|
| Albana di Romagna | Barbera |
| Barbarossa | Bonarda |
| Colli Bolognesi | Cabernet Sauvignon |
| Colli Piacentini | Lambrusco |
| Gutturnio | Malvasia |
| Lambrusco | Merlot |
| Lambrusco di Sorbara | Pinot Bianco |
| Lambrusco Grasparossa di | Pinot Grigio |
| Castelvetro | Pinot Nero |
| Lambrusco Salamino di Santa Croce | Riesling Italico |
| Pagadebit di Romagna | Sangiovese |
| Ronco dei Ciliegi | Sauvignon |
| Sangiovese di Romagna | Trebbiano |
| Trebbiano di Romagna | |

One region, two districts (Emilia in the west and Romagna in the east), three wines, is the simple way to summarize this huge region, stretching almost across northern Italy.

Its northern border, for practically Emilia-Romagna's entire length, is the slow meandering river Po. Most of the region is therefore fertile plain and excruciatingly flat – at least until far south of the east–west motorway that bisects the region, where the Apennines start to rise. The climate is searingly hot and sticky in summer, freezing and damp in winter, and in between fog, fog and more fog.

The plain is rich in milk and milk products (such as Parmesan cheese), meat and meat products (such as prosciutto and salami) and fruit. The place of wine in all this is revealed most eloquently by the wine lists of Bologna's many fine restaurants. There will be a long flight of Tuscan reds, whites from Friuli and so on, then just a brace of Lambruscos and maybe one or two other reds and a white from the region.

For decent wine you need slopes, unless the vine happens to be Lambrusco. This is therefore Lambrusco territory. It flourishes over huge swathes of the centre of the region, in Emilia around Modena and Reggio Emilia, where most of it is DOC, and further afield, where it is not.

The second important wine zone is in Romagna in the east of the region and stretches from south-east of Bologna to the Adriatic coast. The area is simply delimited, with three varietals, Albana, Sangiovese and Trebbiano, with 'di Romagna' appended to their name. Production is restricted to south of the ancient Via Emilia, where there are the first, faint beginnings of the Apennine foothills, except for Trebbiano, which is allowed to flourish north across the plain almost to Ravenna.

The third wine zone, Colli Piacentini, is set well apart, in uplands (hooray), tucked away in the far north-west of Emilia. With Lombardy next door, and Piedmont just a hop away, these wines are north-west Italian in style, with indigenous Bonarda and Barbera presiding over a clutch of local and French grape varieties. As a little icing on the three-zone cake, there are blobs of viticulture scattered around elsewhere, particularly by the coast (Bosco Eliceo) and on the low hills around Parma and Bologna (Colli di Parma and Colli Bolognesi).

## ELBA DOC
TUSCANY

🍷 Sangiovese, Canaiolo, Trebbiano Toscano, Biancone

🥂 Trebbiano Toscano and others

It is rather fun getting to Elba if you avoid the ferry. You squeeze into a tiny eight-seater plane at Pisa airport which bumps and sways along the coast and across the narrow strait to the island, flying so low you follow your path with a road map. Those of a nervous disposition are advised to avoid travelling on windy days. It is a fascinating little island, the shape of a corkscrew with a cork in and well endowed with wines. The whites are no duller than most Tuscan whites, the reds are usually on the light side and Chianti-esque. The estate to go for is La Chiusa, or track down a small grower called Lupi Rocchi.

## ELEGIA
Vino da tavola
TUSCANY

🍷 Sangiovese

Calling a wine Elegia either means that its producer has been more carried away than usual by his vinous masterpiece or they are beginning to have real trouble in Tuscany thinking up new, valid names for their proliferating super-Tuscans. Its producer, Federico Carletti, guided by his consultant winemaker, has done a wizard job in raising the level of his Vino Nobile di Montepulciano estate, Poliziano in south-east Tuscany, from an also-ran to a front-runner.

Elegia was first made in 1983, then in '85 and '86. It comes from the same Prugnolo vines, a Sangiovese clone, that form the major part of Poliziano's Vino Nobile, with part of its ageing a year in *barriques* and so tastes like an intense Vino Nobile imbued with massive oakiness. The wine therefore needs plenty of time for its flavours to integrate, soften and harmonize.

## ERBALUCE DI CALUSO DOC
PIEDMONT

🥂 Erbaluce

They told me there was progress afoot in Erbaluce. Since 1980 this small area producing not bad but by no means brilliant lean, flinty dry whites for drinking young and occasional sparklers from the Erbaluce grape has doubled to more than 60 hectares (150 acres), they said, although production has only increased by 15 per cent to 3000 hectolitres. This is another depressing example of how, despite considerable over-production and declining consumption patterns nationwide, a common Italian idea of 'progress' means churning out yet more wine. But at least yields per hectare have decreased, so maybe there's hope of more memorable wine in the future, from around the village of Caluso in north-west Piedmont. Best producers: Renato Bianco, Colombaio di Candia and Luigi Ferrando.

## EST! EST!! EST!!! DI MONTEFIASCONE DOC
LAZIO

🥂 Trebbiano Toscano, Malvasia Bianca, Trebbiano Giallo

If you haven't yet heard the tale, told every time the wine is mentioned, about how Est! Est!! Est!!! got its name, six exclamation marks and all, you will no doubt rush to buy some on learning it came from the testimony of a twelfth-century boozy bishop's servant. Apparently, he was so enthused by the stuff that his normal sign to his master of the best drinking holes was given triple effect. If, by some quirk, the wine at Montefiascone *was* so good 800 years ago, they certainly couldn't have been using Trebbiano to make it, not unless ideas of 'good' were very different then.

Est! Est!! Est!!! at least has the decency to be produced around Lake Bolsena, tucked away in a northern corner of Lazio, sandwiched between Tuscany and Umbria where it won't embarrass Lazio's majority, the Romans. Its standard used to be so poor its producers must have believed they could sell it by legend alone. Thank goodness they appear to have been disabused of that idea. Some of the wine is even tasty. The Montefiascone co-operative is leading the way and has gone for the ultimate turnabout – *serious* triple-Est from a *cru*. Falesco and Mazziotti are also good. Drink young.

## ETNA DOC
SICILY

🍷 🍷 Nerello Mascalese, Nerello Cappuccio and others

🍷 Carricante, Catarratto, Trebbiano, Minella Bianca

Etna is more than just one volcano. In fact, it is a whole clump of them, covering a huge tract of east Sicily, with Etna itself the major peak, 3323 metres (10,900 feet) high. The wine is honestly named. The vineyards do indeed grow on the sides of the volcano, but only on its east side, forming a long, narrow crescent at the comparatively low altitudes of 500–1000 metres (1640–3280 feet). Nevertheless, it is high enough to mean that while you might be sunbathing on the coast you'd need a thick jumper up among the vines. The altitude is a major positive factor shaping the wines, the black volcanic soil another.

If you can't get to grips with traditional Barolo, don't even try traditional red Etna. It is harsh, tannic, alcoholic – a real mouth-attacker. When you recover from the blow you are too stunned to remember if there was any fruit there or not. Some age for 20 years or more before softening, by which time any fruit there was has gone. Others are made in a less aggressive mould, with producers only just getting the hang of making them more approachable yet not more prone to oxidization.

Etna white is the weirdest mixture of acidity and earthy flatness – yet it works! It may be just imagination but it really seems to smell volcanic, *not* sulphury. The Superiore has more of the remarkable grape Carricante, up to 100 per cent. The rosé is an also-ran.

Many people (including me) believe Etna, particularly the red, could be a world-beater. (Some local enthusiasts believe it already is.) Winemakers, researchers, technicians, academics – all are homing in on Etna. Barone di Villagrande is the leading producer of 'accessible' wines, Torrepalino (Solicchiata) the leading traditionalist, and Barone Scammacco is fast on the ascendant.

## IL FALCONE
## Castel del Monte DOC
PUGLIA

🍷 Montepulciano, Uva di Troia, Bombino Nero, Sangiovese

This, the best wine from the most esteemed producer of Castel del Monte, the pride of Bari, has been proposed as the best red of all Puglia – a mighty plaudit. The producer is Rivera, with enviably sited vineyards surrounding the thirteenth-century Castle of Monte itself. Il Falcone is his Castel del Monte Riserva and its fortune is in no little measure due to a bumped-up level of Montepulciano – well past the 35 per cent maximum red Castel del Monte should theoretically have. But no-one there seems to mind too much, so why should we? It has good structure and keeping power and is a 'serious', earthy, minerally, liquorice-like wine with a ten-year ageing potential. But Puglia's number one? I don't reckon so. Look for 1984, '83.

## FALERNO DEL MASSICO DOC
CAMPANIA

🍷 🍷 Aglianico, Primitivo, Piedirosso

🍷 Falanghina

The fabled wine of the Roman heyday was Falernum, so documents tell us. The nearest we can get to it is a wine called Falerno, which may or may not bear more relation to its illustrious forebear than its name and area of production, which straddles the south of Lazio and the north of Campania. Or straddled, I should say, because after 25 years of discussion and intensive recent advocacy by the men from Villa Matilde (one of the only two estates worth taking seriously, Moio is the other) 'ancient' Falerno has been recognized as a 'modern' DOC, with its approved coastal territory kept firmly the Campanian side of the border. Red Falerno is rich, full, earthy, truffly, sometimes verging on baked, and has a strong bitter finish. I'm not convinced it ages as well as it is supposed to; about six years seems the limit. It might stand a better chance with less wood ageing, say down to the one year minimum. The broad, milk-like white comes from the under-exploited, anciently noble Falanghina grape which, if handled well, ought to make you sit up and take notice – which it doesn't often enough. There is also a milky, strawberry, rose-like rosé and a Primitivo-only version of the red.

## FARA DOC
PIEDMONT

🍷 Nebbiolo, Vespolina, Bonarda

Up in the Novara-Vercelli hills, Fara has given its name to the 15 hectares (37 acres) or so of vineyard around it. A scant 600 hectolitres of wine comes from them, at its best firm and violetty four or more years from the vintage. Best producers: Ferrardi, Bianchi, Castaldi. Best vintages: 1988, '86, '85, '82.

## FARO DOC
SICILY

🍷 Nerello Mascalese, Nerello Cappuccio, Nocera and others

I suppose it makes sense to call a wine that comes from the rocky north-east tip of Sicily where it nearly joins mainland Italy, 'Lighthouse' (*faro* in Italian). And I suppose it is reasonable to keep a DOC alive for just one or two small producers – after all, there are others, in Piedmont at least, in the same situation. But from what little Faro is made, it is not all that easy to assess the potential quality of the zone. Bagni keeps the flame ignited. The seriousness of his approach isn't in doubt, neither his dedication or conviction. He devotedly makes his wine as he always has, and pours his older samples with pride. But I do find them rather too oxidized for most modern wine drinkers.

## FELDMARSCHALL
Vino da tavola
ALTO ADIGE

🍷 Müller-Thurgau

To be able to claim you have Italy's highest vineyard at over 1000 metres (3300 feet) and one of Europe's highest too is no bad thing. To plant the Germanic Müller-Thurgau variety there is inspired thinking. To turn out one of the purest, most elegant, whistle-clean, floral, aromatic, aristocratic incarnations of that variety is the result of exceptionally careful vine-tending and skilful wine-making. Congratulations, Mr Tiefenbrunner, and long may your Feldmarschall vineyard thrive.

If you can get your hands on a bottle, either try it young when it rather shyly shows its potential or have patience for at least three years during which time it will be closed and ungiving. Then you can revel in its brilliance when it emerges from its chrysalis. If the vintage isn't good enough, the wine isn't made.

## FIANO DI AVELLINO DOC
CAMPANIA

♀ Fiano, Greco, Coda di Volpe, Trebbiano Toscano

Either you go completely crazy about Fiano or you fail to see what all the fuss is about. The major producer in the area, around Avellino just inland from Vesuvius, is Mastroberardino. The true glories of the wine are revealed in the *cru* version, Vignadora. Very young, it is distressingly anonymous; young it is of little more than passing interest; but by a year or so old it is fabulous. Its charms are quite restrained, just a subtle, but concentrated, peachy-nutty-creaminess. But, oh how those understated flavours can beguile you, how they can get more and more alluring with each sip, how they can take hold of your attention and enrapture you. The non-fans don't know what they are missing. In the late 1980s a newcomer, Vadiaperti, started to make Fiano worthy of comment too. Perhaps his style will attract the unconverted.

## FIORANO
### Vino da tavola
LAZIO

♟ Merlot, Cabernet Franc, Cabernet Sauvignon

♀ Malvasia di Candia, Sémillon

◄ Herbert Tiefenbrunner's ornately designed cellar-building with its intricate woodcarvings, just south of Bolzano, hides serious wine-making endeavour, not least of which is his Feldmarschall, from Müller-Thurgau grapes grown on one of Europe's highest vineyards.

If you had a name as aristocratic sounding as Boncompagni Ludovisi, and if you were Prince of Venosa and possessed a beautiful estate called Fiorano about 15km (9 miles) from Rome along the old Appian Way, you wouldn't necessarily feel obliged to follow the viticultural practices of lesser mortals, would you? Even so, it must have caused a bit of a stir among the Romans 50 odd years ago when Boncompagni planted the Bordeaux Cabernet/Merlot grape blend, though there was a nod to local sensibilities by giving Merlot, not unknown in Lazio, a 50 per cent stake. More outlandish still must have seemed the planting of Sémillon (the Sauternes grape) which he used to make one of his two white wines. The local Malvasia di Candia was used to make the other.

The wines, white as well as red, spend two to three years in chestnut barrels then the same time again in bottle. Eccentricity seems to run in the family and the Prince's descendant waits at home until buyers come, by appointment, to persuade him to part with them – cash sales only permitted. I suppose he reckons wines of such noble origin will have a certain cachet and be much in demand, however disappointing they taste.

## FIVE ROSES
### Vino da tavola
PUGLIA

♟ Negroamaro, Malvasia Nera

Five Roses has been called both Italy's greatest rosé and a rip-off. Neither is true. Its claim to fame, apart from its extraordinary name (apparently a wheeze of some American GIs: a translation of its source, Cinque Rose), is as Italy's first bottled rosé (1925). Its Unique Selling Proposition, in marketing speak, is that it is bottled over a year after its harvest. But in today's rush to drink wines indecently young, this is no great advantage. Whatever the other consequences of this policy, one is that once Five Roses is in bottle it is more than ready for drinking. Its producer is Leone de Castris, its origin the Salento peninsula, alias Italy's heel.

## FLACCIANELLO
### Vino da tavola
TUSCANY

♟ Sangiovese

Officially entitled Flaccianello della Pieve, it's the super-Tuscan to end all super-Tuscans. It's the best or at least nearly the best nearly always. Its credentials are impeccable: it comes from Panzano, a most classic Chianti Classico commune; the estate is Tenuta Fontodi, which produces high-class Chianti Classico; the grape variety is 100 per cent

Sangiovese and the winemaker is Franco Bernabei, one of the most skilled in Tuscany. The wine is also aged for around nine months in *barriques* and about the same time again in large casks. But this check list doesn't explain the wine's brilliance, why its punchy, plummy, cedaryness has that extra touch of complexity and a superb sense of harmony. Thank goodness you don't have to understand it to enjoy it. The first vintage was 1981. All the vintages appearing since (none was made in 1984) have been well up to scratch.

## FONTALLORO
### Vino da tavola
TUSCANY

🍷 Sangiovese

Just how many stunning wines is the brilliant winemaker Franco Bernabei responsible for? He should be very proud of Fontalloro, a super-Tuscan from Fattoria di Felsina at Castelnuovo Berardenga towards the south of the Chianti Classico area. The estate is owned by Giuseppe Mazzocolin. He is young, full of energy, enthusiastic and inspires Bernabei to make some wonderful wines.

Fontalloro, from 100 per cent Sangiovese (the Sangioveto clone), is a big, rich, spicy, plummy, chunky number, big enough to wear its mantle of oak lightly. First made in 1982, the evidence that it will age slowly and remarkably finely is already accumulating. 1986, '85 (particularly) and '83 (delicious now, better later) are all impressive.

## FRANCIACORTA DOC
LOMBARDY

🍷 Cabernet Franc, Barbera, Nebbiolo, Merlot

🍷 Pinot Bianco, Chardonnay

I've always thought the mixture of grapes for red Franciacorta was weird and no explanation for it, however rational, has yet convinced me that it isn't. Nevertheless it works. From Piedmont, to Franciacorta's west, come Barbera, giving zest and acidity, and Nebbiolo, giving grip and backbone. From Friuli and/or eastern Veneto, to Franciacorta's east, come Cabernet Franc, giving stylishness and grassiness, and Merlot, giving roundness and suppleness. Put that lot together and you get something very individual, almost indescribable, and, in the right hands, rather good. 1986, '85, '83, '82 all have their merits.

The white, from less incongruous grapes, is less idiosyncratic, but can turn out to be a much classier white, steely and flintily crisp, than is habitual in Italy and fine at two to three years old. One reason is Franciacorta itself, west of Brescia. It is humid territory, containing both east- and west-facing hills, with well-nigh perfect drainage. The other reason is that there are comparatively few estates, most producing smallish quantities of wines and nearly all of which are firmly devoted to quality, not the quick buck. 1987 is good, '88 better. Bellavista is hard to beat. Ca' del Bosco is in a class of its own. Cornaleto, Faccoli Lorenzo, Il Mosnel, Longhi-de Carli, Maggi are others to look for.

## FRANCIACORTA SPUMANTE DOC
LOMBARDY

🍷 Pinot Bianco, Chardonnay

'I used to fight shy of Italian *spumante* until I discovered . . .' Not quite, but sparkling Franciacorta at its best has an elegance, a refinement, and a creamy, grassy, salty classiness that is hard to upstage. On the other hand, sparkling Franciacorta not at its best would have a struggle proving its superiority against the big guns of Trentino or Piedmont. At its most basic it doesn't even have to be *metodo classico*, *charmat* will do. Only if made by *metodo classico*, though, can it declare a vintage or carry the tag *nature* or *pas dosé*, both meaning super-dry. There is also a pink version, which gets its colour from a little Pinot Noir juice in the blend. Ca' del Bosco tends to be the benchmark but I'd go for Bellavista any day – it is superb. Or else there is Faccoli Lorenzo, Monte Rossa, Cavalleri, Berlucchi – all good. I like to keep non-vintage Franciacorta Spumante for a year before broaching it; vintage I prefer at two to four years. But sometimes the temptation to drink it sooner is irresistible.

## FRASCATI DOC
LAZIO

♀ Trebbiano Toscano, Malvasia di Candia, Malvasia del Lazio, Greco

Frascati is one of the few Italian wines that practically everyone has heard of and most people have tried at some time or another. It is also the wine that is most often cited to show all that is bad in the Italian wine scene. It is accused of being colourless and practically tasteless, or of having a taste but a fat, nasty one. It is held up as *the* example of over-production, slipshod wine-making, tendency to oxidation, lack of regard for patrimony, and so on, that used to be the scourge of Italy. Can it really be so wicked?

Certainly, the standard house plonk you get in restaurants and *trattorie* in and around Rome, Frascati's homeland, is not noticeably worse than elsewhere in Italy – and streets better than some. This 'frascati' may be the real thing, but is more likely a Frascati-lookalike, coming from anywhere in the Castelli Romani, an extensive ridge of hills south-east of the city. Whatever it is, when drunk on the spot it has the right sort of style, it goes down well enough and is drunk with everything, even with what we would consider red wine foods.

It is when you try various Frascatis in the cold grey light of home that you realize that the criticisms can be true, although there are some, and an increasing number, that are perfectly OK – going on good, and one or two that are excellent. Frascati, best young, should taste soft, creamy and nutty. Or should it? If you look at its grape variety regulations you realize they are a mess. The wine can be all Trebbiano – great for neutral background vinous swill but not much else; or all Malvasia – too prone to oxidation if not handled right, but peachy, nutty, flavoursome and characterful. To make matters worse, of the two Malvasia varieties permitted, the better one (del Lazio) is restricted to 30 per cent, the less good one (di Candia) can be used as liberally as you like. The decent companies make a reasonable commercial compromise and mix Trebbiano and Malvasia in varying proportions, the best ignore the law and bump up the Malvasia del Lazio.

Colli di Catone, the company that is the byword for the best Frascati, now has a *cru* wine, Colle Gaio. It's pricy, but shows what can be done when quality is the only consideration. Fontana Candida, a sound, reliable producer, also has a single-vineyard, super-smart wine called Santa Teresa. Il Marchese and Villa Simone are good. Goodish producers include Cantina Sociale di Monteporzio Catone, Colli di Tuscolo, Conte Zandotti, Gotto d'Oro.

## FREISA

This is the sort of stuff we should be seeing more of. Grapes that are quintessentially Italian, grapes that no-one else in the world would dream of handling, grapes that turn out supremely characterful and drinkable wines. Yet Freisa, once understandably popular in its native Piedmont, was in decline, its vineyards being turned over to more 'saleable' varieties such as Dolcetto, Barbera, and even Cabernet and Chardonnay – as if the world doesn't have enough of those already. Now, we can breathe a sigh of relief – Freisa has been rediscovered and producers such as Scarpa, Roberto Voerzio, Clerico, Gaja, Aldo Conterno, Giacomo Conterno, Gigi Rosso, Sebaste, Vergnano, and, particularly, Vajra need no longer proffer their Freisa reluctantly and apologetically.

It produces wine that is often paleish red, with a firm, raspberry-like aroma. It can be lightweight, slightly sweet, a bit fizzy; more often it is dry and combines soft raspberry fruitiness with high acidity and the almost-rasping austerity that is the hallmark of southern Piedmont. You get a tug of war between grip and grace that can be really exciting. It is grown mainly around Alba, as Freisa delle Langhe, and around Chieri and Asti, where it is DOC.

# FRIULI-VENEZIA GIULIA

The region of Friuli-Venezia Giulia, often called just Friuli for short, is the true Italian north-east. Bordered by Yugoslavia to the east and Austria to the north, and suffering down the centuries from wars as it is one of Europe's major crossroads, Friuli has become a meeting place of three cultures: Slavic, Teutonic and Venetian (from the west). Yet the atmosphere in its scattered villages and sedate towns remains undeniably Italian.

The wine zones of Friuli cover much of its southern half. There are three DOCs of major importance (Collio, Colli Orientali and Grave del Friuli), three of minor importance (Latisana, Aquileia and Isonzo) and one relative newcomer (Carso) whose influence remains to be seen. The high – and increasing – reputation of Friuli for its wines hinges on two small districts next to the Yugoslav border: Collio and Colli Orientali. Despite the rivalries, there's not a lot to choose between them, the distinction being provided by provincial boundaries rather than by great differences in soil or climate. Their pre-eminence over other Friuli DOCs is due to their situation on hill terrain. So much importance is placed on this asset that only wines from proper hill slopes are allowed to use these

highly regarded names. Most of the rest of south Friuli is flat. Grave del Friuli is the biggest zone and the only one producing large quantities of wine. It is responsible for its fair share of basic wine, much of it still issuing forth in large bottles declaring 'Tocai' (white) or 'Merlot' (red). But it is possible to achieve a more-than-decent level of quality, with a lot of self-restraint in yields and a lot of care in the cellar.

There is a wide range of grape varieties grown in Friuli, each usually vinified and bottled separately. A count at the end of 1987 revealed 68 different combinations of district and grape for DOC wines alone and the number is growing.

The essence of the Friuli wine style is varietal purity, but subtlety; the understated approach. When it works, as it frequently does, they have an elegance and a classiness that are hard to beat. Most grape varieties are white, and Germanic Traminer and Riesling rub shoulders with French Sauvignon and Chardonnay as well as with the local Ribolla, Verduzzo and Malvasia, to name but a few. Reds are fewer, less highly regarded and may have suffered from a predominance of white wine-making expertise in the region. But advances with reds are now coming thick and fast.

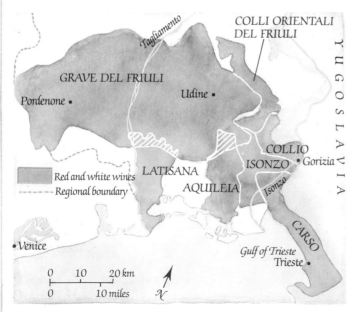

► The steep slopes of Collio are green and lush and produce some of Friuli's best wines.

| WINE ENTRIES | GRAPE ENTRIES | Riesling Renano |
|---|---|---|
| Aquileia | Cabernet Franc | Sauvignon |
| Carso | Cabernet Sauvignon | Tocai |
| Colli Orientali del Friuli | Chardonnay | Traminer |
| Collio | Malvasia | Verduzzo |
| Grave del Friuli | Merlot | |
| Isonzo | Pinot Bianco | |
| Latisana | Pinot Grigio | |
| Picolit | Pinot Nero | |
| Schioppettino | Refosco | |
| Trevenezie | Ribolla | |
| Vintage Tunina | Riesling Italico | |

## GALESTRO
**Vino da tavola**
TUSCANY

♀ Trebbiano, Malvasia, Vernaccia and others

Back in the bad old days of the late 1970s when Chianti was still legally supposed to contain a hefty whack of white grapes there was suddenly a glut of white grapes on the market. This was probably because producers did not want to dilute their red wine with white, whatever the DOC regulations said. Several big producers, Antinori, Frescobaldi, Ruffino and their ilk, in an unprecedented show of mutual co-operation, got together to forge a solution. The answer revealed splendid marketing acumen for the times: a lowish alcohol (10·5 per cent), slightly *frizzante*, light, crisp, fresh wine for drinking young, which each producer made and bottled individually using the common name of Galestro. Pretty successful it was too, in Italy at least. Galestro producers now number about a dozen. They have formed themselves into something akin to a *consorzio* and the wine is well established. But it isn't particularly cheap or characterful. I've often found it much like drinking dilute lemon juice. Agricoltori del Chianti Geografico, Ricasoll, Antinori, Frescobaldi, Rocca delle Macie, Ruffino typify the mould. Perhaps the newly permitted Vernaccia in the blend will add character.

## GAMBELLARA DOC
VENETO

♀ Garganega, Trebbiano di Soave, Trebbiano Toscano

I was never able to work out what was so different about Gambellara, lying adjacent to Soave, to warrant its own DOC. It always seemed to me just like Soave and, if anything, not quite as good. Then I had a good look at the map and noticed a dotted line indicating a provincial boundary, which the border between the two zones appeared to follow. Bureaucracy strikes again! For the record, Gambellara DOC also encompasses a Recioto (in still, *frizzante* and *spumante* versions), and a Vin Santo too. Decent producers: La Marescialla and Maule.

## GARGANEGA

Garganega is the main grape for Soave. I'm not sure if that is a commendation or a criticism. No, it must be the former because it means it is responsible for the honeyed glories of Recioto di Soave too, as well as the few really *nice* Soaves around. It isn't responsible for much else, apart from Gambellara, which is as near as dammit Soave anyway, and it isn't found much outside the Veneto region. It's a sturdy little monster, vigorous as anything, which is just what most of the Soave producers like, as they can get super-high yields out of it without it squealing, or going all weak and feeble the following year; it just comes back for more. If reined in with a firm hand, Garganega will furnish the delicious, concentrated, elegant Soave with an almondy touch that I wish we saw more of.

## GATTINARA DOC
PIEDMONT

♟ Nebbiolo, Bonarda

Gattinara is a small area, 92 hectares (227 acres), up in northern Piedmont, in the Novara-Vercelli hills, with a reputation that seems disproportionate to its size. Then you learn that it has more than its fair share of documents attesting to its 'ancient renown', and that a number of large companies invested heavily in vineyards in the area 20 years ago to preserve their supplies of what was reckoned the best wine of the area. Gattinara produces lightweight Nebbiolo wines. At their best they can be elegant and violetty, with a touch of spice and a lightly bitter finish, which age well, drinking well from five to 15 years old or more (minimum legal ageing is four years). All too often, though, they are mediocre in quality, fat and chocolaty, tending to oxidation much sooner than that. Which is why the news that Gattinara has received the go-ahead for DOCG is thoroughly depressing. Good years: 1986, '85, '83, '82, '79, '78, '74. Best producers: Le Colline, Antoniolo, Ferrando, Nervi, Travaglini.

## GAVI DOC
PIEDMONT

Cortese

People still praise Gavi to the skies. But for all that, it is almost always only a pleasant, firm, ripe but steely white wine made in and around the village of Gavi in south Piedmont. Why it has such an overblown reputation I cannot say, and I certainly wish it didn't have the prices to match. And yet Gavi *can* rise to meet its image, even if it is still too expensive. It develops a subtle but engaging, delicate fruit character that, though restrained, impresses more and more with every sip, especially at one to two years after the vintage. La Scolca (but ouch! what prices!) and La Giustiniana certainly reach this level. Other estates that might rise above the norm include Castello di Tassarolo, La Battistina, La Chiara, Bergaglio and Broglio.

Usually the wine is called just Gavi; sometimes Cortese di Gavi after its grape variety. This may be because a producer thinks it sounds more special that way or, if an estate makes two quality levels of Gavi, the simpler wine will be dubbed Cortese di Gavi. To make Gavi seem even more important the idea was hatched of calling it Gavi di Gavi. But the only estates permitted to do so are those with vineyards in the village of Gavi, which is but one of several in the DOC area. Others naughtily call theirs just Gavi Gavi separated by a curlicue to give the same effect.

## GHEMME DOC
PIEDMONT

Nebbiolo, Vespolina, Bonarda

Like Gattinara, Ghemme is another Nebbiolo-based red wine from the Novara-Vercelli hills of north Piedmont. While lighter in style than big brothers Barolo and Barbaresco from the south of the region, Ghemme certainly has more guts than the better-known Gattinara, more balance and better overall quality. Quality-wise the area is dominated by one producer, Antichi Vigneti di Cantalupo, who have divided up their 18-hectare (44-acre) estate on the prime Cantalupo hill into two *crus* to which, idiosyncratically, they have given Latin names: Collis Breclemae and Collis Carellae. On sale after four years' minimum ageing, it is best for the next six years or so. Best years: 1985, '83, '82, '80, '79, '78, '74.

## GHIAIE DELLA FURBA
Vino da tavola
TUSCANY

Merlot, Cabernet Sauvignon,
Cabernet Franc

Ghiaie, that mouthful of vowels following a hard 'g', refers to the gravelly soil of vineyards in the rolling hills of the Carmignano district, outside Florence, belonging to the Contini Bonacossi family of the impeccable Tenuta di Capezzana estate. The wine, made in roughly equal proportions from each of the two Cabernets and Merlot, is neither copy-cat Bordeaux, nor aggressively super-Tuscan. It is mellow, blackcurranty and has plenty of weight, body and staying power, yet with a lightness of touch that gives it some refinement. One of the earliest and still one of the most exciting Cabernet-based Tuscans. Best years: 1983 and '81 are good now, '88, '86 and '85 to keep.

## GOLDMUSKATELLER
Alto Adige DOC, Trentino DOC
TRENTINO-ALTO ADIGE

Moscato Giallo

Goldmuskateller (or Goldenmuskateller) is German for the grape variety Moscato Giallo. Up in German-speaking Alto Adige (Südtirol) its wine is usually on the sweet side (for example, from Lageder), but the most famed Goldmuskateller is dry, from Herbert Tiefenbrunner – and jolly good it is too. Below the great Italo-German divide, in the Trentino half of the region, Moscato Giallo is grown more widely, and the best producers are Conti Martini (sweetish version) and Spagnolli (dry). There are, however, fewer producers in Trentino than one would expect for the acreage given over to the grape. Why? Because a lot of that much lauded, teutonically pure Südtiroler Goldmuskateller has trundled up from Trentino, that's why. The sweeter Goldmuskateller (DOC in both Trentino and Alto Adige) is best in its first flush of youth; the dry version (not DOC) improves for four years, sometimes longer.

## GRAVE DEL FRIULI DOC
FRIULI-VENEZIA GIULIA

🍷 Cabernet Franc, Cabernet Sauvignon, Merlot, Pinot Nero, Refosco dal Peduncolo Rosso

🍷 Cabernet Franc

🍷 Chardonnay, Pinot Bianco, Pinot Grigio, Riesling Renano, Sauvignon, Tocai, Traminer Aromatico, Verduzzo

▲ From the hills of Colli Orientali, the vast plain of Grave del Friuli stretches beyond the horizon. The odd undulation is prized as vineyard land. Colli Orientali growers, whose land stretches down from the hills, are only allowed the name Grave del Friuli for their wine from flat lands.

It is easy to go on about the glories of the classy wines of Friuli with their restraint and pure varietal tone, forgetting that these wines are mainly from just two small areas (Collio and Colli Orientali), forming no more than a third of Friuli's DOC production of over 400,000 hectolitres. Grave del Friuli, the great gravel plain that stretches across most of the southern half of the region, turns out about half its DOC wine (and about three times as much *vino da tavola*) and pretty unexciting much of it is too. There's tons of Merlot and heaps of Tocai and the interest factor of both is little more than a stifled yawn. There's no shortage of technology, so no shortage either of a succession of clean, faultless whites, all declaring various grape variety names on the labels – and all tasting much the same. And yet . . . there *are* good wines from Grave: Refosco, Verduzzo, even the dreaded Merlot and Tocai can reach surprising heights, particularly from those who make full use of whatever gentle slopes there are and *restrict* their yields – the usual story. Let's keep our fingers crossed that the stunning 1988 vintage will spur more producers on to better things.

Collavini are coming more and more to the fore. Plozner is improving by leaps and bounds. Duchi Rota-Badoglio, Vigneti Le Monde, Vigneti Pittaro, Conti di Maniago, Conti di Porcia e Brugnera, Pradio, Russolo are others to watch. Drink the whites and rosé young, and reds up to five years old (Refosco possibly more).

## GRECHETTO

Some years back Grechetto was just another also-ran Italian white grape languishing in Umbria and partially responsible for Orvieto, itself not much more than another also-ran Italian white wine. Then someone had the wheeze of trying it out for a wine in its own right. What a revelation! Not only does it have a wonderful deep, nutty character with green fruits, it also is a natural for harmonizing with the wood of the fashionable *barriques*. Smart Orvieto producers Bigi were the first to bottle a 100 per cent Grechetto, called Marrano, aged in *barriques*. Antinori have been far more cautious, going for a Chardonnay-Grechetto blend (called Cervaro).

Traditionally, apart from its minor role in Orvieto, Grechetto appears in small part in white Torgiano (alias Torre di Giano), Colli del Trasimeno and Colli Perugini; and predominates in Bianco d'Arquata (Adanti's stands out) and Grechetto di Todi, all of which are Umbrian wines. It also can make superb Vin Santo (Lungarotti and Avignonesi). It is not the same grape as southern Italy's Greco.

## GRECO

Greco or 'Greek' has its light kept firmly under a bushel for its home is in south-west Italy (Campania, Calabria) where few are yet skilled or caring enough to bring out the best from this ancient white variety of eminently classy potential. Hints of its dry, smoky, minerally richness come from Greco di Tufo or occasional bottles of Cirò. Its magical qualities as a sweet wine are more apparent, displayed by Greco di Bianco.

## GRECO DI BIANCO DOC
CALABRIA

♀ Greco

Let's first sort out the name. No, it hasn't been written back to front; it just happens that there is a coastal village called Bianco in the extreme south of Calabria where they grow the Greco grape. Greco di Bianco is a *passito* wine, with minimum 14 per cent alcohol and another three per cent worth in sweetness. More importantly, it can be wonderful. Neither big, nor sticky, it is more a delicate, floral sweetie that gets drier and more intense as it ages (it is brilliant young, though). Ceratti's is the one to hunt down with its ethereal bouquet, all flowers and dried fruits, and its elegantly balanced taste.

## GRECO DI TUFO DOC
CAMPANIA

♀ Greco, Coda di Volpe Bianco

Greco is *the* white grape of south-west Italy. Its best manifestation is as Greco di Tufo from Campania's Avellino province. Such a high proportion of the area's Greco grapes find their way into producer Mastroberardino's cellars, their style has to be the one we take as representative. Their *cru* Vignadangelo is noticeably superior to their straightforward version but Greco di Tufo has never excited me nor convinced me it is worth its price the way Fiano di Avellino (from contiguous vineyards and the same producer) has. It's just a good, smoky, minerally, flavoursome white which needs a year to show its potential and then may age gracefully. A fizz version exists too.

## GRIFI
Vino da tavola
TUSCANY

♀ Sangiovese, Cabernet Franc

A super-Tuscan with a healthy dash of Cabernet but with two differences from others of that ilk. First, the Cabernet is the grassy Franc type rather than the more usual blackcurranty Sauvignon; second, the grapes don't come from Chianti but from the vineyards of the impeccable Avignonesi estate in Montepulciano, further south. This also means the Sangiovese clone used for the heart of the wine is Montepulciano's Prugnolo Gentile. Weighty and impressive, the plums and liquorice wine, *barrique*-aged of course, is almost in the top rank. First made in 1981 and consistently good since, it needs five to ten years to peak.

## GRIGNOLINO

Grignolino's name comes either from the dialect word *grignè* meaning grin, or from a similar word meaning 'pippy'. The grape was once held in high repute. It has now shrunk, both in renown and amount planted. Nowadays it is found mainly in south Piedmont where it is DOC in Asti and Monferrato Casalese. Is it just coincidence that this, Asti in particular, is sparkling-wine country, given that Grignolino is light-coloured, lightweight (though with Piedmontese austerity) and tends to be fizzy? It can be hard to love, with a bitter tang, although it can cut through rich food with aplomb.

Best producers: Fenocchio, Scarpa, Bruno Giacosa, Pio Cesare, Vietti, Bricco Mondalino, Coppo, Bologna, Rivetti, Il Milin, Nuova Cappelletta and Tenuta dei Re.

## GRILLO

There is no doubt that Grillo is an ace grape. It ripens well under the burning sun; it doesn't over-yield; it gets packed with sugar; it oxidizes easily (a benefit for Marsala); and it has incomparable flavours. So what do Marsala producers do? Rip it out, that's what. I almost cried when they told me. So why? Well, it's that low yield. Who gives a toss about quality when you can get at least four times as much from other grapes? Who worries about quality anyway when the product sells however lousy it is? One day they will come to their senses – if it is not too late.

## GUTTURNIO
## Colli Piacentini DOC
EMILIA

♟ Barbera, Bonarda

I wonder who was the first to realize that sharp, lively Barbera and soft, round Bonarda were electric together. I salute that person and would, if I had one, raise my *gutturnium* (traditional Roman imbibing cup) and drink a toast to him/her with youthful cherries-and-chocolate Gutturnio, the result of such a blessed marriage. Usually with about 60 per cent of Barbera and from Emilia's far west it can age a few years but is more exhilarating young. Fugazza's is the best, Romagnoli's and Zerioli's not bad. Strangely, across the border in Lombardy, they usually keep their Barbera and Bonarda separate. Killjoys!

## ISCHIA DOC
CAMPANIA

♟ Guarnaccia, Piedirosso, Barbera

♟ Forastera, Biancolella and others

No, I'm not going to wax lyrical about Guarnaccia or Forastera. I'm sure they are very fine and noble local grape varieties whose distinctive qualities you will appreciate fully without my help while lazing in the sun or dozing under the pine forests of the island of Ischia in the Bay of Naples. If you still believe the story about wine not travelling Ischia is one of the few wines that will back you up, because it sure won't taste as inviting when you get it back home. D'Ambra's wines are well thought of locally.

## ISONZO DOC
FRIULI-VENEZIA GIULIA

♟ Cabernet Franc, Cabernet Sauvignon, Franconia, Merlot, Pinot Nero, Refosco dal Peduncolo Rosso

♟ Chardonnay, Malvasia Istriana, Pinot Bianco, Pinot Grigio, Riesling Italico, Riesling Renano, Sauvignon, Tocai Friulano, Traminer Aromatico, Verduzzo

A Friuli DOC with a string of grape varieties as long as your arm and, no doubt, still increasing. Isonzo, though, has an important role if you happen to have vineyards stretching south from the top-rated Collio DOC. You can then produce two qualities of wine, with a pretty smart name for each.

Isonzo has some pretty good grassy Cabernet and supple, cherries-in-fruit-cake Merlot, usually for drinking before their fifth birthday; the other reds have little track record. There is some attractive peachy Malvasia Istriana and floral Riesling Renano, but both are delicate, verging on ephemeral and need drinking young, as does the broader Pinot Bianco.

Best years: 1988, '86, '85. Best producers: Attems, Eddi, Stelio Gallo, Pecorai, Prandi d'Ulmholt, Gianni Vescovo and Zampar.

## LACRYMA CHRISTI DEL VESUVIO DOC
CAMPANIA

🍷🍷 Piedirosso, Sciascinoso, Aglianico

🍷 Coda di Volpe, Verdeca, Falanghina, Greco

Variously written as Lacrima, Lachryma and Lacryma, it's the latter which appears to have settled as the correct, though somewhat un-Italian spelling of the 'Tear belonging to Christ'. There are several versions of how this wine got its name. The most common is that when Lucifer was booted out of heaven he grabbed a piece of it as he fell, then let it go. It landed around the Gulf of Naples. God recognized his lost territory, cried, his tears landed on target and as they did so vines appeared. Another story is that Christ, looking down on the Gulf of Naples from heaven, wept to see its beauty. (Must have been before the Neapolitan urban sprawl developed.)

The stories are the best thing about the wine. The wines' usual name is just Vesuvio and the Superiore versions are 'honoured' by the name Lacryma Christi. Sweaty reds that age quickly and earthy whites, sometimes sweet or fortified, are the norm. Mastroberardino's are the best of a bad bunch.

## LAGO DI CALDARO DOC
TRENTINO-ALTO ADIGE

🍷 Schiava, Pinot Nero, Lagrein

The wine from Caldaro, a lake surrounded by vines near the upper reaches of the Adige river, may be called Kalterersee by the local German speakers but Lago di Caldaro is too pretty a name to be abandoned – let's stick up for it. The wine's pretty nice too. Only lightish red, sometimes no more than deepish pink, it is low in alcohol (ten per cent minimum), with the smoky, strawberry-yogurt flavours of Schiava grapes. Young and fresh it's a perfect lightweight quaffer. As there's a lake-full of it (around 200,000 hectolitres), there's plenty there to quaff too, even if Germany, Austria and Switzerland nobble more than their fair share. And don't let those Südtiroler folk kid you it all comes from around the lake. Only the Classico version does. Otherwise vineyards entitled to the name stretch from north of Bolzano right down the Adige valley into Trentino.

There's a Superiore with half a degree more alcohol and, with yet another half degree, a version called Scelto or, for the Germans, Auslese. Despite the term, though, it has nothing to do with sweet German Auslese. All Lago di Caldaro is dry. Best producers: Hofstätter, Kuenburg, Lageder, Laimburg, Muri-Gries, Rottensteiner, Schloss Schwanburg, Tiefenbrunner.

## LAGREIN

It would be easy to dismiss Lagrein as 'of minor interest only' and I'm sure many do. But Lagrein should be of major interest because it is one of Italy's grape gems. It ripens late; only in Trentino and Alto Adige are summers just right for it to flourish without over-ripening, but there it turns out succulent, weighty, ripe reds. At their best they are like the finest, darkest melted chocolate, but as concentrated as the strongest *espresso* coffee. Lagrein can produce a deep-coloured beast called Lagrein Scuro or Dunkel, which ages well if you can find any that hasn't been drunk in its first enticing flush of drinkability. It also makes a pretty neat rosé called Lagrein Rosato or Kretzer.

## LAGREIN DUNKEL
Alto Adige DOC, Trentino DOC
TRENTINO-ALTO ADIGE

🍷 Lagrein

What a wonderful word is *doonkl* (meaning 'dark') – the Italian equivalent, *scuro*, isn't nearly as expressive. If you don't drink the wine youngish when its dark chocolatiness mingles with fresh, ripe fruit to make a resoundingly moreish drink wait until after four or five years. Then, if well made, it can blossom as a mature wine, still with its deep, dark chocolate but with a complex bitter fruits overlay. Best years: 1988, '86, '85, '83, '82. Best producers: Cantina Sociale Colterenzio, Conti Martini, Foradori, Grai, Lageder, Niedermayr and Tiefenbrunner.

## LAGREIN KRETZER
**Alto Adige DOC, Trentino DOC**
TRENTINO-ALTO ADIGE

♀ Lagrein

Much as I might go a long way to taste a wine called Dunkel, one called Kretzer I might avoid. So I would miss out on a really good rosé and more fool me for being word-prejudiced. The Kretzer or Rosato version of Lagrein is lightly coloured, but more penetrating in flavour than you would expect from its delicate pink hue. Dry and quite firm, its strawberries and plums fruit make you want to return for more, while it has enough lightweight fleshiness to give it interest. The younger you drink it the better. Best producers: Conti Martini, Foradori, Grai, Lageder, Tiefenbrunner.

## LAMBRUSCO

Lambrusco grows from one end of Italy to the other. Tank loads of its wine trail across the country to huge anonymous bottling plants in odd locations. But it is at home only in Emilia, grown high on modified pergolas, producing in its rashly prolific way on Emilia's flat, or at best barely undulating, countryside. Lambrusco is the butt of more wine snob jokes than probably all other grapes and wines put together, but it has resulted in more glasses being swished down *pleasurably* than it is possible to imagine, and has switched many a soul on to the fun of wine-drinking.

It wasn't just some clever marketing hunch to turn this red grape into something sweetish, lowish in alcohol, cherry-like and fizzy-ish; the wine has always had the tendency to fizz and Emilians have long known they needed to tie their corks down firmly and beware of exploding bottles. Lambrusco also had a tendency for its fermentation to 'block' in winter, leaving natural residual grape sugar. The rest was just careful honing of a natural tendency. The wine was often a bit *brusco*, or sharp in the mouth in the old days. So the vine (feminine) became known as La Brusca and therefore . . .

## LAMBRUSCO
EMILIA AND ELSEWHERE

♀ ♀ ♀ Lambrusco

▶ Much Lambrusco is now harvested by machines. But some of the high-trained vines with plentiful foliage are still picked by hand. It may require a ladder to reach the grapes, but at least it isn't back-breaking work. The black grapes are put in small plastic buckets to stop them being crushed under their own weight too soon.

Lambrusco, as a name on a bottle, can mean more or less anything. The wine can be from more than 60 sub-varieties of the vine. It can come from one or more regions around the country. It could be from vines grown by one group of farmers, made by someone else somewhere else, and bottled by someone else again. Or it could be just from Emilia in central Italy, or an area within Emilia, such as Reggio or Modena; from just one sub-variety; and could be DOC. It can be red, rosé, 'blush' or white; more fizzy, less fizzy; sweeter, less sweet; low-alcohol, and so on. Yet, it is usually recognizable for what it is. So whatever Lambrusco may be, it certainly isn't anonymous. It drives the producers of Modena, Lambrusco's heartland, mad that all these other wines from vines grown wherever are allowed to be sold as Lambrusco. For them, Lambrusco is only its true self when it comes from its traditional lands, where the best sub-varieties, Sorbara, Grasparossa and Salamino, are found. And you can see their point. For how many of us know that Lambrusco di Modena (not DOC) and Lambrusco Reggiano (DOC) are better than plain Lambrusco di 'Nowhere' but not as good as the three other names? Do we realize that it is a skilled and quite costly job to extract good white juice from the naturally red Lambrusco grape so that it just can't be too cheap? And if it *is* dirt cheap it might be made from Trebbiano instead of from Lambrusco?

At the other end of the scale, there is 'real' or 'traditional' Lambrusco, only occasionally found and only in Emilia. Cavicchioli are the most vociferous 'real' Lambrusco campaigners, firstly with their *dry*, bitter-sharp, morello-like Lambrusco Tradizione, now also with the low-yield, white-heart cherry Vigna del Cristo. Even more 'traditional' is the *metodo classico* Picòl Ross from the Il Moro estate.

Lambrusco won't have a vintage date and it is not for keeping. The cherry-like red, an ideal match for the rich, buttery, cheesy sauces and the fat salami and sausages of Emilia, is the real taste of Lambrusco; the whites and pinks are no more than thirst quenchers.

## LAMBRUSCO DI SORBARA DOC
EMILIA

Y Lambrusco

Sorbara, north of Modena, is believed to be the place where Lambrusco originated and is still recognized as the home of today's best wine. From the central part of the delimited Lambrusco territory in the province of Modena, Sorbara is the name both of the particular sub-variety of the grape and the zone in which it grows. Occasionally dry, usually semi-sweet but made a little drier than other types, Sorbara's particular characteristics are a pronounced and elegant perfume and good acidity. Drink it, don't keep it. Cavicchioli is the leading producer. Giacobazzi, Chiarli, Fini, Riunite follow.

### LAMBRUSCO GRASPAROSSA DI CASTELVETRO DOC
EMILIA

🍷 Lambrusco

The Grasparossa sub-variety of Lambrusco grows south of the town of Castelvetro in the province of Modena. Its wine has more tannin than the other 'superior' sub-varieties; it is also often fuller in flavour, deeper in colour and therefore suitable for wines with more sweetness rather than less. The extra amount of oomph means that it usually gains approval among wine cognoscenti (those who are not sniffy about all Lambrusco). Drink it, don't keep it. Cavicchioli, Chiarli, Giacobazzi, Riunite are reliable producers.

### LAMBRUSCO SALAMINO DI SANTA CROCE DOC
EMILIA

🍷 Lambrusco

The third of the trio of 'best' Lambruscos, all in the province of Modena, the Salamino sub-variety is grown north of Modena itself, in the area of Santa Croce, which stretches northwards to the border with Lombardy. The lands are lower lying than the zones of the other two Lambrusco sub-varieties and the wines consequently richer and fatter, though with enlivening good acidity. Drink it, don't keep it. Cavicchioli and Chiarli are reliable producers.

## LATISANA DOC
FRIULI-VENEZIA GIULIA

🍷 Cabernet Franc, Cabernet Sauvignon, Merlot, Refosco

🍷 Refosco

🍷 Chardonnay, Pinot Bianco, Pinot Grigio, Sauvignon, Tocai, Traminer Aromatico, Verduzzo

Latisana is one of the Friuli districts making numerous varietal wines, which felt it worthwhile to distinguish its identity by means of its own DOC. In the south-west of Friuli, bordering the Tagliamento river and the boundary with Veneto to its west, it is one of the smaller districts with 600 hectares (1482 acres). Not all is planted, however, and it produces disproportionately little wine, only around 10,000 hectolitres a year. Merlot is the most prolific variety, while Tocai, the other Friuli giant, is relegated to third place by the irrepressible advance of Cabernet. Few Latisana producers have come to the fore; little Latisana wine gets exported, neither is it well distributed in Italy. The DOC was no doubt a cause for self-congratulation; I can't see what other benefit it has bestowed on these pleasant but not particularly outstanding wines. Best years: 1988, '86, '85 for reds. Drink the whites young. Best producer: Isola Augusta.

## LAZIO
CENTRAL ITALY

*Wine entries:* Castelli Romani, Cerveteri, Est! Est!! Est!!! di Montefiascone, Fiorano, Frascati, Marino, Montecompatri Colonna, Orvieto, Torre Ercolana, Velletri, Zagarolo

◀ The characteristic reddish soil of Frascati, Lazio's most important wine zone, in the hills of the Castelli Romani south-east of Rome, produces sturdy vines that thrive on the gentle slopes. The Colli Albani are in the background.

Lazio is Rome. Or so it often seems. And Rome's is the easiest image to stamp on this longish, disparate region of 17,200 square km (6640 square miles) which, at its northern end, skirts Tuscany and Umbria with their enthralling scenery, their calm and cultured existence; while its southern part mingles with the laid-back, disordered, wilder, much hotter *mezzogiorno* (south) and stretches nearly to the chaos of Naples. There is also a large mountainous spur of Lazio which stretches eastwards into the Apennines. But the hub of the region is Rome.

Even the wine districts seem to be drawn to the Eternal City. Most skirt its east and south, where there is a vast semi-circular ridge of hills. Those nearest Rome are called the Castelli Romani (Roman castles) and, apart from vineyards, embrace cool, shady summer homes for Rome's moneyed citizens (and the Pope). Further round the curve the hills are called Colli Albani and Colli Lanuvini. It is the Castelli Romani that house the most typical and most widely available wines of Lazio: Marino, Montecompatri Colonna, Zagarolo and, most famed of all, Frascati. All these are white, usually dry, mostly from various combinations of tricky-to-handle Malvasia and unexciting Trebbiano, and keep both Romans and tourists well lubricated. Reds around here form a small minority, not often highly regarded and not DOC. To find the Roman reds you have to travel 'sunwards' on the Autostrada del Sole. Then you hit the area where Cesanese, Lazio's red claim to fame, is cultivated and the wines are all called Cesanese di 'Something'. Down near the coast, in Aprilia, Sangiovese and Merlot get a look in, although the whites stay staunchly Trebbiano. And further north the zone of Cerveteri produces decent red blends of Montepulciano with Sangiovese and Cesanese (even here the white is unswervingly Trebbiano/Malvasia).

For something different you have to look right up in the northern corner by the lake of Bolsena, where there's sweet, strong, red Aleatico di Gradoli. In the same corner there is also Est! Est!! Est!!!, until recently a Roman embarrassment, and a little bit of the Orvieto zone, claiming refugee status from Umbria, its main homeland.

## LESSINI DURELLO DOC
VENETO

🍷 Durella

Well, I eventually managed to taste the wines of Lessini Durello. After all, you should always give a new DOC (1988) a fair hearing, especially when its grape variety, Durella, has been described as 'worthy' and it hails from next door to Soave and Gambellara but isn't just a copycat version of these more famous wines, having eschewed their grape varieties. Sadly, the wines I tasted, both still and sparkling, were such marvels of over-zealously used technology that any character they might have had had been squeezed right out of them. Perhaps it is just growing pains.

## LESSONA DOC
PIEDMONT

🍷 Nebbiolo, Vespolina, Bonarda

Just three growers in a slip of an area with a mere 5 hectares (12 acres) to its name up in northern Piedmont are poor credentials, one would think, for any greater notoriety than a listing of its name among DOCs. But one grower is Sella who, as with his other holding in adjacent Bramaterra, plods doggedly along in the most traditional of ways. He makes admirable medium-weight, not overly tannic wine with violets, strawberries and coffee cut through with a good bite of acidity. Then there is Paolo de Marchi, a gifted Chianti producer, whose family has land in Lessona which was once planted with vines, and who is determined to replant there and show just why the zone used to have such an exalted reputation. Best years: 1988, '86, '85, '83, '82.

## LIGURIA
NORTH-WEST ITALY

*Wine entries:* Cinqueterre, Pigato, Riviera Ligure di Ponente, Rossese di Dolceacqua

▶ When the mountains of Liguria fall almost sheer to the deep blue sea, as here at Cinqueterre, there is no choice but to plant vines on narrow terraces. Ligurians need sturdy legs and had better not suffer from vertigo.

I went to Bibe, a wine fair in Genoa, a few years back. Since Genoa lies neatly in the middle of the slim arc of craggy, flower-bedecked Liguria – 'Italy's Riviera' – I was keenly anticipating enlightenment on the hitherto mysterious wines of the region. The large international Italian companies were there for all to see, as were numerous small, well-regarded estates from many parts of Italy. But finding the real McCoy from local producers was not so easy. The few, very few, Ligurian stands were of the hidden-in-the-corner, food-in-the-background, cigarette-in-mouth, puddle-of-long-opened-wine-in-tiny-plastic-cup-type. I returned home with precious little experience of Pigato, Vermentino and the like, let alone unearthing a Cinqueterre or Rossese di Dolceaqua.

Three years later at VinItaly, Italy's major annual wine fair held at Verona, three sets of keen, young, energetic Ligurian producers sharing a stand, took great delight in letting me compare and contrast their Vermentino, Pigato and Ormeasco. This time there were no cigarettes, real glasses and even a spittoon! Liguria has grown up.

Most Ligurian wines, often from very small producers who sell only to their friends, come from the Riviera di Ponente, the lefthand half of the Ligurian arc, west of Genoa. The most important grapes cultivated are the light, delicate, white Vermentino; the floral, peachy, white Pigato; red Ormeasco (more usually known as Dolcetto), which also comes, called Sciac-trà or Sciacchetrà, as a deep rose; and the succulently fruity red Rossese. Rossese grown in the hills right by the French border has a separate DOC, Rossese di Dolceacqua, which was Liguria's first. The righthand, east, side of the arc of Liguria is called the Riviera di Levante. The pattern of viticulture is similar, although here the wines still wait for DOC to arrive. The sole exception is the tiny, idiosyncratic, zone of Cinqueterre right at the eastern end of the region, with its rare, sought-after whites, which are sometimes *passito*, from the little-known Bosco grape.

## LISON-PRAMAGGIORE DOC
VENETO

🍷 Cabernet Franc, Cabernet Sauvignon, Merlot, Refosco dal Peduncolo Rosso

🍷 Chardonnay, Pinot Bianco, Pinot Grigio, Riesling Italico, Sauvignon, Tocai, Verduzzo

Lison-Pramaggiore is in Veneto's far east, part surrounded by Friuli. The locals certainly seem to have taken to heart the Friulian way of doing things. Until recently, the district comprised three DOCs: Cabernet di Pramaggiore, Merlot di Pramaggiore and Tocai di Lison. Having reorganized themselves with just one name, albeit hyphenated, they clearly decided to get as many varietals included under it as they could, perhaps to save them having to apply for additions later on. So Chardonnay, the winemaker's crutch, got its gong, as did the hardly common Pinot Bianco, Pinot Grigio and Riesling Italico, and the newly fashionable (but not often successful) Sauvignon. If you feel, as I do, all this is stretching the DOC criterion of 'local tradition and practice' too far, stick to the Cabernet, Merlot and Tocai (especially its Classico). At least producers are used to handling these varieties and the wines are usually OK, if rarely distinguished. Look out for wines from La Fattoria, Russolo, La Fornace, Tenuta Sant'Anna. Drink the whites young and the reds from 1988, '86, '85.

## LOCOROTONDO DOC
PUGLIA

♀ Verdeca, Bianco d'Alessano, Fiano and others

Locorotondo might not claim to be anything extraordinary but there seems to be a tacit acceptance in Puglia's Salento Peninsula, where the wine comes from, and in neighbouring Basilicata, that Locorotondo is quite simply *the* white to go for. It is, too. No-one wastes time trying to discover great complexities in it – but its refreshingly light, lively, almondy apricotty fruit makes it a delight to drink, as young as possible, either icy cold in the heat of a Puglian summer, or chilled with more restraint for a good glug in northerly gloom. You could do a lot worse than try the version from the Locorotondo *cantina sociale*, a co-operative which puts most of its fellows to shame. Other recommended producers are Borgo Canale, Calella, De Castris, Distante, Nuzzo. There is a Locorotondo *spumante* too.

## LOMBARDY
NORTH-WEST ITALY

*Wine entries:* Franciacorta,
Franciacorta Spumante, Lugana,
Oltrepò Pavese, Riviera del Garda
Bresciano, Ronco di Mompiano,
Valcalepio, Valtellina

Arrive at Milan airport, if it isn't fog-bound, head through the city, if you
can see through the pollution, start trundling along the factory-lined,
lorry-clogged, east-west motorway, and you might not be too enam-
oured of Lombardy. But get away from the city and the region takes on
a totally different aspect. To the north there are alpine foothills, in the
north-west the lakes: Maggiore, Como and Varese and the east brings
tranquil Lake Garda. So there's plentiful compensation for the strains of
life in the city.

The Po river is Lombardy's southern boundary for most of its extent
(hence the freezing-in-winter, stifling-in-summer Po valley climate that
southern Lombardy suffers). There's just a small triangle, in the west,
that crosses the river, known as Oltrepò Pavese. This is also one of

◄ The tranquil Santuario della Sassella dominates vineyards of the same name, a sub-denomination of Valtellina Superiore in Lombardy. Viticulture is only possible on these steep, uneven pieces of land near the Swiss border with the shadowy presence of the Alps in the background, because they are above the Adda river which keeps the air moving and chases away the clouds.

Lombardy's most important wine areas, with assorted varieties like Barbera, Bonarda, Moscato, Riesling, Pinot Grigio and Pinot Nero jostling for position on the gentle hills that seem to belong neither to Lombardy, nor to neighbouring Emilia.

At the other end of the region, in the far north, there is a long, thin strip of vineyards, the Valtellina, making Nebbiolo-based wine in Piedmontesque styles. In the extreme east is Lugana, which somehow squeezes character from Trebbiano. But the most Lombardian of Lombardy's wines are produced in the middle. There's Franciacorta, with a red from a strange Veneto-Piedmont grape blend, a Pinot-based white and a potentially stunning *spumante*. And next door is Valcalepio, until recently with wines little seen away from their origin, but now spreading its wings. There are numerous others, especially from near Lake Garda. So there's no need to go to one of Milan's sophisticated *enoteche* to get something decent to drink.

## LUGANA DOC
LOMBARDY

♀ Trebbiano di Lugana and others

How do the good folk of Lugana turn out decently characterful, floral, appley, nutty wines when the grape is the uninspiring Trebbiano, king of neutrality? I would like to believe that their Trebbiano di Lugana clone is a different variety mis-named, but people who know about these things say otherwise. I would harbour doubts about sneaky dollops of personality-packed must being added to the brew, but the artisanal nature of many producers knocks that idea on the head. I wish producers elsewhere would plant Trebbiano di Lugana to see how it fares. You never know, we might end up admiring the grape. Best producers: Ca' dei Frati, Co' de Fer and Zenato. Drink it young.

## MALVASIA

So widespread is Malvasia that practically every region of Italy has at least one wine made from the grape, in one or another of its sub-varieties. It was one of the first grape varieties to arrive in Europe via Sicily and still flourishes there – on the Aeolian (Lipari) islands, in particular. Malvasia likes the sun and isn't too keen on the rain, suffering from rot and mildew in the damp. So the south suits it fine. It is a natural for making sweet or strong wines, or, best, strongish-sweet wines – particularly *passito* and *liquoroso* styles, most typically from Sicily and Sardinia. At its best Malvasia has the aroma and taste of ripe, fresh apricots, is packed full of flavour, but charms you gently rather than attacking you with power – it can be absolutely brilliant. Sometimes it is dry, like the aromatic, but not all that characterful, Malvasia Istriana from Friuli, or the more perfumed, more flavoursome, more characteristic Colli Piacentini and Oltrepò Pavese Malvasia from Emilia and Lombardy (Fugazza's Romito and La Muiraghina's are particularly good), which may be sweetish and/or lightly fizzy too. Or it may be *frizzante* or *spumante*, typically in north-west Italy. It ought, though, always to be redolent of apricots.

Although the grape is normally white, it can have quite reddish skins. It is then called Malvasia Nera and often gets used in red wines, especially in Puglia, where its contribution to perfume is indispensable.

In central Italy Malvasia flourishes in Lazio, Umbria and Tuscany. Lazio, in particular, boasts two important sub-varieties: the workhorse Malvasia di Candia and the posher Malvasia del Lazio. Apart from Tuscany's (and Umbria's) Vin Santo, though, the grape is kept firmly in control and used for normal strength, dry wines, usually to add character to the ubiquitous Trebbiano base. It is in central Italy, too, that you most often come across Malvasia's disadvantage – it can oxidize easily, going dark, dull and flat.

## MALVASIA DELLE LIPARI DOC
SICILY

♀ Malvasia di Lipari, Corinto Nero

The Lipari or Aeolian islands form a volcanic archipelago off the north-east coast of Sicily. Apart from local pastimes like sliding down a cliff of pure powdered pumice (you're supposed to do it naked) into a brilliant aquamarine sea, with blobs of pumice bobbing around in it, there are vines to cultivate, mostly the ancient Malvasia variety.

There are three styles of wine: simply sweet (*dolce naturale*), fortified (*liquoroso*) and *passito*. The Malvasia delle Lipari doled out to tourists is usually fortified and is heavy, sticky-sweet and cloying. Avoid it. The island of Salina, though, boasts Carlo Hauner whose Malvasia delle Lipari is irreproachable. For apricots, honey, citrus, candied peel and other tastes of Sicilian *pasticceria* (pastries) bound up in a liquid, these are the wines; they are ready once bottled. There's now a small co-operative on Salina, called La Ginestra, with a group of young lads doing their best to turn out an ace Malvasia *passito*, without any of Hauner's modern technology, just by old-fashioned ways. There may be only 2500 bottles of it, it may not be all that refined, but it is keeping alive thousands of years of tradition and it lets the wonders of the grape speak for themselves. Keep at it boys!

## MALVASIA DI BOSA DOC
SARDINIA

♀ Malvasia di Sardegna

Bosa, a small, hilly area on the west coast, is the home of Sardinia's best Malvasia, so admired that Bosa folk don't let it escape their clutches too easily. When you manage to locate some, one bottle isn't enough – there are four versions you have to try before deciding its worthiness: sweet (*dolce naturale*) and dry (*secco*), fortified sweet (*liquoroso dolce*) and fortified dry (*liquoroso secco*), in increasing order of the amount of alcohol they contain. Rich and almondy-apricoty, they have most perfume when freshly bottled. Salvatore Deriu Mocci has the best reputation. To avoid the two-year ageing requirement some make the otherwise equivalent *vino da tavola* Malvasia di Planargia instead. Best producers: Josto Puddu, Naitana.

## MALVASIA DI CAGLIARI DOC
SARDINIA

♀ Malvasia di Sardegna

Unlike Sicily, where Malvasia cultivation has been pushed out to its satellite islands, Sardinia still has plenty of house room for its ancient friend. Most is produced by co-operatives and quality, need I add, is variable. Just like its smarter version from Bosa, there are four types, sweet and dry, fortified and not, and you'll have to go to Sardinia to try some. Best as soon as bottled. Best producers: the Marmilla and Dolianova co-operatives.

## MARCHE
CENTRAL ITALY

*Wine entries:* Rosso Conero, Rosso Piceno, Verdicchio dei Castelli di Jesi, Verdicchio di Matelica

The Marche stretches, long and lean, along the Adriatic coast, from south of Romagna and the bodies-on-beaches stretch of Rimini, Riccione and Cattolica to Ascoli Piceno and the beginning of Abruzzo, and with it the south. It has always seemed to me a particularly blessed region. It is not highly populated, rarely on tourist itineraries, yet with a landscape of such beauty I gasp every time I see a photo, let alone the real thing. The sea looks the bluest of blue, the beaches are small, hidden and not covered with roasting flesh, the glorious rolling hills of dark green, lighter green and straw-coloured patches stretch for miles, the spasmodic stone-built old villages have a quiet and reflective air; it really does approach rural bliss.

I bought some sandals and had my hair cut in Jesi. 'Where?', said my winey friends. The name of the small town means nothing without its 'Verdicchio dei Castelli di' precursor. It was reassuring to see that Jesi does indeed still have its ancient *castelli* (castles), well at least one, right by the hairdresser. The Verdicchio wine zone starts just outside the

town. Yet, despite its being the one wine that has put the Marche on the wine map, it certainly isn't the most extensive DOC area. That privilege goes to Rosso Piceno, followed by other little known Trebbiano-based wines like Bianco dei Colli Maceratesi and Falerio dei Colli Ascolani. But the Castelli di Jesi zone is certainly the most intensively cultivated and produces about 160,000 hectolitres of wine a year, accounting for as much as 60 per cent of the region's DOC total. Verdicchio is also grown further south around Matelica where it is DOC and around Montanello and Serrapetrona, where it isn't.

Rosso Piceno is also the most prolific red. The best known red, on the other hand, is Rosso Conero, from a smallish area on the massif of Monte Conero, behind the port of Ancona. For those who like odd wines, the Marche has Vernaccia di Serrapetrona: a perfumed, fizzy, dark red, made dry, medium or sweet.

▼ An idyll of rural bliss. A solitary stone house in shady surroundings in the quiet calm Marche, with Verdicchio vineyards on nearby slopes.

## MARINO DOC
LAZIO

♀ Malvasia, Trebbiano, Bonvino, Cacchione

Marino is a soft, cream-and-nuts Frascati lookalike for drinking young, from the Castelli Romani hills next door. It is rarely as good as Frascati's front runners, though rarely as expensive either. The co-operative, with the brand name Gotto d'Oro, is about as typical as you can get. Marino's potential, though, is something else, as you can see if you get your hands on the version made by Paola di Mauro called Colle Picchioni.

## MARSALA DOC
SICILY

🍷 🥂 Catarratto, Inzolia, Damaschino and others

When we think of the great fortified wines of the world, we think of sherry, port, Madeira, stop. Why don't we think of Marsala? Because, although it was, and still could be, a great fortified wine, very, very little of it is anywhere approaching great now. And why is this? Because some Marsala producers knew they could make a very nice living churning out rubbish while swearing the wines were still 'great'. They realized they were dealing in a profitable commodity and started playing it for all it was worth. How short-sighted! Nearly everyone else in Italy has understood that to survive in the 1990s you have to aim for quality or change jobs. In Marsala, though, they seem to think about today, or possibly yesterday, and shut their eyes to the possibility of apocalypse. Why, they are even uprooting the one grape, Grillo, that could ever give them the quality they will one day need.

Despite the much vaunted 1984 revision of the DOC, it basically just reduced the production area a bit and gave 'Marsala all'Uovo' and other nasty flavoured Marsalas another title, 'Cremovo'. You can use up to eight grape varieties in any proportions for Marsala DOC, as if even the law says, 'Chuck in what you like, it doesn't matter'.

Good Marsala still exists in the tiny, and diminishing, stocks of Marsala Vergine. This brings us to the classification of Marsala, which is not a model of simplicity. There are numerous types, split mainly by the minimum wood-ageing requirement which ranges from one year for Fine and two for Superiore up to ten. Then there's an optional subdivision by colour, be it *oro* (gold), *ambra* (amber) or *rubino* (ruby). And there's a sweetness split too, into dry, semi-dry, or sweet. Vergine Marsala (five years' ageing) is dry and is a cut above the rest as it depends on small amounts of fine, old wines and slow ageing. This is expensive and after the horrors further down the Marsala chain few are brave enough to fork out for it. So Vergine is pretty scarce.

Is there any good news? Just a bit. Marco De Bartoli's powerful, dry-toffee, chestnut and woodsmoke, sweetish 20-year-old Marsala Superiore (which nearly didn't get DOC approval because the authorities thought it was 'too good'), and his younger Vigna La Miccia (which has cocked a snook at the law by being so light, fresh and creamily perfumed that it is almost unrecognizable as a Superiore) show what can be done. Best of the rest: Lombardo, Rallo, Curatolo. Marsala is ready to drink once bottled. Drink Vergine before a meal and the sweeter styles after.

## MARZEMINO
### Trentino DOC
TRENTINO

🍷 Marzemino

Although Marzemino is now also grown in Lombardy, there's no doubt where its home is: the southern half of Trentino. It is, quite rightly, incredibly popular there because it has all the fresh fruit gluggability of Beaujolais, but is softer, rounder and more redcurranty. It is best youngish, at about two years old, and its style is reassuringly consistent since the recent formation of a go-ahead *consorzio*. Best years: 1988, '86, '85. Best producers: De Tarczal (*the* Marzemino specialist), Simoncelli, Longariva, Bossi-Fedrigotti, I Vini del Concilio.

## MELISSA DOC
CALABRIA

🍷 Gaglioppo, Greco Bianco, Greco Nero and others

🥂 Greco Bianco, Trebbiano Toscano, Malvasia

The big wine name in Calabria is Cirò. Melissa is just next door to the south, on the ball of Italy's foot. It is quite similar to and often just as good as Cirò. Living under its shadow, though, it tends to get ignored and no-one in Melissa seems to be doing much about it. The co-operative, Torre Melissa, is the prime source; the fresh, minerally white for drinking young is better than the punchy earthy-sweet red which needs a few years to soften but can risk oxidation. The other main producer is Ippolito.

## MERLOT

Merlot has avoided the wave of fashionable popularity besieging Cabernet Sauvignon, its Bordeaux counterpart, probably because its reputation is for large quantities of rubbish. This is unfortunate because, when looked after properly, Merlot can turn out wines that would disgrace no-one. Its dishonour stems from north-east Italy, where there have long been large quantities sold as a commodity, sometimes in large bottles, often bearing little more than the legend 'Merlot' and a huge *vino da tavola* region. On the other hand, Merlot, with its rounded, brambly, fruit-cake fruit and clean, lean finish, is responsible for some of Friuli's most attractive reds, especially in the hill zones. It crops up in Trentino, is scattered around in Lombardy's Bergamo and Brescia too, and along the Emilian Po valley foothills. The quality is usually reasonable, though not particularly inspiring. Then south of Rome there's Merlot di Aprilia about which it is kinder to say nothing. All in all, it is not the most auspicious of backgrounds to propel Merlot into star status in the 1990s.

## MOLISE
SOUTHERN ITALY

*Wine entries:* Biferno, Pentro

If you haven't heard of Molise, don't worry. Neither, it seems, have many Italians. It is a small region of just 4483 square km (1731 square miles), nestling under Abruzzo. Molise, small and sparsely populated (less than 350,000 people) though it is, can – and does – pride itself on its hard wheat, which makes fabulous pasta and long-lived bread, its oil, honey and any number of other agricultural crops. Until the mid-1980s only one thing was missing: it suffered the ignominy of being the only region in Italy without a single DOC for its wines. Then two were awarded at once: Biferno and Pentro. Mind you, DOC doesn't seem to have inspired many producers to create elevated wines even though the potential is there; Di Majo Norante is the honourable exception.

## MONICA DI SARDEGNA DOC
SARDINIA

Monica

Sardinia is associated with big, heavy, alcoholic, often sweetish wines such as Monica di Cagliari. But Monica di Sardegna is different. It is just the easiest, most quaffable red around; at least it is when made by the Cantina Sociale di Dolianova. Lots of ripe, damson-like fruit, a touch of pepper, a touch of chocolate – but why analyse it? Just drink it dry, young and fresh or up to four years old.

## MONTECARLO DOC
TUSCANY

Sangiovese and others

Trebbiano Toscano, Sémillon, Pinot Gris and others

No, this wine doesn't come from the casino. Montecarlo is a small hilly area in northern Tuscany near the olive oil town of Lucca. There are a few decent, creamy, nutty, appley white wines, such as Vigna del Greppo, and some depressing examples of neutrality. The good ones clearly stem from liberal use of the unlikely other grapes allowed (Sémillon, Pinot Gris, Pinot Bianco, Vermentino, Sauvignon and Roussanne). Fattoria del Buonamico is well ahead of the field among producers making reds, but then it had been getting plaudits for its oak-aged, plummy, dusty Rosso di Cercatoia, for years before DOC recognition. Drink the whites young, the reds from 1988, '86, '85.

## MONTECOMPATRI COLONNA DOC
LAZIO

Malvasia, Trebbiano, Bellone, Bonvino

Montecompatri Colonna lies next door to Frascati in the Castelli Romani south of Rome. It is remarkably similar to cream-and-nuts Frascati but less famous with a less accessible name and a lower price. Labels may say just 'Montecompatri' or 'Colonna' as well as the full name. The wine may be *amabile* or sweet but is usually dry. A *frizzante* version exists too. The major producer, and jolly reliable, is the Montecompatri co-operative. Drink it young.

## MONTEFALCO DOC
UMBRIA

🍷 Sangiovese, Trebbiano Toscano, Sagrantino and others

What a pity that the international reputation of Umbria has become tied up with Orvieto, Torgiano and Lungarotti and not also with Montefalco. Set right in the middle of this land-locked region, between St Francis's watering hole of Assisi and Spoleto, Montefalco is well worth a try. Despite being condemned to suffer 15 to 20 per cent of white Trebbiano which must damp down its tea-fruit-spice, middle-Italian Sangiovese character, the Sagrantino saves the day, even though there can be no more than ten per cent of it. It hauls the wine back from the mire of mediocrity and gives it a real boost of richness, plums, prunes, dark cherries and so on and an enlivening swipe of acidity. Best years: 1988, '87, '86, '85, '83. Best producers: Adanti (especially), Caprai, Paolo Bea, Rocca dei Fabbri.

## MONTEPULCIANO

First let's get the confusion sorted out. Montepulciano, the grape, grows widely in the southern half of eastern Italy, from Marche down to Puglia. Montepulciano is also the name of a town in Tuscany in western Italy, giving its name to a wine called Vino Nobile di Montepulciano. The grape Montepulciano is not used for this wine, nor is it commonly found in Tuscany at all. The grape is most widely planted in, and ideally suited to, the conditions in Abruzzo and only occasionally outside this region is it used unblended. Montepulciano is high-yielding. Even when not restrained too much it produces a deeply coloured rich wine, dominated by brambly fruit, with pepper and a touch of spice. When its yield is held properly in check, it can be a delicious monster, filling your mouth with a great surge of concentrated ripe fruit which is prevented from getting totally out of control by its peppery-spicy dry finish. Such a grape, making wine that is good when it is ordinary and great when it is special, just has to be one of Italy's greats. Other Montepulciano-based reds include Rosso Conero (Marche); Biferno, Pentro (Molise); San Severo (Puglia); and Cerveteri, Cori, Velletri (Lazio) with Rosso Piceno (Marche) containing a substantial minority of the grape.

## MONTEPULCIANO D'ABRUZZO DOC
ABRUZZO

🍷 🍷 Montepulciano, Sangiovese

▶ Somebody has to put the bottled wine into cartons – only the very largest companies have automated the process. Usually reckoned to be women's work – as here at Illuminati's cellars in Abruzzo – in areas of high unemployment men have begun to take over.

Vast swathes of Abruzzo in central-southern Italy are planted with Montepulciano; a huge 230,000 hectolitres of DOC Montepulciano d'Abruzzo is produced, not to mention *vino da tavola* Montepulciano too. The DOC zone extends the whole length of the region, for good or ill, stretching from the Adriatic coast inland to the Apennines. The wine is rarely less than respectable, sometimes wonderful. Red Montepulciano, brambly, peppery, spicy, is naturally deep in colour. Yet there is also a rosé version, called Cerasuolo, made by giving the grape juice the merest contact with its dark-coloured skins.

Worthy producers range from the terrific Valentini (almost unbelievably restricted yields) and the idiosyncratic Pepe through to the very good Cornacchia, Illuminati, Cicio Zaccagnini, Cataldi Madonna. There are also exemplary large-scale producers like Casal Thaulero and C.S. di Tollo whose top of the range wines (Orsetto Oro and Colle Secco respectively) are much better than you might suppose. Best years: 1988, '87, '86, '85, '83, '82, '81, '80, '79, '77.

## MONTESODI
### Chianti Rufina DOCG
TUSCANY

🍷 Sangiovese, Canaiolo, Trebbiano Toscano and others

Although classified as Chianti Rufina, Montesodi seems to have taken on a life of its own, more or less being regarded as a super-Tuscan. It is from a prime 12-hectare (30-acre) site on the prestigious Castello di Nipozzano estate belonging to the Marchesi de' Frescobaldi, who have been making wine since the 1300s. First made in 1974, Montesodi comes from 30-year-old vines with stringent yield controls, a well-exposed site above the Sieve river, the natural good acidity of Chianti Rufina and 20 months of *barrique*-ageing. Put that lot together and you come up with a powerful, damson, peppery, rich wine that matures over ten years to a refined, perfumed gem. Best years: 1988, '86, '85, '83, '82, '79, '78.

## MORELLINO DI SCANSANO DOC
TUSCANY

🍷 Sangiovese

A few years ago everyone in Florence had latched on to Morellino di Scansano. If you went out to dinner and the occasion didn't warrant the grand presence of a super-Tuscan those in the know eschewed simple Chianti and drank Morellino. I suppose it was nice to have something fresh, cherry-like and peppery, not too worryingly different from the Chianti on which Florentines are weaned, but with 100 per cent Sangiovese. Or perhaps it was one-upmanship by those with holiday homes on the coast in south Tuscany, south of Grosseto. Morellino comes from the hills behind, where old time residents retreated to survive the mosquito-infested summers. Best years: 1988, '87, '86, '85, '83, '82. Erik Banti is the leading producer, Fattoria Le Pupille good and Mantellassi and Motta up and coming.

## MOSCADELLO DI MONTALCINO DOC
TUSCANY

🍷 Moscato Bianco and others

Way back, too long ago to recall, there was plenty of Moscato planted around Montalcino in southern Tuscany and it was pretty highly rated. So when the huge American firm Villa Banfi, decided to stake a mere 100 million dollars' worth in Montalcino, buying up 1700 hectares (4200 acres) including the odd castle, they thought that it would be a good idea to revive the Moscato. They planted masses of it. They also revived the local name, Moscadello. Lightly fizzy, with the grapiness that is Moscato's strongest asset, low in alcohol and pretty sweet, it is no hardship to force down a cool, young glass or three. Sweet, fortified and still versions are permitted too. Tenuta Il Poggione also makes it. Drink the wine young.

## MOSCATO

Grape or grapes? There are actually two varieties of Moscato grown in Italy, Moscato Bianco and Zibibbo, but as the theoretically inferior variety, the latter, turns out some rather superior wines I wouldn't get too worried about which is which. Moscato is a rather wonderful grape variety. It is just as suitable for making sweet wines as dry; sparkling wines or still; light delicate floaters or strong, weighty plodders. It can make fabulous wines at seven per cent alcohol and wines just as fabulous at 17 per cent. The wine's colour can be the palest of green-tinged straw, deep yellow-gold or proper rosé pink. Throughout all this variation one thing is constant: wine from Moscato has a heavenly musky perfume and smells and tastes like fresh, ripe grapes – the only variety that does.

► Tasting is the surest way to see how a wine is getting along. Gianni Voerzio takes a vat sample of his still slightly cloudy, unfinished Moscato d'Asti.

## MOSCATO D'ASTI DOC
PIEDMONT

♀ Moscato Bianco

Moscato d'Asti confusingly covers two different wines, Moscato d'Asti Spumante and Moscato Naturale d'Asti, both from the same area in southern Piedmont as Asti Spumante. Moscato d'Asti Spumante is rather like Asti Spumante – frothy, musky and deliciously grapy and, from a half decent producer, can be just as good. The only major difference is that it isn't necessarily quite as fizzy.

Moscato Naturale d'Asti is part-fermented Moscato grape must, like Asti before it gets its fizz. Usually producers reserve their best grapes for it. It only reaches about seven per cent alcohol, sometimes a little more, frequently even less; the rest of its grapy sweetness stays as just that, and there may be a touch of bubble to help it along. A good glass of Moscato d'Asti, *naturale* version, is sheer heaven, the essence of delicacy, with all Moscato's trade mark of grapiness, dashes of roses and apples too, and a purity of taste which seems almost virginal. Thank goodness good producers are legion. Arione, Ascheri, Bera, Giacomo

Bologna, Duca d'Asti, Dogliotti, Fontanafredda, Le Colline, Rivetti, Saracco, Traversa, Vietti, Vignaioli Santo Stefano, Roberto Voerzio are some. Drink both wines young.

## MOSCATO DI CAGLIARI DOC
SARDINIA

Y Moscato Bianco

Although Moscato for Moscato di Cagliari can grow anywhere in the southern third of Sardinia, only about 1000 hectolitres of wine are produced and most of it stays strictly local. It is richly grapy, always sweet, usually *passito*, strong and sometimes fortified too. It can be unexciting but, even then, it usually slips down easily enough. Once bottled it is ready for drinking. Best producer: Cantina Sociale di Dolianova.

## MOSCATO DI PANTELLERIA DOC
SICILY

Y Zibibbo

Pantelleria is an unbelievable island off the south-west coast of Sicily, lying nearer to Tunisia in Africa than to Sicily itself. It is small, rocky, with one green part covered with pines and their scent, the odd tatty small town, weird round-domed houses, endless small terraces mostly growing capers, and the wind. The wind always blows, nay batters, be it from south (unbearably hot), north (shiveringly cold, even in an African August), east or west. Hence Pantelleria's name, derived from 'Island of the Winds'. Among everything else there are vines, low trained, to withstand the buffeting. The vines are Moscato all right, but Zibibbo, a different variety from the Moscato Bianco of most of the rest of Italy.

The most typical Pantellerian Moscato wine is *passito*, the grapes being dried out of doors as quickly as the sun's strength will allow – the quicker the better for quality. Moscato Passito di Pantelleria at its best, like De Bartoli's Bukkuram, has been called liquid sunshine. Grape, raisin, oak, toffee flavours, all combine to a terrific luscious whole. His Kam is even better and his ace Moscato di Pantelleria, made with one foot in the modern technology camp, the other firmly in tradition, is as fresh as a daisy and with a gentle, ripe sweetness. The DOC permits a number of styles, both *passito* and non-*passito*, with differing amounts of alcohol, some fortified, some sparkling. Many are almost never seen. Other good producers are Murana and the island's co-operative, with its toffee-like fortified *liquoroso passito* called Tanit.

## MOSCATO DI STREVI
PIEDMONT

Y Moscato Bianco

Strevi is on the eastern edge of the Asti zone in southern Piedmont near Acqui. Its wines are in the grapy Asti Spumante mould, usually *frizzante* or *spumante*, with more body and more refinement than their more famous neighbour. Strevi probably wouldn't have attracted as much interest as it has were it not for Domenico Ivaldi whose contribution is a superb *passito* wine, achieved by drying the grapes so much that the amount of wine he gets is tiny but terrifically concentrated. It ages remarkably too. Since 1985 another Ivaldi, Giovanni with son Gianpaolo, has been following the same route. Other good producers are Bruni, Mangiarotti and Villa Banfi. Drink non-*passito* wines young.

## MOSCATO ROSA
Alto Adige DOC, Trentino DOC
TRENTINO-ALTO ADIGE

Y Moscato Bianco

Ever smelled a wine that smelt exactly like rose petals and tasted like rose water too? Moscato Rosa (or Rosenmuskateller as they say up in German-speaking Alto Adige), achieves this and it is an unworldly experience. *The* producer is Walter Tapfer of Graf Kuenberg (Schloss Sallegg). Apart from the rose petal aromas, most penetrating when the wine is young, some of Tapfer's Moscato Rosa can last for 15 years or so (1983 will be such a one). When it is *amabile* or semi-sweet, Moscato Rosa is DOC. Tiefenbrunner's version is dry so it is *vino da tavola* but it still absolutely stinks of roses! Best years: 1988, '86, '85, '84, '83.

## NEBBIOLO

If you like to see a good argument develop ask a few wine folk about Nebbiolo. There will be those who sigh and go misty-eyed in appreciation of this small, round, dark grape, espousing the sheer brilliance of the wines it produces and applauding its ability to make wines of such complexity without the help of other grapes. Others will treat it as a quirky pest, moaning that the winemaker has to do this, that and the other to get decent wines, *despite* their coming from Nebbiolo. The problem, if a problem it be, is that Nebbiolo packs in a lot of acidity and a lot of tannin. And it doesn't always cede an awful lot of fruit to its wines. This means its wines are not *fun* to drink, particularly early on in their lives. On the other hand, they can be some of the most wonderful, sensational wines. From anywhere. Ever. All this tannin and acidity is just a cocoon for the chrysalis of violets, truffles, raspberries, liquorice, prunes, chocolate and goodness knows what else.

Nebbiolo reaches its greatest heights in the southern half of Piedmont, around Alba. In the north of Piedmont the wines get less intense, more violetty but often more chocolaty too. Apart from Carema these northern Piedmont wines may have the Nebbiolo attack softened by small amounts of less tannic red grapes such as Bonarda and Vespolina. Nebbiolo also has a reasonable presence in Lombardy, in the wines of Valtellina and in a supporting role in red Franciacorta.

Nebbiolo has to be grown on south-facing slopes. Even with the full ration of sun this gives, it still ripens late, occasionally even as late as November by which time there is plenty of fog around. Fog in Italian is *nebbia*, hence the grape's name. It has, though, two very different names in other parts: Spanna in north Piedmont and Chiavennasca in north Lombardy. Whatever its name, Nebbiolo is great. Don't forget it.

## NEBBIOLO D'ALBA DOC
PIEDMONT

♟ Nebbiolo

Nebbiolo d'Alba is ideal if you feel like proper, south Piedmont Nebbiolo but don't feel the occasion, your pocket or your mood merits the full works of Barolo or Barbaresco. It is grown in lands around the big Bs but doesn't have their long ageing requirement; a year is enough. You end up with a small-but-perfectly-formed younger brother type wine: lighter, less intense, more accessible and less expensive too. Any decent Barolo or Barbaresco producer's Nebbiolo d'Alba from 1987, '86 or '85 should be worthwhile. They can be kept for a few years too. The DOC eccentrically also encompasses rare sweetish and sparkling versions.

## NEBBIOLO DELLE LANGHE
Vino da tavola
PIEDMONT

♟ Nebbiolo

If you are a winemaker in south Piedmont's Langhe hills, Nebbiolo delle Langhe is a convenient title to use if you don't want to have to subject your wine to even the one year's ageing it needs for Nebbiolo d'Alba; if you want to try unconventional vinification techniques; if you want to sell off third-rate Barolo or Barbaresco; or if you are unfortunate enough to have your vines outside the Nebbiolo d'Alba area but still in the Langhe. Nebbiolo delle Langhe, then, is a hotch-potch. Wines can be good or indifferent, typical or strange, exciting or dull. If you see one imported, give it a whirl – it might be good news. In Piedmont, be more chary.

## NOSIOLA
Trentino DOC
TRENTINO

♀ Nosiola

Nosiola is a white grape variety, found only in Trentino, and planted in small amounts. Its flavour is so strange it is esteemed just by those who grow it and a few 'in the know'. Dry, with lots of hazelnuts, oil, apples, a touch of honeysuckle and lemon, and a strongly bitter finish, sometimes it seems quite rustic. Nosiola is also used for Trentino's Vino Santo, a sweet *passito* wine. Best producers: Fanti, Madonna delle Vittorie, Pojer & Sandri, Poli, Pravis and, for Vino Santo, Pisoni. Drink young.

## NURAGUS DI CAGLIARI DOC
SARDINIA

♀ Nuragus, Trebbiano, Vermentino and others

If you want to sum up today's white wine scene in Sardinia, all you need is a glass of Nuragus di Cagliari, from the southern third of the island. It is by far the most prolific white DOC with over 27,000 hectolitres produced. Light, crisp and appley, for drinking as young as possible, it is the complete antithesis of old-style Sardinian wines, so big and alcoholic they'd knock you out quicker than a *maquis* bandit. Nuragus is not hugely characterful, though. *Amabile* and *frizzante* versions exist. The Cantina Sociale di Dolianova sets the tone.

## OLTREPÒ PAVESE DOC
LOMBARDY

♟ Barbera, Bonarda, Pinot Nero

♟ Pinot Nero

♀ Cortese, Moscato, Pinot Grigio, Pinot Nero, Riesling Italico, Riesling Renano

▲ Even though the Oltrepò Pavese zone rises above the plain of the Po valley it is still subject to mists and fogs which soften the outlines of the scenery, giving it a gentle air.

Just a tiny corner of Lombardy lies south of the long, ambling Po river, which nearly bisects Italy, dividing its continental north from the peninsula proper. It is called, with unassailable clarity of description, Oltrepò (over the Po) Pavese (in the province of Pavia). It is not until you get into the Oltrepò that you get any relief, that is hills. And where these nice, gentle, curvy hills start, so does the wine zone in a cultural melting pot surrounded by Piedmont, Liguria and Emilia-Romagna.

Basic Oltrepò Pavese Rosso or Rosato is a two- to four-grape blend (Bònarda with Barbera, Uva Rara, Ughetta). The same blend makes three 'special' wines from restricted parts of the zone, all *frizzante*. Barbacarlo is probably the best, dry, substantial and almondy. Buttafuoco is a touch sweeter, dark and punchy; and Sangue di Giuda (or 'Judas Blood'!) is semi-sparkling, distinctly sweetish, deep, rich and not for the unadventurous. Then there is a whole string of single grape varieties. Best and most typical are soft, raspberry, mocha Bonarda and firmly acidic, redcurrant, smoky Barbera. Grapy Moscato leads the whites. But beware. With all these, there is a tendency to fizz: they like it that way there. For the British, the wise producers remove the bubbles. Hardly surprisingly in this land where sparkle is king, there is an Oltrepò Pavese Spumante, usually made with Pinot-type grapes. Think Oltrepò; think bubble. Drink the whites young, the reds from 1988, '86, '85. Best producers: Ballabio, Ca' Longa, Casteggio, Fugazza (Castello di Luzzano), Frecciarossa, La Muiraghina, Lino Maga (Barbacarlo), Mazzolino, Monsupello, Pegazzera.

## ORVIETO DOC
UMBRIA, LAZIO

♀ Trebbiano Toscano, Verdello, Grechetto and others

Orvieto in the south-west of Umbria is a curious but beguiling town atop a mass of hill that rises so sheer from the surrounding countryside you wonder how anybody ever manages to get to the top. Remnants of the ancient Etruscans are all around; you can almost feel their presence – even without copious draughts of the local hooch to aid your imagination. But it is unkind to call Orvieto's wine hooch. It isn't nearly that bad, rarely descending below dull, and sometimes is a real joy. Orvieto used to be seen outside Italy mainly as a medium-dry or *abboccato* wine. There still is a little *abboccato* around, some *amabile* and even on occasions some quite delectable honeyed sweet Orvieto, made by grapes affected by noble rot. Usually though, it is now dry.

Trebbiano (locally called Procanico) at the head of the list of grape varieties ought to sound the death knell for any expectations of character or personality. But all is not lost. There is Grechetto which can add a quota of nuttiness and green fruits to the wine. By using Verdello too, Trebbiano need represent no more than half the wine. Try Bigi's *cru* Torricella (dry) and your hopes will be more than realized. It will age for a couple of years. Drink other Orvietos young. With the right vineyard site in the central, Classico, area, the right yields and the right care and attention Orvieto certainly can pull something out of the bag. Other wines worth a look are from Barberani and Decugnano dei Barbi while Bigi (non-*cru*), Barbi and Antinori are all quite acceptable.

## PAGADEBIT DI ROMAGNA DOC
ROMAGNA

♀ Pagadebit

'Paga-debit' pays the debts. This paragon of money management was every Romagnan vine-grower's dream because it always managed a healthy crop of grapes. Until, unfortunately, complacency and the prodding search for something new drove it into extinction. Enter the saviour of the day, Commendatore Pezzi of Fattoria Paradiso. He found an old stump in his vineyards, consulted experts, propagated it, selected the best cuttings and so on until his gentle, nutty, greengage Pagadebit, first a touch sweet, now dry, was drawing admiring crowds of visitors. The recent DOC (1989) includes dry, *amabile*, and *frizzante* versions as well as a sub-denomination, Bertinoro, where Fattoria Paradiso, still the best producer by a long chalk, lies. Drink it young.

## PALAZZO ALTESI
Vino da tavola
TUSCANY

♟ Sangiovese

This is a super-Tuscan made by the classy Brunello di Montalcino estate of Altesino. It uses the Brunello clone of Sangiovese, pruned really hard to give about half the normal yield. But, unconventionally, 20 per cent of the grapes are kept separate, undergo a carbonic maceration and are then added in to the normally made wine. It also spends up to a year in *barriques*. Results are convincing. There's no shortage of Brunello's powerful, spicy style, the *barriques* give the oaky roundness that makes the wine easy to enjoy, while the dominant impression is of drink-me blackberry fruit. Try it at three years old and lively, or more mellowed several years on. But try it.

Palazzo Altesi now has a brother. In 1985 Altesino first made Alte d'Altesi from a blend of Brunello with 30 per cent Cabernet Sauvignon, giving it one year's *barrique*-ageing, and following more in the mould of other new-wave Tuscan wines. It is a big chunky number, but with no rough edges, and has gone straight into the super-Tuscan top bracket. Best years: 1986, '85.

## PENTRO DOC
MOLISE

♟ ♟ Montepulciano, Sangiovese and others

♟ Trebbiano Toscano, Bombino Bianco and others

When Molise eventually received its first DOC allocation in 1984, long after every other region, it seemed only fair that each of its two provinces (Campobasso and Isernia) should get one each. So Isernia was awarded Pentro (sometimes called Pentro di Isernia). But Pentro covers two completely distinct and well-separated areas. One is at the region's extreme west, nearer to the Mediterranean than Molise's own Adriatic coast; the other area is more central. When the wines become worth drinking we can worry about what comes from where.

## LE PERGOLE TORTE
Vino da tavola
TUSCANY

♟ Sangiovese

An intense, rich, weighty super-Tuscan, well imbued with oak and therefore best not drunk until it has softened and harmonized, from six years old onwards. From the Monte Vertine estate in Chianti Classico, it was the first super-Tuscan made solely from Sangiovese to be aged in *barriques*. Today, after spending six to 12 months in large oak barrels it stays in *barrique* for a year, followed by a few months in bottle before release. First made in 1977, Le Pergole Torte is still one of the classiest of its genre. Best years: 1986, '85, '83, '82, '79, '78.

## PIAVE DOC
VENETO

♟ Cabernet Franc, Cabernet Sauvignon, Merlot, Pinot Nero, Raboso

♟ Pinot Bianco, Pinot Grigio, Tocai, Verduzzo

The valley of the Piave, north of Venice, is broad alluvial plain and there is no shortage of wine that is just as dismal as this uninspiring terrain would lead you to expect. But good old Italy is always full of surprises and there is plenty of lively enough wine to raise a few eyebrows. One reason is that the top viticultural research station of Conegliano is nearby and uses Piave for its investigations into maximizing quality from flat lands. Piave's most exciting wine is Raboso. Well, it would be, wouldn't it? An indigenous grape that hasn't spread far afield can usually be relied on to give a worthwhile taste, and red Raboso, all earthy, herby fruit and tannic clout, is no exception. The other reds, apart from dull Pinot Noir, aren't bad either, tending to the fleshy and grassy; the whites are less engaging. Rechsteiner is probably the only producer who has whites that suggest you sit up and take notice. His reds are among the best too, along with those from Castello di Roncade and Collalto. Drink whites young, Raboso up to eight years, the others up to four. Best years: 1988, '86, '85, '83, '82.

## PICOLIT
Colli Orientali del Friuli DOC
FRIULI-VENEZIA GIULIA

♟ Picolit

Picolit has been called a hype and a rip-off. It is neither. It started with a misguided attempt to present it as Italy's answer to Bordeaux's barley-sugar-like Sauternes. Anybody expecting that and getting Picolit's subtle, floral, honeyed sweetish flavours was bound to be disappointed. And Picolit is expensive. One reason is the distressing-sounding affliction, floral abortion, which prevents the vine flowering properly. Not all the grapes develop fully and the amount of wine produced is tiny. Plantings are not widespread, also keeping the price high. 'Rip-off' is too strong though. Picolit is revered for real in its homeland and is totally alluring from a good estate such as Volpe Pasini, Ronchi di Cialla, Dri, Ca' Ronesca, Sgubin (not DOC), Abbazia di Rosazzo, Ronco del Gnemiz and Gradnik. Best years: 1988, '86, '85, '83, '82, '79.

# PIEDMONT

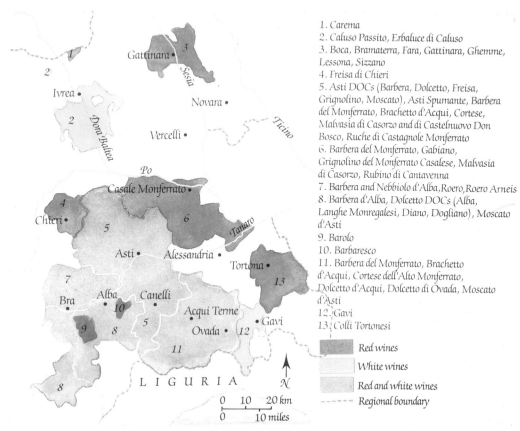

1. Carema
2. Caluso Passito, Erbaluce di Caluso
3. Boca, Bramaterra, Fara, Gattinara, Ghemme, Lessona, Sizzano
4. Freisa di Chieri
5. Asti DOCs (Barbera, Dolcetto, Freisa, Grignolino, Moscato), Asti Spumante, Barbera del Monferrato, Brachetto d'Acqui, Cortese, Malvasia di Casorzo e di Castelnuovo Don Bosco, Ruche di Castagnole Monferrato
6. Barbera del Monferrato, Gabiano, Grignolino del Monferrato Casalese, Malvasia di Casorzo, Rubino di Cantavenna
7. Barbera and Nebbiolo d'Alba, Roero, Roero Arneis
8. Barbera d'Alba, Dolcetto DOCs (Alba, Langhe Monregalesi, Diano, Dogliano), Moscato d'Asti
9. Barolo
10. Barbaresco
11. Barbera del Monferrato, Brachetto d'Acqui, Cortese dell'Alto Monferrato, Dolcetto d'Acqui, Dolcetto di Ovada, Moscato d'Asti
12. Gavi
13. Colli Tortonesi

Red wines
White wines
Red and white wines
Regional boundary

| WINE ENTRIES | Gavi | Moscato |
|---|---|---|
| Asti Spumante | Ghemme | Nebbiolo |
| Barbaresco | Lessona | |
| Barbera d'Alba | Moscato d'Asti | |
| Barbera d'Asti | Moscato di Strevi | |
| Barbera del Monferrato | Nebbiolo d'Alba | |
| Barolo | Nebbiolo delle Langhe | |
| Boca | Roero | |
| Brachetto d'Acqui | Roero Arneis | |
| Bramaterra | Spanna | |
| Bricco Manzoni | | |
| Caluso Passito | GRAPE ENTRIES | |
| Carema | Arneis | |
| Dolcetto d'Alba | Barbera | |
| Erbaluce di Caluso | Dolcetto | |
| Fara | Freisa | |
| Gattinara | Grignolino | |

Tucked away up in the north-west corner of Italy, Piedmont has no coastline nor does it have a city as wondrous as Rome or Venice to attract the crowds, but for many wine lovers a visit to the region is more like a pilgrimage. For Piedmont is the home of Nebbiolo, super-grape *extraordinario*, whose merits are more hotly contested than any other, and of Nebbiolo's most prestigious wines, Barolo and Barbaresco.

The alpine foothills in north and west Piedmont often have too harsh a climate for vines but grapes can ripen only where river valleys bring air movement and so extra sunshine. The Dora Baltea, flowing south through Ivrea, carves out the Nebbiolo zone of Carema and the area of white Erbaluce di Caluso and sweet Caluso Passito. The river Seisa brings viticulture to the Novara and Vercelli hills, south of Lake Maggiore around Gattinara.

It is the south of Piedmont, though, that harbours most of the region's wines. South-east of Turin the landscape becomes characterized by angular hills with perfectly straight rows of vines stretching horizontally across the slopes. This is the heart of Nebbiolo country, with the wine zones of Barolo and Barbaresco on either side of the little town of Alba, also famous for its fabulous white truffles. There, as elsewhere in

▲ The steep Langhe hills in Piedmont, with their neat serried rows of vines, are even more stunning in autumn.

the region, the late-ripening Nebbiolo is planted on the sunniest, south-facing slopes, leaving other slopes for less particular varieties or other crops (mostly maize). A hilltop vineyard site, called *bricco* in dialect, is particularly prized.

Barbera and Dolcetto are widely planted too. There are smaller amounts of Grignolino and Freisa, once in decline but now expanding again. All these red varieties, despite their wide differences, have a common core of austerity (especially when their wines are young) that makes them typically Piedmontese.

White wines take very much second place in the region. Apart from fashionable Gavi in the south-eastern corner, made from Cortese, it was only in the 1980s that interest was shown again in the native varieties, Arneis and Favorita. Yet the strangest thing about south Piedmont is that just next door to probably the harshest, most mouth-attacking reds from anywhere in Italy are the lightest, most delicate mouthfuls of grapiness you could ever hope to find. The province of Asti is home to Asti Spumante and Moscato d'Asti from the Moscato grape: sheer, elegant bliss.

## PIGATO
**Riviera Ligure di Ponente**
**DOC**
LIGURIA

♀ Pigato

There's not a vast choice of white grapes with which to regale a visitor to Liguria but if you are someone's guest it is with Pigato they will fill your glass, just as your pasta will come dressed with their best *pesto* sauce (basil, pine nuts and garlic). Pigato is reckoned a full strong-flavoured white, but it isn't all that powerful, only when compared with its Ligurian compatriot, Vermentino. Pigato's floral, peachy greengagey, nut-milk character doesn't exactly grab you by the braces but fills your mouth quite nicely with flavour and does get rather moreish. Best producers: Alessandri, Anfossi, Riccardo Bruna, Cascina Feipu, Feola, Lupi, Ramoino, Vio. Drink young.

## PINOT
NORTH ITALY

♀ ♀ ♀ Pinot Bianco, Pinot Grigio,
Pinot Nero

Pinot is probably the most gloriously imprecise wine description in Italy. It can be white, rosé or red; from any or all of three grape varieties (sometimes with Chardonnay too); and sparkling or still. However, if you just ask for 'Pinot' without specifying further, what you will get is a white wine, usually still and usually from the Pinot Bianco grape, sometimes with a bit of Pinot Grigio and occasionally white juice from Pinot Nero thrown in for good measure. The word Pinot for sparkling wine has a special cachet: it is well known in Italy that the three Pinots and Chardonnay make the best quality sparklers.

## PINOT BIANCO

Wine made from Pinot Bianco is tangy, creamy and slightly salty. It is usually drunk young, lacking the reputation for ageing potential, but when its acidity is high enough and its maker good enough it can be fabulous at 15 years old or more. Its varietal character is most acute in Alto Adige and northern Trentino, its subtlety best revealed in Friuli. The grape also grows in Veneto where the wine is a little rounder, with a firmer finish, Lombardy and western Emilia. There are outcrops in Tuscany and near Bologna, even, thanks to modern technical know-how in Puglia where it ought to be too hot for the grape. In other parts of the world Pinot Bianco is rather looked down on. Unfortunately, even in Italy there are plenty of people still disdainful of it, even though it realizes its finest potential there. The all-powerful Chardonnay has claimed their allegiance instead. The two wines when made without oak ageing are quite similar when young. So much so that one or two producers from Alto Adige (and elsewhere for all I know) have labelled vats of good Pinot Bianco as in-demand Chardonnay and sold them as such. Don't forget Pinot Bianco's seminal role, though, in Italian dry sparkling wines.

## PINOT GRIGIO

Pinot Grigio thrives in Friuli-Venezia Giulia, the Veneto, Trentino and Alto Adige. It can shine in Lombardy, Emilia and Tuscany too. Despite its name (*grigio* means grey), the wine is certainly not grey, although the grapes can take on a greyish hue. The grapes can also be anything from greenish-yellow to red – Pinot Grigio is nothing if not capricious. The darker grapes come in handy for a copper-coloured wine called *ramato* ('coppery'), typical of Friuli but currently out of vogue. Pinot Grigio also suffers, or perhaps enjoys, a split identity. On the one hand, it is a name to be reckoned with and is the standard-bearer for the north-east in the rest of Italy. On the other, it is deemed an unremarkable, rather fat wine of little interest. As so often with a grape grown on hundreds of sites over vast tracts of land, both opinions can be justified. It is broad, sometimes oily, sometimes like almond and walnut shells, sometimes a bit like marzipan, sometimes like freshly cooked fish, sometimes just squeaky-clean and super-fresh. And in the hands of star growers these different flavours all come together to produce something really stylish

## PINOT NERO

Pinot Nero is the devil of a grape to deal with. It is happy in France (there called Pinot Noir), especially in Burgundy, but elsewhere it is horribly fussy and needs inordinate amounts of tender loving care to make wine anywhere near up to its capabilities. So the battle has been on in Italy, as in the rest of the world, to conquer Pinot Nero, until recently without success. With the bottling of each new trial and its proud but nervous launch for the waiting pundits, suspense hung in the air. But the vote was always 'no'; another good attempt, interesting in its own way but not Pinot Noir as the French have taught us to recognize it.

Suddenly all has changed. From Franciacorta in Lombardy two estates have emerged with the real McCoy: Ca' del Bosco with Pinero and Bellavista with Le Casotte. From Colli Piacentini there's La Stoppa's Alfeo. Now the mould is broken others are sure to follow. Nevertheless, superb and unique as 'archetypal' Pinot Nero is, with its opulent and ethereal perfumed raspberry, beetroot and earthy, vegetal flavours, it begs the question why should so many people spend so much time and effort on a vine long-established in Italy to make a wine which apes its style in France.

## POMINO DOC
TUSCANY

🍷 Sangiovese, Canaiolo, Cabernet Sauvignon and others

🍷 Pinot Bianco, Chardonnay, Trebbiano Toscano and others

Perhaps I am being ungenerous but I have always reckoned that getting a DOC for Pomino Rosso was nothing more than a copy-cat move, after a glance over the shoulder at Carmignano. Both areas are in Tuscany but outside Chianti Classico; Carmignano in Chianti Montalbano, Pomino in Chianti Rufina. Both were mentioned in the Bando, a document of 1716 defining the boundaries of the four most illustrious wines of the time. Both have Cabernet in their Sangiovese-based blend. Both areas are dominated by one large estate owned by aristocracy. But while Carmignano's Conte Ugo Contini Bonacossi slogged away for years to get recognition for Carmignano (with Cabernet included because he had strong evidence that traditionally it always had been – as it might have been in Pomino), the Marchesi de' Frescobaldi's plummy Pomino Rosso followed without too much hassle in 1983, eight years later, by which time Cabernet was already high fashion.

Pomino Bianco is another matter. It had already been produced for a number of years by Frescobaldi as a *vino da tavola*. It was well known in Tuscany and abroad and highly rated. Frescobaldi also made, and still does, a version from specially selected grapes called Il Benefizio which goes into *barriques*. It comes out oak sodden but when left a year or two to calm down can blossom into a magnificent toasty, buttery number. Therefore, although Pomino Bianco seems like a private Frescobaldi DOC, the spirit of the main DOC objective, to enshrine local tradition and practice, was sure as anything respected. Best years: 1988, '86, '85, '83, '82 for both red and white. There is a Vin Santo too.

## PRELUDIO
Vino da tavola
PUGLIA

🍷 Chardonnay

In mid-1988 a glossy brochure flopped on to my doormat, announcing the arrival of wines of a certain Tenute Torrebianco in Puglia and, in particular, a Chardonnay called Preludio n.1. Oh no, I thought, someone else on the Chardonnay bandwagon, and from far too far south, the wine will be a technologically light, fresh glass of nothing at an elevated price. Then I tasted the wine and had to eat (or drink?) my words. There was a nice, smoky, earthy whiff and gentle but rich, creamy fruit with a dry, stony end. Then I started to believe the bumph about a carefully chosen site 200 metres (650 feet) high and the difficult-to-cultivate, calcareous tufa soil well suited to Chardonnay. From 1988, the second vintage, more has been produced (950 hectolitres) and its quality is even better.

## PRIMITIVO DI MANDURIA DOC
PUGLIA

🍷 Primitivo

Ask any wine student to name one wine from Puglia and the answer you are most likely to get is Primitivo di Manduria. Not because the wine is so brilliant, so rare, so odd or so widely sold, but because it is part of the learner's catechism that the Primitivo grape is believed to be the origin of California's Zinfandel variety, now more or less reckoned indigenous to the United States. The hows and whys of this remain a mystery. But it has benefited the more go-ahead Puglian Primitivo producers who have decided to export to the United States labelling it as Zinfandel.

The land around Manduria (east of Taranto in the Salento peninsula) is flat and sun-baked. The vines are planted in small, individual, *alberello* bushes, close to the ground where their dark grapes can get incredibly ripe, meaning liver-frighteningly high levels of potential alcohol. Most of the grapes are used to bump up the weedier offerings of elsewhere (except no-one actually admits to buying them). Those that are used for Primitivo di Manduria proper make a dark purple, dry or slightly sweet, mega-gutsy blackberried beast with at least 13·5 per cent alcohol. There is also a fully sweet version, a fortified sweet and a fortified 'dry', which is still sweet, but stronger! Clued-up producers like Soloperto and Savese prefer to avoid all this and simply classify their wines by their alcoholic strength. Vinicola Amanda is also highly rated.

## PROSECCO

If the Pinot family of grapes is the backbone of Italian sparkling wine, Prosecco is its soul. The two give their all in two totally separate types of *spumante*. Pinot-type is usually serious and aiming for refinement; Prosecco *spumante*, all milky, appley froth, equals frivolity. Prosecco is another of those Italian grapes that knows where it thrives and stays there, in this case about midway between Treviso and Belluno in eastern Veneto. It is also one of those grapes that tends to produce fizz, sometimes whether you want it to or not. So what Prosecco does best is produce *frizzante* and sparkling wine that is just like the still version but with bubbles. Getting the fizz into Prosecco has to be as swift as possible to avoid the normal yeast-induced changes. So you bottle it as soon as the yeasts have worked up the pressure you want. So crucial to Prosecco folk was this that they took on the rest of Europe, fighting in the portals of the EC to ensure the nascent pan-Community sparkling wine law granted Prosecco the right to undercut the minimum ageing requirement demanded of everyone else. They won.

## PROSECCO DI CONEGLIANO-VALDOBBIADENE DOC
VENETO

🍷 Prosecco, Verdiso

This must be one of the longest and hardest to pronounce wine names in the book, especially with six-syllable Valdobbiadene demanding the stress on its fourth syllable. Valdobbiadene and Conegliano are towns at the western and eastern edges of the wine zone, lying between Treviso and Belluno, and the wine may take the name of just one of them, an option that most producers thankfully use. At the Valdobbiadene end is a zone called Cartizze, credited with producing the finest wines and so granted its own sub-denomination, Superiore di Cartizze. Prosecco di Conegliano-Valdobbiadene can be still, but is usually *frizzante* or *spumante*. All three styles can be dry or sweet. So there is plenty to keep the label printers happy and confuse the customers.

Prosecco's natural market is nearby Venice. If when in Venice you pop into a local hostelry for a moment's respite from the continual tramp of tourist feet, Prosecco, with its soft, appley, milky flavours will taste absolutely great. Back home it won't taste as good – you can't export atmosphere – but it will still be a refreshing glass of simple, soft wine with bubbles. Carpenè Malvolti is the best known name; Zardetto, Canevel and Le Case Bianche the best. Drink young.

## PUGLIA
SOUTHERN ITALY

*Wine entries:* Brindisi, Castel del Monte, Il Falcone, Five Roses, Locorotondo, Preludio, Primitivo di Manduria, Salice Salentino, Squinzano

▲ No-one is quite certain of the origins of these strangely-shaped *trulli* in Puglia. The Locorotondo vineyards with their ochre-brown soil and bush-like, *alberello* vines are occasionally interspersed with other crops.

Puglia, the heel of Italy, is a big region – 19,374 square km (7470 square miles). Its northern limit is on the same latitude as Rome; its south level with Corfu. If you are a tourist your main interests are probably the Gargano peninsula, the spur, a huge mass of high rock and pine forest with some gasp-worthy sights and astounding bathing, and the *trulli*, strange-looking round houses with conical roofs whose origins are uncertain, found mainly in Alberobello (near Locorotondo and Martina Franca for those who travel by the drinking posts). You'll also probably want to go to 'Land's End', Santa Maria di Leuca, where helpful locals tell you, 'Either you jump in the sea or you turn back'.

If it is DOCs you are after there are three areas to target. The first is in the north of Puglia, inland from the Gargano so you'll have to sacrifice the aesthetics, where there is San Severo and Cacc'e Mmitte di Lucera. (Don't even attempt to pronounce this unless you have had lessons in the local dialect.) A little further south is a large cluster of which Castel del Monte is the least obscure and that mainly because one producer, Rivera, has put it on the map. Then there's a long haul down to the Salento peninsula – the bit of Puglia with both an east and a west coast – where the others are scattered.

This is to date the most successful area for wine. The Salento has sea all round to temper the climate; it has the Negroamaro grape for its reds and Verdeca, which turns out snazzy Locorotondo, for its whites (and one or two others too). So as Puglia continues to flex its vinous muscles and starts to realize its great potential, despite strong claims from its northern and central wines the current lead from the Salento may well continue.

## RAPITALÀ
### Alcamo DOC, vino da tavola
SICILY

🍷 Nerello Mascalese, Nero d'Avola, Perricone

🍷 Nerello Mascalese

🍷 Catarratto, Trebbiano

If Sicily could be said to have a model estate Rapitalà is it. Apart from the winery's brilliant setting, in a gentle dip in the Alcamo hills in north-west Sicily, green and tranquil, surrounded by vines which receive excellent exposure to the sun, no expense has been spared in the pursuit of ever-increasing quality. In this case that means hiring the services of Gigi Lo Guzzo, Sicily's leading winemaker, and giving him his head. His attentions at Rapitalà were first directed to the white, officially DOC Alcamo – not that it really matters, and by the beginning of the 1980s it was already receiving praise as fresh, floral and terrific value. Then, in 1988, came a delicate, strawberries and almonds rosé that is up with a fighting chance of rivalling Cellaro, Sicily's best. Then he persuaded the estate to let him put his experiments with red into practice with terrific punchy, fleshy, brambly results that I hope aren't just a flash in the pan. Drink white and rosé young, the new red from a year old onwards.

## RAVELLO
### Vino da tavola
CAMPANIA

🍷🍷 Piedirosso, Aglianico, Merlot

🍷 Coda di Volpe, San Nicola, Greco

Strange, isn't it, how of the three Campanian Amalfi Coast 'resort' wines (the others are Ischia and Capri) the best, Ravello, is the one without the DOC. You could credit this superiority to the grape blends. Me, I reckon there are more real people living along this glorious, craggy coast, not tourists I mean, than there are on the holiday islands and that there are enough of them who won't accept any old rubbish as their daily slurp to ensure that the major producer, Episcopio, doesn't let his standards slip too far. If they did drop, he might then need DOC to persuade the tourists to buy the wine instead.

## REBO
### Vino da tavola
TRENTINO

🍷 Rebo

Rebo is rather like the proverbial needle extricated from the haystack. It is a cross between Merlot and Marzemino which emerged in 1948 after countless experiments by Rebo Rigotti. The aim had been to find a grape which would replace Merlot in Trentino, where it is prone to downy mildew and problems at the time of flowering. Rebo more or less did, its Marzemino side adding zesty, lively, fresh fruit to Merlot's softness. Promising as it is, I can't see it taking over from Merlot yet, while Cabernet-Merlot blends are all the rage. Drink it two to three years old. Leading producer: Dorigati.

## RECIOTO DELLA VALPOLICELLA DOC
VENETO

🍷 Corvina, Rondinella, Molinara and others

Ears in Italian are *orecchie*, in Veronese dialect, *recie*. No, this is not a bilingual anatomy lesson, just the most popular explanation of how Recioto came to get its name. A bunch of grapes often has one large cluster and two shorter ones sticking out on either side. These 'ears' get more sun and are less subject to rot so their grapes, according to Veronese wisdom, are better quality. Recioto used to be made just from the ears, but these days it is made from any part of the bunch, as long as the grapes are of super-high quality (and quite a job it is selecting the best too). It is basically a *passito* wine, the grapes drying for up to four months or more, in an airy room before fermenting. If the fermentation stops naturally before all the sugar turns to alcohol or if it is stopped by human hand, the wine, dark and strong, remains sweet. If the wine ferments to dryness it gains the additional name Amarone.

Recioto is a far cry from ordinary Valpolicella – you could be excused for not even recognizing it as a version of the same wine. But when you taste its luscious, intense, bitter cherries, plums, smoke and meat stock flavours, then imagine extracting from a top notch Valpolicella the essence of its flavours, the common origin becomes clear. Recioto in all its sweet glory is less often seen than its dry partner. So make the most of the odd occasions when a bottle comes your way. Ignore the fortified and sparkling versions. At the end of a meal when you are not in a hurry to go anywhere try the real thing, from starry producers such as Quintarelli, Allegrini, Le Ragose, Masi, Serègo Alighieri, Tedeschi, Ferrari, from 1986, '85, '83. Take it slowly and wait for it to win you over.

## RECIOTO DELLA VALPOLICELLA AMARONE DOC
VENETO

Corvina, Rondinella, Molinara and others

► Grapes undergoing the *passito* process to make Recioto della Valpolicella are carefully arranged on shallow trays, piled one above the other, with plenty of space for the all-important air to circulate. With luck the weather will be dry, no rot will form and by January the shrivelled purple grapes will be raisin-like, concentrated and sugar-packed.

Amarone means strongly bitter. Vinously it means that Recioto della Valpolicella has been left to ferment to dryness. Except that it never seems absolutely dry; when you take a sniff you get such rich, opulent fruit you get the feeling that you are about to taste something quite sweet. The initial sensation is fruit-sweet too, then bitter-sweet, then you get a final explosion of taste, now strongly dry and with a flourish of bitter chocolate. Amarone fills your mouth with all the wonderful bitter cherries, plums, smoke and meat stock flavours of sweet Recioto but in 'the bitter one' they are even more intense and focused. It is a pretty strong beast too. In short, Amarone is just amazing stuff. From producers such as Quintarelli, Allegrini, Le Ragose, Masi, Serègo Alighieri, Tedeschi and Tramanal, in years like 1986, '85, '83, '81, '79, '78, '77 it can be mind-blowing. But beware. Not every bottle warrants such eulogies and such experiences don't come cheap.

As for that long title, the wine has recently been rechristened Amarone della Valpolicella. In addition, since the decent stuff only comes from the hilly Classico zone and it is therefore helpful to know which wines do, 'Classico' can now be cited where appropriate. Good news.

## RECIOTO DI SOAVE DOC
VENETO

Garganega, Trebbiano

Whoever would have thought of Soave as a softly honeyed, peachy, apricotty, almondy, appley, delicious, lightly sweet wine? But that is what Recioto di Soave is. The *passito* process wreaks a transformation from ugly duckling to swan. Most Soave producers can't be bothered to make it. But those who care about quality, like Pieropan (classic!) and Anselmi (aged in oak: more barley-sugar-like) *do* bother; as do Allegrini, Masi, Tedeschi and Quintarelli, only their vineyards fall outside the Soave area so their Recioto is *vino da tavola*, unrevealingly named Fiorgardane, Bianco Campociesa, Vin de la Fabriseria and Il Bandito respectively. Tedeschi's also contains a proportion of traditional, but no longer officially permitted grape varieties. Drink it at two to five years old. Ignore the sparkling and fortified aberrations.

## REFOSCO

Wine made from Refosco or, to give it its full name, Refosco dal Peduncolo Rosso is, at its best, deeply coloured and has a tangy, tarry, grassy, summer-pudding flavour with a bitter-dry finish. Or it can be lean and dull. The grape is a stalwart Friulian resident, the best examples being found in Collio and Colli Orientali. A less good clone called Refosco Nostrano crops up in small amounts in the Carso, by Trieste. Anyway, it is called Terrano there. Best years: 1988, '86, '85, '83, '82.

## REGALEALI
### Vino da tavola
SICILY

🍷 Nero d'Avola, Perricone

🍷 Nerello Mascalese, Nero d'Avola

🍸 Inzolia, Catarratto, Sauvignon

Regaleali must be one of the last bastions of old-style Sicilian aristocracy. How the driver who had accompanied me over vast tracts of that craggy, part-barren island fumed when he was put to sit in the kitchen with the servants while the rest of us lunched formally in Conte Tasca d'Almerita's dining-room. Arm-flailing gestures and a stream of unrepeatable language marked our winding return from this deserted spot bang in the middle of Sicily. Lifestyle apart, the Count and his family have a firm grip on their 200 hectares (495 acres) of vineyard; both red and white wines have been acclaimed the best in Sicily. The site helps: high and kept from over-heating by breezes and night-time mists.

The foremost red is Rosso del Conte, all punchy plums, coffee and tobacco flavours from selected late-picked grapes. The 1980 is still going strong. Regaleali white is enlivened by 30 per cent Sauvignon. There is also a special white, Nozze d'Oro with even more Sauvignon. The first vintage was 1985 (the year of the Count's *Nozze d'Oro* – golden wedding) and its lemony, leafy, herby taste – like nice non-sweetened, non-spirity vermouth – meant it was snapped up fast. 1988 followed. Drink straight Bianco young, the Rosso at two to four years.

## RIBOLLA

In looking for something good it can be all too easy to ignore what is under your feet. Ribolla, one of Friuli's native varieties, produces wines which are subtle, lemony, a touch creamy and with fresh acidity; when well made they can be minor gems. They may not be like the fashionable, international stars Chardonnay or Sauvignon but that is no reason to decry them as many Friulians do. It was only those in Colli Orientali who originally thought kindly enough of the grape to include it on the DOC list. Collio has now followed suit, which is only right as Ribolla reaches its peak up in Collio's hills right on the Yugoslav border. Otherwise it provides a useful acidic bite in Ribolla/Malvasia/Tocai blends in DOC Collio. Ribolla, full name Ribolla Gialla, has not so far strayed into the rest of Italy. It has a red partner, Ribolla Nera, whose more usual name is Schioppettino.

## RIESLING ITALICO

Widely grown in eastern Europe where it is called variously Welschriesling, Laski Riesling (or Rizling as the EC now insists we write it), Olasz Rizling/Riesling and so on, Riesling Italico produces vast quantities of plonk, at best easily quaffable, at worst unspeakable. Yet in Italy it really isn't too bad at all. It sometimes hides inside bottles labelled just 'Riesling', which is naughty because it makes you think of the aromatic, far superior Riesling Renano (German Rhine Riesling). Still, Riesling Italico can be quite aromatic in its own right, with good refreshing acidity tweaking up its soft, gentle flavours. It mainly appears in the north-east; to its advantage in Friuli and Veneto, but to its disadvantage in Trentino-Alto Adige in whose climate and altitude it really is not happy. In Lombardy's Oltrepò Pavese it is more than respectable and in Emilia's Colli Bolognesi it can be even better. You'll also find fair quantities scattered around elsewhere.

## RIESLING RENANO

Those making wines from Riesling Renano (Rhine Riesling) look to Germany for the model versions of this highly perfumed grape. But while Riesling reaches tremendous heights of refinement in the slaty vineyards of the Rhine and Mosel, I am not alone in claiming that it achieves the essence of its most purely varietal style in Teutonic Italy: Alto Adige, and the hilly parts of Friuli near the Yugoslav border. Usually bone dry (Germany's Rieslings tend to be sweeter), steely fresh, with a pot-pourri of fruits and flowers, at its best it is almost shockingly, cleanly, pure-tasting. Up in Alto Adige, Tiefenbrunner's standard setter is piercingly exhilarating; east in Friuli, Jermann and Schiopetto lead the field with their more restrained, enticing nerve-tinglers. Those who are less daring still make attractive crisp wines, abundantly perfumed but less exciting. Riesling Renano is DOC in most of the north-east. Where it isn't, the *vino da tavola* versions can be just as good: it all depends on the producer. Elsewhere it is thin on the ground.

## RIVIERA DEL GARDA BRESCIANO DOC
LOMBARDY

🍷 🥂 Groppello, Sangiovese, Barbera, Marzemino

🥂 Riesling Italico, Riesling Renano

I'd be tempted to think that Riviera del Garda Bresciano was a mind-over-matter wine, the 'mind' along the lines of 'we must have something for all these tourists (mostly German) who fill our resorts along Lake Garda every year and our wine will be worth much more as a DOC', were it not for there being some substance to the 'matter'. The Groppello grape more or less belongs to this area around the western bank of the lake. Its reds are chunky and lively but more fun are the delicate rosés, called Chiaretto. The whites are as yet unproven as DOC was only granted in 1989. Best producers: Ca' dei Frati, Costaripa, La Torretta, La Pertica, Pasini.

## RIVIERA LIGURE DI PONENTE DOC
LIGURIA

🍷 🥂 Ormeasco, Rossese

🥂 Pigato, Vermentino

They have been talking about getting DOC for the western (*ponente*) side of the Ligurian riviera for so long I began to think it would never materialize. But at last it arrived, just in time for the spankingly good 1988 harvest. The whole of the coastal area from Genoa to the French border is included, and all the grapes are traditional. Vermentino is the light, white quaffer; Pigato the fuller, more serious white. Ormeasco (the local name for Dolcetto) is the mouth-filling, vibrantly fruity red, which also, called Sciac-trà or Sciacchetrà, supplies the rosé no Mediterranean coastal area can be without. Then Rossese adds a lighter, more perfumed touch to the repertoire and a bit of elegance. Alessandri, Anfossi, Boiga, Riccardo Bruna, Colle dei Bardellini, Cascina Feipu, Feola, Lupi, Ramoino, Vio are all worthy of attention.

## ROERO DOC, ROERO ARNEIS DOC
PIEDMONT

🍷 Nebbiolo

🥂 Arneis

Those fortunate enough to have vineyards in southern Piedmont's Cuneo province, but unfortunate enough to have them on the north side of the river Tanaro with its sandier soils spent many years feeling pretty miffed. Not only were Barolo and Barbaresco on the south side but all the folklore of the area referred to that side, the Langhe, too. The big wide world knew next to nothing of their side, the Roero. Their red wine may have been entitled to DOC Nebbiolo d'Alba, but that had to be shared with the Langhe folk. They wanted their very own DOC. Nothing else could placate their ruffled feathers. So in 1985 Roero DOC was born, individualized by minimal differences from Nebbiolo d'Alba. All very fine. And very fine some of the wines are too, showing the lighter, more easily acceptable raspberry, violets face of youngish Nebbiolo. Best years: 1988, '86, '85. Best producers: Almondo, Deltetto, Malabaila Malvirà, Pezzuto-Malot, Rabino. In 1989 came the white partner, from Arneis, ending the need to label it 'Arneis dei Roeri *vino da tavola*'. White Roero

Arneis should be subtle, restrained and alluring, with nutty, pears, apples and liquorice flavours. Best producers: Deltetto, Malabaila, Malvirà. Castello di Neive's is great too, but not DOC as it is from outside the zone. Drink within a year or two of the vintage.

## RONCO DEI CILIEGI
**Vino da tavola**
ROMAGNA

🍷 Sangiovese

Ronco dei Ciliegi is one of three separate plots (the others are Ronco delle Ginestre, Ronco Casone) of the estate Castelluccio in a hilly bit of southern Romagna. Three things mark the wines out. Firstly, the Sangiovese used is the pukka Sangiovese Grosso from Tuscany instead of the so-so local Sangiovese di Romagna. Then the ageing is carried out in small barrels of 350 litres, instead of the trendy 225-litre *barriques*. Probably most important of all, the consultant winemaker is Vittorio Fiore, one of a handful of top wine magicians in Tuscany. Perhaps it is hardly surprising, then, that the wines taste far more Tuscan than Romagnan with plenty of rich, pruny, spicy fruit – and they're jolly good. Ronco dei Ciliegi is usually the best of the trio. Five years old is still considered 'young' here: the 1983 will be starting to drink well in 1990 – by which time it will all have been sold. 1986, '85, '83, '82 and '81 are all worthy vintages – if you can find them. There is also a tiny amount (600–700 bottles per year) of oak-fermented Sauvignon Blanc called Ronco del Re.

## RONCO DI MOMPIANO
**Vino da tavola**
LOMBARDY

🍷 Marzemino, Merlot

Some people love experimenting. Mario Pasolini just can't stop. He always has some ideas buzzing round in his mind for his steep vineyards near Brescia, be they new varieties, different techniques (sparkling, *passito* . . . ) or both. Ronco di Mompiano was his first wheeze, a blend of Marzemino, with a third of Merlot, neither commonly found in Lombardy. After a decade of tinkering it appeared in 1967. It was a bold move considering that it was before the craze for smart *vini da tavola* set in. But, lively, zesty and fleshy, it worked. And it still works. Best years: 1988, '86, '85.

## ROSSESE DI DOLCEACQUA
**DOC**
LIGURIA

🍷 Rossese

Goodbye Rossese di Dolceacqua? Less than 2500 hectolitres have been made in recent years and the area is now inside the new Riviera di Ponente zone which threatens to swallow it up. It won't matter as long as there is still some refreshing, perfumed, floral, lowish-in-acid Rossese to quench the thirst of folk on the French border in the far west of Italy's rocky and riotously colourful Riviera of Flowers. It is terrific when drunk very young, which most of it is these days and it can become all soft and cuddly after two or three years. The best come from tiny, artisanal producers whose wines you won't get your hands on – unless you know one of their friends, or get friendly with them yourself. So go for Giobatta Cane, Guglielmi, Lupi.

## ROSSO CONERO DOC
MARCHE

🍷 Montepulciano, Sangiovese

▶ The heartland of Rosso Conero is on the slopes of Monte Conero, a massif just inland from the port of Ancona. The name comes from a particular type of cherry tree (called Conero by the Greeks) that grows on the stony white soil of its peaks.

Rosso Conero is the Marche's best red wine, primarily because it is made almost entirely from the gutsy Montepulciano grape variety. True, I've had some bottles that made me think they had been squeezing the grapes with a steamroller to get every last morsel, bad flavours as well as good, out of them; but the general level is pretty reliable. Rosso Conero, a smallish area near the coast, is towards the northern limit of where the Montepulciano grape will thrive, so its almost voluptuous brambly fruit gets a sharper edginess along with its pepper and spice. Best producer: Marchetti; talented up-and-coming youngsters: Moroder, Serenelli; rank and file goodies: Garofoli's Vigna Piancarda and Umani Ronchi's San Lorenzo. Best years: 1988, '87, '86, '85 and '83.

# ROSSO DI MONTALCINO
## DOC
TUSCANY

🍷 Sangiovese

Brunello di Montalcino is a big wine, a serious wine, a slow-maturing wine and a wine that has to receive four years' ageing before it can be bottled. There is nothing wrong with any of this but it does mean that, even if you live in the heart of Montalcino and love Brunello dearly, you wouldn't want to drink it every day. And if you are a producer of Brunello your cash flow is an accountant's nightmare. So whoever had the idea of Rosso di Montalcino and manoeuvred it into existence just as Brunello di Montalcino was upgraded to DOCG deserves a hearty round of applause.

It is like a less intense Brunello di Montalcino (from the Brunello clone of Sangiovese) that can be sold by its first birthday. Those who feel that Brunello's ageing period is too long look to Rosso di Montalcino with broad grins as evidence for their claims. This is not the point. Both wines are valid. Rosso di Montalcino, though, has an extra shot of lively, cinnamon-plummy fruit: what it loses on matured complexity, it gains with youthful excitement. It is affordable too. Any bottle is worth a gamble but those from the best producers such as Altesino, Caparzo, Case Basse, Cerbaiona, Col d'Orcia, Lisini, Il Poggione, San Filippo, Talenti, Villa Banfi will have the edge. Best years: 1988, '87, '86, '85. Brusco dei Barbi is along the same lines but richer. As it has a unique and non DOC-approved vinification method it is *vino da tavola*.

## ROSSO DI MONTEPULCIANO DOC
TUSCANY

♟ Sangiovese, Canaiolo, Malvasia and others

'Me too'! That is the cry that went up among the producers of the beefy Vino Nobile di Montepulciano as they looked across from their hill-top enclave in southern Tuscany and saw producers in nearby Montalcino reaping all the benefits of being able to sell a quicker-maturing Rosso di Montalcino while the ultra-serious Brunello di Montalcino still slumbered in its barrels. 'We want something like that', said the Montepulciano folk. And set about getting it. It took a while but at last Vino Nobile producers can select their best grapes for the 'noble' wine, safe in the knowledge they have a good home in Rosso di Montepulciano for the rest. And at last they have a young, less intense, fruitier wine to drink when the occasion doesn't call for the big stuff. We'll have to wait until more wines appear, though, to see whether the practice matches the theory.

## ROSSO PICENO DOC
MARCHE

♟ Sangiovese, Montepulciano, Trebbiano, Passerina

I reckon that if the Montepulciano content of Rosso Piceno could creep higher, so would the wine's prospects, even though the 60 per cent Sangiovese it has to have imparts breadth and some elegance to the robust Montepulciano, particularly when producers age their wines in large oak casks. With the exception of the most northerly province of Pesaro, the zone covers the entire Adriatic side of the Marche region. The wine is made spasmodically throughout, with the fluctuations in quality that you would expect from such a basic store cupboard wine.

Go for the Superiore. For once Rosso Piceno Superiore does not just imply slightly higher alcohol; it comes from a small, high-quality area by Ascoli Piceno, in the extreme south of the region – more like a 'Classico' really. Best years: 1988, '87, '86, '85, '83. Best producers: Villamagna (for the normal), Cocci Grifoni (Superiore).

## SAGRANTINO DI MONTEFALCO DOC
UMBRIA

♟ Sagrantino

I can't understand why Sagrantino isn't better known. More people deserve to try this deep, plums, prunes, dark cherries, liquorice wine. Admittedly not a lot is produced; most, by far, of the less than 6500 hectolitres of DOC red wine from this mid-Umbrian zone is straight Montefalco (a Sangiovese/Sagrantino blend) not the far superior version made solely from Sagrantino. If you do get some and think it tastes as if there is a sweet wine in there somewhere bursting to get out – you are right. Sagrantino grapes can be semi-dried in *passito* style, yielding a remarkable concentrated *abboccato* version. 1985 and '86 are the years to go for, '88 the year to wait for. Best producers: Adanti (especially), Caprai, Paolo Bea, Rocca dei Fabbri, Fongoli.

## SALICE SALENTINO DOC
PUGLIA

♟ ♟ Negroamaro, Malvasia Nera

♟ Chardonnay, Pinot Bianco, Sauvignon

Although the name Salento is given to the whole peninsula which forms Italy's tall heel, the wine zone Salice Salentino ('Salentine Willow' – how pretty!) covers only a small part, on the Adriatic coast, south of Brindisi. The most important wine is red, mainly from the anciently noble Negroamaro variety, as black and bitter when young as its name describes and tannic too. But give it a dose of soft, aromatic Malvasia Nera to add charm and perfume; give it a good five years to settle down and mollify its mouth-attackers; in short, wait for the tearaway, unkempt adolescent to grow into a refined young adult, and Salice Salentino ought to be rave-worthy. But there's been too much complacency to permit much improvement yet. There are also new varietal wines, from Aleatico (red, also *liquoroso*), Chardonnay and Pinot Bianco (white). Candido and Cosimo Taurino are the best producers, but even they make their best wines as *vino da tavola*: Cappello di Prete (excellent) and Notarpanaro respectively. Also good: De Castris, Vallone. Best years: 1987, '86, '85, '83, '82.

## SAMMARCO
**Vino da tavola**
TUSCANY

🍷 Cabernet Sauvignon, Sangiovese

Castello dei Rampolla has embraced the wave of Cabernet Sauvignon worship as well as any. Thèir Chianti Classico always has the seductive whiff of a sizeable dollop of Cabernet Sauvignon in it. So it is hardly surprising that for Sammarco, Rampolla's super-Tuscan wine, Cabernet has dominated, to the tune of 75 per cent. Of course, *barrique*-ageing plays its part too. The end result is superb blackcurranty Cabernet with a strong Tuscan accent. Best years: 1988, '86, '85, '83, '82, '81. All can be kept, 1985 and '88 should be.

## SANGIOVESE

With Sangiovese Italy struck lucky. It is Italy's most widely planted red grape variety, almost its most prolific and the variety that most people associate as 'the taste of Italy'. This is not just chance. Well before Italy's recent wine renaissance began, and before wine legislation stabilized what was grown where, the choice of a vine for most growers depended mainly on its yield. Sangiovese was usually the best of whatever was available locally for giving gratifyingly abundant crops without the wines getting too thin and tasteless. This was the stroke of fortune for, unlike neutral Trebbiano – the white in equivalent circumstances – Sangiovese does fulfil claims for its venerability.

However widely it travelled, though, Sangiovese's real stomping ground was and remains central Italy: Tuscany, Umbria, Romagna and the Marche, with, less eminently, Lazio. Without Sangiovese, there would be no Chianti as we know it, no Brunello di Montalcino, no Vino Nobile di Montepulciano, no Carmignano. Umbria would have no Torgiano to take its place on the world stage; the Marche would have to rely on Montepulciano, there teetering on the edge of a too-cool climate, in wines like Rosso Conero. Romagna would be almost without red wine. It is a dismal prospect. Even worse we would never have discovered the joy of low-cropped Tuscan Sangiovese on its own, nor its exciting affinity with Cabernet Sauvignon.

Like all plants long grown in different soils, climates and regions, there is not just one Sangiovese vine. The significant difference is between the traditional Tuscan Sangiovese with its clones such as Brunello, Prugnolo or Sangioveto, and Sangiovese di Romagna, from across the Apennines. Sangiovese di Romagna is the real high yielder. And it was Sangiovese di Romagna that was planted everywhere, even in Chianti, when the drive for ever-higher quantity went mad in the 1960s. Still, that is all being put right now as the vines are now being replanted. So by the turn of the century Romagnan Sangiovese should be all back in Romagna where it belongs. And Tuscan Sangiovese? Still in Tuscany, for sure, but there are already at least two plantings in Romagna so don't expect all the complications to fade away.

## SANGIOVESE DI ROMAGNA
**DOC**
ROMAGNA

🍷 Sangiovese

Sangiovese di Romagna (the grape) is the big bad wolf of Sangiovese clones because when it overproduces, which it does with consummate ease, its wines are but gaunt shadows of what you might expect from the variety. Most wine made from Sangiovese di Romagna isn't that bad but it isn't too brilliant either. Yet if it gets a proper, hilly slope instead of Romagna's usual extensive plains sites; if the vineyards have good aspect and exposure; and if the yields are held in check by hard pruning, Sangiovese di Romagna can metamorphose into an aristocratic glassful, racier and less chunky than the Tuscan versions, with a long, steady ageing potential. Only Fattoria Paradiso with his *cru* Vigna delle Lepri hits the mark with unerring precision. Foschi, Nespoli, Casetto dei Mandorli, Le Calbane, Spalletti, Canepella can also be good. Best years: 1988, '86, '85, '84, '83, '82.

## SANTA MADDALENA DOC
ALTO ADIGE

🍷 Schiava, Tschaggele, Lagrein, Pinot Nero

From central Bolzano you can be among the vines of Santa Maddalena in ten minutes — on foot! A cardiac-arresting ascent quickly brings you into a dense cluster of vine-green, pergola-covered, conical hills. The transformation is as exhilarating as the climb, the views fascinating — vineyard bliss one way, the city of Bolzano, seemingly dominated by a huge railway junction, the other.

Mussolini once declared Santa Maddalena one of Italy's four greatest wines. The zone has been trying to shrug off the *duce* connection ever since. For even the staunchest Santa Maddalena fan would not place the wine in that category. It is, with few challenges, the best wine made from the red Schiava grape, but that is another matter. It is light red in colour and for glugging the younger the better, with the smoky, strawberry-yogurt flavours of the Schiava sometimes given a teensy boost of Lagrein. The wines of Grai, Hofstätter, Lageder, Rottensteiner (Hans or Heinrich) or the incomparably named Glögglhof should set you on the right lines. For those who incline more to German terms (this being a bi-lingual zone) yours is Sankt Magdalener.

## SARDINIA

*Wine entries:* Anghelu Ruju, Malvasia di Bosa, Malvasia di Cagliari, Monica di Sardegna, Moscato di Cagliari, Nuragus di Cagliari, Torbato di Alghero, Vernaccia di Oristano

If you are stuck in the wilds of Sardinia's remote interior with its rugged *maquis* and tales of banditry stubbornly refusing to get out of your mind, you probably feel you need something hefty to keep you going. Most people stay near the fabulous coastline of the Costa Smeralda with its clear blue-green sea, and coves, rocks, bays and beaches where light quaffers are more the order of the day. Both heft and quaff are exactly what Sardinia provides.

Traditional Sardinian wines are big, fat and strong; some dry, and a goodly number sweet and sticky. Give a Sardo (never Sardino, unless you want to get thumped) half a chance, it seems, and he will come up with some knock-out drops. Well, there is plenty of Malvasia and Moscato around which lends itself admirably to that sort of thing. But now temperature-controlled fermentation is all over the island, resulting in an abundance of light, fresh and amazingly cheap gluggers of all colours, mostly from co-ops.

The influences on Sardinia are not quite what you might expect from a glance at the map. After all, apart from its northern tip it is not all that close to Italy, nearer Africa and closest to France's Corsica. Yet its character is Spanish, at least in the north, which spent many years under Castilian domination. In the south the Moors had control, which explains the strange-sounding names like Deriu Mocci, Porcu, Marrubiu that abound. The Spanish influence accounts for Sardinia's major red grapes being Cannonau, which is none other than Spain's Garnacha, and Monica, also from Spain. And why its important whites include Vermentino and Torbato, both originally Spanish; not to mention Vernaccia with its sherry-like wine. Of Sardinia's other leading grapes only white Nasco seems to have originated on the island. Nuragus came with the Phoenicians, Malvasia and Moscato from Asia Minor.

## SARMENTO
Vino da tavola
TUSCANY

🍷 Sangiovese and others

'We need something', said a Chianti producer one day, 'to give sluggish summer sales a boost, to use up excess grapes, to help cash flow. Why not a lightweight wine, made with Chianti grapes, vinified to be ready for the beginning of June and — we can make a big selling point of this — only on sale until the end of September.' 'And,' added another, warming to the theme, 'we'll recommend that it is served chilled a bit. That should get them drinking it instead of white.' The idea enthused everyone and the first bottles, called Sarmento, duly appeared in June 1988. Well, that is how I imagine it happened, anyway.

## SASSICAIA
**Vino da tavola**
TUSCANY

🍷 Cabernet Sauvignon, Cabernet Franc

Sassicaia started the Cabernet Sauvignon craze in Tuscany. First made in 1968 on the estate of the Marchesi Incisa della Rocchetta at Bolgheri near the Tuscan coast, the wine astounded everyone with its wonderfully seductive, fruit-dominated, blackcurrant and mint flavours. Odd bottles appeared abroad and were proclaimed 'Italy's greatest wine', especially by those who used France as the standard for judging all wines, but others raved too. Its star has not diminished.

Sassicaia gets 18 months to two years of *barrique*-ageing and another two in bottle before it is let loose on its awaiting public. It still needs ages before it peaks: five, ten, or even 20 years say some. Vintages vary but all are at least good, otherwise it isn't sold. 1985, '82, '81, '72 and '68 merit the highest glory. It is a startlingly good example of the Cabernet grape at its most assertive and it shows what fine Cabernets Tuscany can produce. Horribly expensive, I never find it as exciting as the top *native* Italian reds.

## SAUVIGNON

The Sauvignon Blanc grape used to lurk rather shyly in small quantities in a few vineyards in Friuli, Alto Adige and Veneto. Then the fashion for Chardonnay took off and a rush of interest in Sauvignon followed in its wake. The grapes have similar credentials: both turn out some highly regarded wines in their native France and both have been widely adopted in the New World. Plantings are growing but not too fast. Which is just as well, judging by the average standard. Wine from Sauvignon at its most exhilarating has a zippily refreshing acidity and a gooseberry or asparagus or blackcurrant bush, grassy flavour. Italian Sauvignon all too often has the shape and style of Sauvignon without all its immediately succulent flavours. Part of the problem is using vines that are too young, part is poor clones. Those who have succeeded are mainly in the Collio district of Friuli (Jermann, Schiopetto, Ca' Ronesca, Radikon and Venica). Apart from Alto Adige and Veneto, plantings of note are now found in Emilia-Romagna, Tuscany, Puglia and Sicily.

## SCHIAVA

A grape that makes wine that tastes of strawberry yogurt and bacon sounds a strange concept, yet that is what Schiava produces – and very nice it can be too! It is grown extensively in Alto Adige, less widely in Trentino, and practically nowhere else. In Alto Adige, where the German speakers call it Vernatsch, Schiava dominates to the extent that the district's red wine production dwarfs its white even though its reputation hangs on the latter. For wines that actually taste of anything it is better to stick to DOC versions like Lago di Caldaro and Santa Maddalena where yields are controlled (although not far enough). Schiava is also a permitted variety in numerous other Alto Adige and Trentino DOCs. Another influence on the quality of Schiava wines is the clone used. Schiava Grossa is the most common, Schiava Grigia one of the best.

## SCHIOPPETTINO
**Colli Orientali del Friuli DOC**
FRIULI-VENEZIA GIULIA

🍷 Schioppettino

Saved from extinction! Bravo! The Schioppettino grape with its wonderfully intense brambly, minerally tone was dying out from lack of interest in the face of more amenable varieties when Paolo and Dina Rapuzzi of the Ronchi di Cialla estate in Colli Orientali in Friuli came to the rescue and reinstated it. They weren't put off by the small quantity it yielded and they gave the wine a judicious ageing in *barriques* which suited it down to the ground. Others in the area were spurred on by their success to replant the variety too but Ronchi di Cialla's wines still head the pack. Occasionally called Ribolla Nera, it needs around five years to show its colours. Best years: 1988, '86, '85, '83.

# SICILY

On my first visit to Sicily I found the island harsh and barren. Travelling through the interior seemed to take forever, with not a sign of habitation, just an endless succession of mountainous rocks with lower slopes varying in colour from tarry black to sulphurous yellow. The lack of enchantment lasted precisely 48 hours. Those craggy lumps stopped looking bleak and started to appear austerely magnificent. I discovered the island's proudly-maintained villages where life is lived openly on the street, the vivid colours and flowers that abound everywhere (even along the central reservation of motorways), the stunning straw-coloured swathes of wheat (Sicily used to be called the bread basket of Europe), and the vistas of olive trees with their silver-grey-green leaves glistening under the burning sun.

The Sicilians have certainly shown themselves astutely, politely dismissive of the DOC system. How else can you explain that of the six DOCs (excluding Marsala and those of Sicily's satellite islands), none of which looks insignificant on the map, one exists only in theory, one is so obscure you need both tenacity and luck to track a producer down, and one exists through the medium of a single producer only? While important wines of Sicily, such as Corvo, Regaleali, even Rapitalà (which does, in fact, have a DOC for its white), have made their name on their own merits without even the need for a super-*vino da tavola* tag.

Despite wine lore that cooler climates are better for white wines, hotter zones for reds, Sicily's greatest success has been with its light, crisp whites from indigenous grapes such as Catarratto or Inzolia, which suit its climate, grown mainly in the west of the island. Up until now the red wines have been less successful, not because the local varieties, Nero d'Avola, Nerello Mascalese, Frappato, Perricone and so on, are inferior but because there has been a reluctance to take up modern wine-making methods quite as enthusiastically. Part of this is the local esteem given to wines that are *marsalesi* (Marsala-like) and therefore what we would call oxidized and faulty, nothing like the firm, fruit-packed wines we crave. Just you wait,

though – things are improving fast!

Marsala is one of Italy's most famous wines and, theoretically, one of the world's great fortified wines but most of it is nowhere near being great now. Sicily's real wine gems come instead from the islands off Sicily: Moscato di Pantelleria from Zibibbo grapes (a Moscato variety) grown on Pantelleria to the south-west towards Tunisia, and Malvasia delle Lipari from the Aeolian (or Lipari) archipelago to the north-east. They are gems not just because they are (when properly made) delicately sweet and delicious but because they are the true heritage of Sicily. The *passito* versions, the most typical, have millennia of tradition behind them and are an intrinsic element of those rocky islands, scorching under the blistering sun.

Red wines
White wines
Red and white wines
Fortified wine

0    25 km
0    25 miles

Aeolian Islands    FARO

MALVASIA
DELLE LIPARI    Messina

Egadi
Islands    Trapani    •Palermo    Mt Etna    •Taormina
ALCAMO    Simeto    ETNA

Enna•

Marsala    Belice    Salso    •Catania
Sambuca    MOSCATO
DI SIRACUSA
Caltanissetta•

MARSALA    Agrigento    MOSCATO
DI NOTO    Siracusa
•Noto

Vittoria
CERASUOLO    Ragusa
DI VITTORIA

N

MOSCATO DI
PANTELLERIA

CONTE TASCA D'ALMERITA

REGALEALI

PRODOTTO E IMBOTTIGLIATO DALL'AZIENDA AGRICOLA REGALEALI
DEL CONTE TASCA D'ALMERITA - S.p.A.

75 CL ℮    VINO DA TAVOLA DI SICILIA - PRODOTTO IN ITALIA    12% VOL

Marsala Superiore
Denominazione di Origine Controllata
1984
prodotto e imbottigliato
da Marco De Bartoli Samperi - Marsala - Italia

750 ml    Zuccheri 5%    18% vol

| WINE ENTRIES |
| --- |
| Alcamo |
| Cellaro |
| Cerasuolo di Vittoria |
| Corvo |
| Donnafugata |
| Etna |
| Faro |
| Malvasia delle Lipari |
| Marsala |
| Moscato di Pantelleria |
| Rapitalà |
| Regaleali |
| Vecchio Samperi |

| GRAPE ENTRIES |
| --- |
| Grillo |
| Malvasia |
| Moscato |

◀ In early spring, even the barren
lands of Sicily can be surprisingly
green and flowers spring up beside the
olive trees and vines.

## SOAVE DOC
VENETO

♀ Garganega, Trebbiano di Soave, Trebbiano Toscano

▶ Picturesque though this may appear, you would do better with Soave from a more sloping vineyard and with grapes collected in smaller containers to prevent them getting crushed before they reach the cellars.

I wonder if there is anyone anywhere in the UK who drinks wine but has never drunk Soave. I doubt it. Just think of all the millions of bottles there must be the length and breadth of the country, not to mention other countries (the USA!) and Italy itself; over 65 million a year in all, the statistics tell us.

Yet Soave's area, east of Verona and just east of Valpolicella in western Veneto, is not enormous. The only way to get such an amount is to exploit the vines for all they are worth, in other words, to get high yields from them. This is not difficult, especially on the flat land, where most Soave grows (only the small Classico zone around the village of Soave itself is hilly – and you need hills for quality). Even the DOC regulations are pretty generous on yield limits. Yet a number of producers would still have difficulty honestly swearing that they never exceed them. This is why so much Soave is pretty innocuous swill with little more than an almondy hint (if you concentrate hard) and a slightly bitter finish. Not only that, but have you noticed how similar most bottles of Soave taste, no matter whose name is on the label? Well, a huge proportion of Soave is made by the local co-operative (as much as 90 per cent some say) and bottled for various companies under different labels or sold in bulk to them, so what can you expect?

If you are happy with Soave as it is – fine. It's certainly not expensive. But an increasing number of people in Soave itself are not happy. They know Soave can, and should, be lots better than decent everyday plonk. Leading producers are Pieropan and Anselmi who have kept yields right down, spared no effort to go all out for quality – and achieved it. Their wines may cost a lot more but there is so much more flavour that it's worth it. They can even last longer than the year that exhausts feebler Soave. Other producers who have steered a midway path between affordability and tastability are Boscaini, Guerrieri Rizzardi, Masi, Prà, Santa Sofia, Suavia, Tedeschi and Zenato, and the list is increasing all the time. Even the big-and-boring producers are coming up with *cru* Soaves which are streets ahead of the norm. But if you want Soave with flavour the grapes must come from the Classico zone. Without the hills, there is no hope.

## IL SODACCIO
**Vino da tavola**
TUSCANY

🍷 Sangiovese, Canaiolo

This super-Tuscan was originally created in 1980 by Sergio Manetti of the Monte Vertine estate in Chianti Classico for a super-smart Florence restaurant, but after a while the exclusivity was dropped, giving Monte Vertine the cachet of being a two super-Tuscan estate (the other wine is Le Pergole Torte). Two factors mark out Il Sodaccio. One is the use of some Canaiolo grapes where other super-Tuscans more typically use Cabernet Sauvignon to partner the Sangiovese. The other is a welcome change from 225-litre *barriques*; the oak casks used are three to four times as big, which gives a much less obviously oaky effect and emphasizes the gently penetrating, pruny-mocha fruit. Il Sodaccio matures slowly. Best years: 1986, '85, '83 and '82.

## I SODI DI SAN NICCOLÒ
**Vino da tavola**
TUSCANY

🍷 Sangiovese, Malvasia Nera

The elegant super-Tuscan of the forward-looking Castellare estate in Chianti Classico, whose consultant, Maurizio Castelli, is one of the best known and respected Chianti wine-making wizards. It was Castelli's idea to bring in the aromatic, rich red Malvasia Nera and see what it would achieve when blended with Sangiovese (the Sangioveto clone). It achieved wonders, but Castelli reckoned its sweet perfume was too much of a good thing, so the Malvasia Nera was cut back to under ten per cent. 1982 and '83 will give you a taste of the 'old' style, '85 and '86 that of the new.

## SOLAIA
Vino da tavola
TUSCANY

🍷 Cabernet Sauvignon, Sangiovese

Solaia seems to have set out to ape Sassicaia (the first Tuscan wine made unashamedly in the Bordeaux image) and ended up beating it at its own game. Many reckon that Sassicaia is the classiest expression of Cabernet in Tuscany but Solaia has punchier, rounder, *fruitier* fruit to match its cedary oakiness, tannic structure and weight. It comes from a single vineyard in Chianti Classico, made only in the best years by Marchesi Antinori, one of the most famous Tuscan houses. Solaia is made in tiny quantities. That, and the need to ensure prestige, means prices are on second mortgage levels.

## SOLOPACA DOC
CAMPANIA

🍷 Sangiovese, Aglianico, Piedirosso, Sciascinoso

🍷 Trebbiano Toscano, Malvasia, Coda di Volpe

The area around Solopaca was known from far back as good for viticulture but why the slump in reputation? One reason was that it fell victim to the recent past's frenetic urge for quantity. They are now replanting the vineyards, which is good, but with prolific Sangiovese and Trebbiano, enshrined by DOC, which isn't. Solopaca is fair enough when well made: a zippy and pleasant, chalky, oily white and a lively, tight, jammy, earthy, dry red. But it could be so much better if they used the native varieties, Greco (white) and Aglianico and Piedirosso (red), as wines from La Vinicola Ocone show. Venditti and Volla are foremost in the push to reinstate quality. Best years: 1987, '86, '85, '82.

## SORNI DOC
TRENTINO

🍷 Schiava, Teroldego, Lagrein

🍷 Nosiola, Müller-Thurgau, Sylvaner, Pinot Bianco

In Trentino, where most wines are from single varieties, the blended Sorni does not meet with everyone's approval. But I like it. How clever to mix red Schiava, the proliferating light quaffer, and beef it up with grassy, liquorice-and-plums Teroldego and punchy Lagrein. And, even better, how clever to take the rare, fascinating but sometimes rustic white Nosiola and turn it into a perfumed charmer with a little wine from more aromatic grapes. Both red and white are best young. Sorni is a small zone in north Trentino. Best producer: Maso Poli.

## SPANNA
**Vino da tavola**
PIEDMONT

🍷 Nebbiolo and others

Spanna is purely and simply the name by which everyone refers to Nebbiolo in the north of Piedmont. In practice it is wine made there from the Nebbiolo grape but not graced by DOC – and much of it pretty so-so. Nebbiolo doesn't always ripen too well up here and may well benefit from a plentiful dollop of something softer and rounder to flesh it out. Other local grapes like Bonarda and Vespolina can be used; a rich, ripe, powerful southerner, like Aglianico, is far better. Up to 15 per cent is legal – but more is sometimes used. Shhh! With Aglianico, Spanna is fat and chocolaty and lasts for a decade or more. Without it the wine is lighter, more raspberry-like and fades sooner. Best producers: Brugo, Dessilani, Ferrando, Nervi, Rivetti, Travaglini, Vallana.

## SQUILLACE
**Vino da tavola**
CALABRIA

🍷 Greco Bianco, Malvasia and others

Who could resist trying a wine called Squillace? Mind you, who could imagine living in a place called Squillace? If you did you would be in a village near the sea on the eastern side of the toe of Calabria. Or better, the beach-side Lido di Squillace. Just imagine a glass of Squillace in Squillace in a shady spot after a morning soaking up the sun – light and delicate, young and fresh, dryish, served too cold, maybe from a jug, the glass misting over, then warming up quickly in the heat ... mmm!

## SQUINZANO DOC
PUGLIA

🍷 🍷 Negroamaro, Malvasia Nera, Sangiovese

Squinzano, sandwiched between Brindisi and Salice Salentino, comes from the bit of Puglia making the region's best wines. Its base is the ancient and celebrated, deep, intense, long-ageing Negroamaro with some Malvasia Nera to add perfume and prevent it becoming too dense and unassailable. The red perks up after a couple of years and cocoa and cooked plum skins flavours appear. The rosé is a deep coral colour. The juice and skins stay together for 12 to 24 hours, giving lots of colour, and no shortage of flavour either. Best producer: Valletta.

## TAURASI DOC
CAMPANIA

🍷 Aglianico, Piedirosso, Barbera

Taurasi is often held up as the great red wine of the entire south of Italy and is said to be *the* example of the glories of the Aglianico grape. Yet if you buy a bottle of Taurasi when it appears on the shelves (it will by then be at least three years old, four if a Riserva) I wouldn't be at all surprised if you were thoroughly disappointed. At this stage it sometimes tastes, not too pleasantly, of sour milk; at times it is merely unexciting. Consecutive vintages can have remarkably different characters too. Don't worry, just tuck the bottle away somewhere for a few years because Taurasi really needs to age. In fact, had I not drunk a really well-aged bottle in Milan's nearest equivalent to a wine bar a few years back, which knocked me out (metaphorically, that is), I might be seriously doubting the claims that are made for it. Taurasi comes from well inland of Vesuvius, in well-drained hilly country (providing beneficial cool). Production is almost entirely in the hands of the highly proficient Mastroberardino. Best years: 1985, '83, '82, '81, '77, '75, '73, '71, '68.

## TAVERNELLE
**Vino da tavola**
TUSCANY

🍷 Cabernet Sauvignon

Unlike everyone else who has gone headlong into Cabernet in Tuscany, the American giant, Villa Banfi bullishly did not soften its impact with any other variety. The result, a super-Tuscan from Montalcino, is called Tavernelle and its first two vintages, 1983 and '82, have won prizes galore. It has turned out with more than a hint of Californian style, with its great galumphing blackcurrant richness and unconcealed oakiness. Perfect for Banfi's American customers, perfect for tasting competitions, and not at all bad for everybody else. 1987, '86, '85 continue the promise of the earlier years.

## TERLANO DOC
ALTO ADIGE

♀ Chardonnay, Müller-Thurgau, Pinot Bianco, Riesling Italico, Riesling Renano, Sauvignon, Sylvaner

Terlano DOC is an alternative to Alto Adige DOC for seven varieties grown west of the Adige river, by Bolzano. As such I can't see the point of it. Its only purpose seems to be for straight Terlano, a blend of non-aromatic Pinot Bianco with the other aromatic varieties. For those who like just a hint of perfume in a light fresh white, this halfway house may suit. Drink young. Best producers: Brigl, Lageder, Rottensteiner, Schloss Schwanburg, C.S. di Terlano and St Michael-Eppan.

## TEROLDEGO ROTALIANO DOC
TRENTINO

♟ Teroldego

Italian wine, to be reasonably decent, is supposed to come from hills. Teroldego Rotaliano, from the north of Trentino, is the exception. Where the Noce river joins the Adige there is a large, flat gravelly plain called the Campo Rotaliano. Most of the plain is covered with Teroldego vines – which are seen practically nowhere else. The resulting wine, with grassy, liquorice and plum flavours, needs either to be drunk young and fruity at two or three years old, or kept for six to ten years (sometimes longer) when it becomes mellow and more truffly. In between it is dull. Best of recent years: 1988, '85, '83 and '79. Foradori is the best producer (they made an excellent 1980 and a wonderful '66 – still going strong). Conti Martini, Dorigati, Endrizzi, Istituto San Michele, C.S. Mezzacorona, C.S. Mezzolombardo, Zeni are also good.

## TIGNANELLO
Vino da tavola
TUSCANY

♟ Sangiovese, Cabernet Sauvignon

Every time a new super-Tuscan, exploiting the smart (mainly) Sangiovese – and (some) Cabernet Sauvignon blend, appears there should be a quick thank-you winged to Antinori. For they were the first in the early 1970s to benefit financially from the then novel idea that a *vino da tavola* could sell at a considerably higher price than DOCs from the same area. With 20 per cent Cabernet Sauvignon and 18 months of *barrique*-ageing, this is still one of the most elegant super-Tuscans – and one of the more expensive. Best vintages: 1988, '85, '83, '77, '70.

## TOCAI

Tocai has a split personality. On the one hand it is the vine of the white 'jug wine' of the plains of Friuli spawning far too many large bottles of indifferent stuff, labelled with little more illuminating than the name 'Tocai' itself. On the other, it is one of Friuli's prized native varieties, capable of a quality of wine the large bottle merchants could hardly dream of. The difference between the two is not some matter of clones: there's just one, Tocai Friulano (called Tocai Italico in Veneto). No, it is that standard bug-bear, yields. Only when pruned hard has the resulting wine enough stuffing to allow its alluring, broad, nut-cream, oily, appley, slightly figgy character to emerge and it can improve well past the year that exhausts the feeble bottles. It flourishes throughout Friuli and in central and eastern Veneto. In Veneto, particularly, it can do itself proud (for example, the wines made by La Fattoria, Rechsteiner), or be a disgrace. Tocai is not the same variety as France's Tokay.

## TORBATO DI ALGHERO
Vino da tavola
SARDINIA

♀ Torbato

When the DOCs were dished out in Sardinia it seems Torbato was missed out. Not that this worried Sella & Mosca, a large modern estate in the north-west of the island, who rescued the grape from oblivion (and sure extinction) in the early 1900s and have turned it into their most widely praised white wine. There is now also a more intensely flavoured *cru*, Terre Bianche, which, with its youthful, light but penetrating, creamy, crispness, is Sardinia's best white. Unfortunately its price matches its reputation. It may be well worthwhile in Sardinia but elsewhere you can drink as well for less. There is a fizz too.

## TORGIANO DOC
UMBRIA

🍷 Sangiovese, Canaiolo, Trebbiano Toscano and others

🍸 Trebbiano Toscano, Grechetto, Malvasia and others

Torgiano is a slip of an area in central Umbria, near Perugia. Theoretically it produces Chianti-like reds and ordinary whites rather like a cross between those from Orvieto and Tuscany. But this is purely theoretical because the area is completely dominated by the quality-conscious Lungarotti family, whose wines have a stamp of character that reflects as much their house style as geographical realities. From a wide range, the plummily muscular red Rubesco (now as synonymous with Torgiano as the name Lungarotti itself) with its Riserva *cru* Monticchio and the steely, floral, rounded white Torre di Giano and its Reserva *cru* Il Pino are the standard-bearers. They attain such consistently sound quality that few could contest that the recently approved DOCG for Torgiano has been the right step forward. Best vintages: 1988, '86, '85, '83, '82, '75, '71.

Of Lungarotti's other wines San Giorgio, a Sangiovese/Cabernet super-*vino da tavola* which is continually receiving plaudits, leads a field that includes an oaky Cabernet Sauvignon (di Miralduolo) and Chardonnay (Vigna i Palazzi), a rosé (Castel Grifone), Vin Santo, Solleone (dry and sherry-like), a sparkler and a *frizzante*. And there's *grappa*, oil and honey too.

## TORRE ERCOLANA
Vino da tavola
LAZIO

🍷 Cesanese, Cabernet Sauvignon, Merlot

Torre Ercolana is made by just one producer, Colacicchi, and comes from Anagni, which lies best part of an hour's drive south-east of Rome. Quantities are tiny (1000-1500 bottles per year – and not every year) and the reputation is very high so there is a bit of oneupmanship among the privileged few who have tried it. The end result varies markedly from year to year as each of its three grape varieties suits different weather conditions and contributes more or less strongly to the final result. I've never found Torre Ercolana as marvellous as it is cracked up to be, but when you can get hold of the wine you can't help but admire its dense, sweet-austere style, especially when there is so little other red wine from Lazio that is worth drinking. Best years: 1983, '82, '78.

## TRAMINER

Is Traminer the same grape as Traminer Aromatico (also known as Gewürztraminer)? Yes, and no. There is just the one Traminer variety, but skin colours vary from yellow to light red. Some produce wines – always white – with more perfume, or aroma, and get the Aromatico tag. But if the word Aromatico is omitted, it doesn't necessarily imply the lower perfume type of vine; it may just be convenient local shorthand.

Traminer originally came from the village of Termeno (Tramin in German) in Alto Adige (Südtirol). It can make highly opulent wines, fat, oily, with a perfume that is a dead ringer for lychees and a distinctly spicy taste. This is all far too much of a good thing for any self-respecting Italian, who prefers a much more muted style with an emphasis placed on elegance. The purest examples of Traminer (Aromatico) are still in Alto Adige, even though there isn't an awful lot of it there any more. It is more widely diffused in Friuli and there have been recent plantings as far south as Calabria.

## TREBBIANO

Wherever you are in Italy you are never far from a Trebbiano vine. Only the border regions of Piedmont, Valle d'Aosta and Friuli-Venezia Giulia escape its insidious influence. It originated in central Italy, where it is still most prevalent (even getting into red wines), and slowly and inexorably spread the length and breadth of the peninsula. What magical character trait does this grape have that makes it as indispensable to growers in Veneto as to those in Sicily, to those on the plains as to those in the hills? The answer is nothing – literally. Trebbiano is one of the most neutral grape varieties found anywhere in the world. Its advantage is that it yields as if it had taken to heart, with unabashed fervour, the biblical command to go forth and multiply. In the post-war days when the future of viticulture in Italy was seen to depend on ever more wine, Trebbiano was a boon. Now that the by-word is quality it is a millstone. The best, indeed the only, defence of Trebbiano is that, in a minor role in a wine, it acts as a gentle base, toning down any over-assertive characteristics produced by grapes of greater personality. This has far more validity for Italians who prefer their whites to be quietly restrained, than for north Europeans who crave the assertiveness.

Like other long-settled, widespread varieties, there are numerous different Trebbiano clones, Trebbiano Toscano being the most common. Trebbiano di Lugana on the south shores of Lake Garda in Lombardy, surprisingly, makes wines that actually taste of something.

## TREBBIANO D'ABRUZZO DOC
ABRUZZO

♀ Trebbiano Toscano, Bombino Bianco, Malvasia

◄ Trebbiano frequently yields too abundantly. To make good wine from these Abruzzo grapes all the overripe, brown and underripe, bullet-like ones should be removed.

Despite the abundance of Trebbiano in Italy, there are only two DOCs which make use of the grape's name in their title. But how absurd that one of these, Trebbiano d'Abruzzo, should not necessarily be from Trebbiano. This has arisen because the grape Bombino Bianco is called Trebbiano Abruzzo locally, even though it is a separate variety. Nevertheless, like Trebbiano, Bombino is not shy about showering grapes on the world and it has a similar tendency to neutrality. Most of the 100,000 hectolitres or so of Trebbiano d'Abruzzo made every year, therefore, are not particularly memorable – just cleanish, lightish, with a faint, minerally nuttiness if you try hard to find it. The more Bombino the better the wines and the best are when it is ruthlessly pruned. For, unlike Trebbiano, when Bombino's yields are kept right down something characterful does emerge. Streets ahead of everyone else is Valentini, whose wines can be truly stunning, biscuity, creamy (almost buttery), hazelnuts and ripe lemon gems. Other front runners: Casal Thaulero, Barone Cornacchia, Illuminati, Masciarelli, Montori, Pepe and Tollo (Colle Secco best). Drink young, except Valentini's which ages well.

## TREBBIANO DI ROMAGNA DOC
ROMAGNA

♀ Trebbiano Romagnolo

I am trying very, very hard to think of something good to say about Trebbiano di Romagna. I am not having much success. There is nothing special about the Romagnan clone of Trebbiano. The grape is grown extensively in Romagna, flat as a pancake though most of it is. There is hardly anyone dedicated enough to try to make a silk purse out of a sow's ear with it. In fact, the best that I can come up with is that it shows Trebbiano at its most typical. In short, avoid it.

## TRENTINO

*Wine entries:* Casteller, Goldmuskateller, Lago di Caldaro, Lagrein Dunkel, Lagrein Kretzer, Marzemino, Moscato Rosa, Nosiola, Rebo, Sorni, Teroldego Rotaliano, Trentino, Trevenezie, Valdadige, Vino Santo

Trentino is a province, the southern half of the region called Trentino-Alto Adige. But since Alto Adige is an autonomous province and rather sniffily dissociates itself from the rest of Italy, still, after 70 years, pining to rejoin Austria, Trentino has to be considered separately. The wines of its north are almost indistinguishable from Alto Adige's. Further south the valley of the Adige river gradually widens from its mountain-guarded gorge-like path, the climate becomes less resolutely sub-Alpine and the wines are softer and broader. The result of this is that Trentino's producers can't get away with the over-cropping that both provinces indulge in without the wines losing character. Trentino is strongly dominated by co-operatives too, whose members receive no incentive to reduce yields.

Viticulturally and culturally the province splits at Trento, about a third of the way down. North of Trento the feel of the place, visually and socially, is Austrian; south it is Italian. Wine classifications unfortunately do not reflect this. The most important DOC is itself called Trentino. Respect for DOC in these parts has ensured that even the everyday quaffers Casteller and Valdadige have been brought into the net. More characterful drinking comes from the indigenous red varieties Teroldego (from the north) and Marzemino (from the south) or the cleverly blended Sorni (red and white). Trentino can also be proud of its high quality fizz, mainly from Pinots Bianco and Nero and Chardonnay (leading producers: Ferrari, Equipe 5).

## TRENTINO DOC
TRENTINO

♂ Cabernet Franc, Cabernet Sauvignon, Lagrein, Marzemino, Merlot, Pinot Nero

♀ Lagrein, Moscato Rosa

♀ Chardonnay, Moscato Giallo, Müller-Thurgau, Nosiola, Pinot Bianco, Pinot Grigio, Riesling Italico, Riesling Renano, Traminer Aromatico

You won't get bored drinking in Trentino. Apart from the 17 different varietal wines there are sparkling, fortified, Riserva and even Vino Santo versions as well as Trentino Rosso (Cabernet with some Merlot) and Trentino Bianco (Chardonnay with some Pinot Bianco). All the grapes, except Nosiola for Vino Santo, and Marzemino, can be grown anywhere within the DOC boundaries, be it in the far north, bordering on Alto Adige, or in the far south, bordering on the Veneto – no short distance (approximately 65km/40 miles). The terrain descends inexorably, following the Adige river valley, from its breathtaking sub-Alpine gorge by the Dolomites, south to the low hills of the Veneto. This gives greater scope for variation between bottles.

Red wines, like the fruit-packed Marzemino or succulent Cabernet and Merlot, are often more impressive than the crisp, clean, gently perfumed whites like Pinot Bianco and Chardonnay which epitomize the region. The aromatic Moscato Rosa and Moscato Giallo may be fortified but, thank goodness, rarely are. Both are usually sweetish; Moscato Giallo is also superb when muskily dry. The sparkling wines are also single varietal (the three Pinots, Chardonnay) but most producers prefer using blends so don't bother with DOC. Vino Santo is from Nosiola whose rare dry white wine varies from fascinating to rustic. Drink whites young, reds from two to four years old, Vino Santo when you can get it.

Apart from Conti Martini, all of whose wines are superb, there is no such thing as 'best' producers in Trentino; some are better with some grapes, some with others. Those worthy of attention include De Tarczal

(Marzemino), Dorigati, Endrizzi, Fanti, Fedrigotti (Cabernet/Merlot), Foradori (Teroldego), Gaierhof (Chardonnay), Guerrieri Gonzaga (Tenuta San Leonardo Cabernet), Longariva, Maso Poli, C.S. Mezzolombardo, Pisoni (Vino Santo), San Michele all'Adige (Cabernet/Merlot), Simoncelli (Marzemino), Spagnolli (Moscato Giallo), Vini del Concilio, Vinicola Aldeno, Zeni.

## TREVENEZIE
**Vino da tavola**
VENETO, FRIULI-VENEZIA GIULIA, TRENTINO-ALTO ADIGE

🍷 🍷 🍷

A wine claiming to come from 'The Three Venices' may stretch our credibility, but in the days when the three north-eastern regions of Italy were part of the Republic of Venice, they were called Venezia Euganea (Veneto), Venezia Tridentia (Trentino) and Venezia Giulia (Friuli). Needless to say, it is well nigh impossible for any wine that has been blended across so huge an area to have any personality, useful as it may be for producers. Wines from the Trevenezie, also known as Tre Venezie or Triveneto, are usually the north-east's ubiquitous Merlot (red) and Tocai (white), usually innocuous or worse, and usually cheap.

## UMBRIA

*Wine entries:* Colli Altotiberini, Colli Perugini, Montefalco, Orvieto, Sagrantino di Montefalco, Torgiano, Vin Santo

'The green heart of Italy' is what the publicity posters call the region of Umbria. And it *is* Italy's geographical heart, midway between Florence and Rome, and it *is* green. It is also predominantly hilly, often inducing a feeling of remoteness, and a treasure trove of Etruscan remains. There is no major city; Perugia, its capital, is a town of only 150,000 inhabitants, its hill-top walled medieval centre neatly concealing the urban sprawl below from visitors' sights. There are tourists around, of course, and Perugia is full of young students of Italian in summer, but nowhere (except possibly Assisi) is excessively crowded, and then only in high summer. All of which makes Umbria the ideal place for the sort of holiday that means a quiet potter around calm villages.

The hilliness of Umbria is reflected in the names of some of its wines: Colli del Trasimeno (around Lake Trasimeno), Colli Altotiberini (in the north, along the course of the upper river Tiber which flows through the region on its way to Rome) and Colli Perugini (south of Perugia). These light red and white wines are not the ones to write home about, though. Far more impressive are Torgiano, a tiny area just south of Perugia; Montefalco with its brilliant red Sagrantino grape between Assisi and Spoleto in mid-Umbria; and Orvieto in the south-west of the region on the border of Lazio. Orvieto is one of Italy's best known whites and has more than its fair share of quality-conscious producers among the larger-size companies who are responsible for much of the production.

## VALCALEPIO DOC
LOMBARDY

🍷 Merlot, Cabernet

🍷 Pinot Bianco, Pinot Grigio

Although not the most French area of Italy historically and geographically, it is Lombardy that looks closest at France for its wine culture. This is probably because Lombardy, with its magnet of Milan, pulls together those with business acumen who are acutely aware of how France has created a long-term high quality image for its wines worldwide, whereas Italy's reputation remains chaotic. That surely is why red and white Valcalepio, the wines of the 'Mountain of Grumello' in central Lombardy, are made not from the area's traditional local varieties (Groppello, Marzemino, Rossera and Rossolo) but from newer, French-style grapes. But why have producers not yet seen that in France there is not just image but substance too? Why do they assume that sales in Bergamo and Milan are all that matter? If it weren't for the producers Tenuta Castello di Grumello and La Cornasella, both making fine, elegant wines that can hold their heads high, Valcalepio might as well not exist. Best years: 1988 for the whites; '88, '86, '85, '83 for the reds.

# TUSCANY

For many people central Tuscany represents Italy. Steep rolling hills in all shades of green, tall cypresses, delicate olive trees, sturdy vines and the occasional pretty stone house all combine to form a timeless scene that captivates nearly everyone. Wine is central to the culture – the vine has been cultivated here for nearly 3000 years and Tuscan wines today include some of the highest quality in all Italy. The atmosphere that pervades the region is a heady mix of respect for traditions, regard for quality and enthusiasm for innovation.

That is not to say that all wines are wonderful. Native whites, in particular, rarely aspire to more than decent, the local Trebbiano and Malvasia grapes needing intervention verging on the divine to make them sing, and some reds are no better than okay. But there is enough that is good enough often enough to make drinking your way round Tuscany really exciting.

Striking whites come mainly from the native Vernaccia and the imported Chardonnay, either aged in *barriques* (which can be overdone) or not. For reds, Tuscany is the domain of Sangiovese, in one or other of its clones and sub-varieties. Sangiovese is at its classiest in (apart from Chianti) Brunello di Montalcino, Vino Nobile di Montepulciano and Carmignano and their 'younger brother' wines Rosso di Montalcino, Rosso di Montepulciano and Barco Reale respectively, as well as in most of the growing number of super-Tuscans.

The explosion of super-Tuscans has been the most obvious sign of innovation in Tuscany. The wines are not DOC (mainly because the grape varieties and their proportions differ from those laid down) but *vino da tavola*, however far you stretch the term, gravely underestimates their standard. Super-Tuscans fall mainly into three categories: 100 per cent Sangiovese; Sangiovese with a little Cabernet Sauvignon; Cabernet Sauvignon with some Sangiovese or, maybe, Merlot. Often they are aged in *barriques* which adds a seductive oakiness. Cabernet Sauvignon is hugely popular, so special are the wines it produces in Tuscany.

Its success is unlikely, though, to drive out the most traditional Tuscan wine of all: Vin Santo. This *passito* wine, usually made in small quantities and with tremendous care, is mostly sweet.

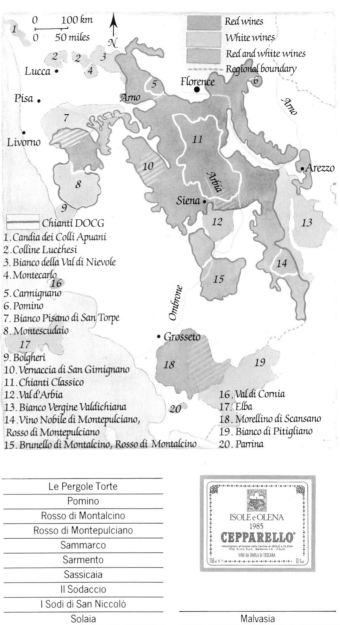

0 | 100 km
0 | 50 miles
N

Red wines
White wines
Red and white wines
Regional boundary

Lucca
Pisa
Livorno
Arno
Florence
Arno
Arezzo
Siena
Arbia
Grosseto
Ombrone

1
2  2  3
4
5
6
7
8
9
10
11
12
13
14
15
16
17
18
19
20

Chianti DOCG
1. Candia dei Colli Apuani
2. Colline Lucchesi
3. Bianco della Val di Nievole
4. Montecarlo
5. Carmignano
6. Pomino
7. Bianco Pisano di San Torpe
8. Montescudaio
9. Bolgheri
10. Vernaccia di San Gimignano
11. Chianti Classico
12. Val d'Arbia
13. Bianco Vergine Valdichiana
14. Vino Nobile di Montepulciano,
Rosso di Montepulciano
15. Brunello di Montalcino, Rosso di Montalcino
16. Val di Cornia
17. Elba
18. Morellino di Scansano
19. Bianco di Pitigliano
20. Parrina

▲ A quiet village, rows of cypresses and peaceful hills – it is no wonder that so many people fall in love with the Tuscan countryside.

| WINE ENTRIES | | |
| --- | --- | --- |
| Bianco Vergine Valdichiana | Le Pergole Torte | |
| Brunello di Montalcino | Pomino | |
| Ca' del Pazzo | Rosso di Montalcino | |
| Carmignano | Rosso di Montepulciano | |
| Cepparello | Sammarco | |
| Chianti | Sarmento | |
| Coltassala | Sassicaia | |
| Elba | Il Sodaccio | |
| Elegia | I Sodi di San Niccolò | |
| Flaccianello | Solaia | Malvasia |
| Fontalloro | Tavernelle | Sangiovese |
| Galestro | Tignanello | Sauvignon |
| Ghiaie della Furba | Vernaccia di San Gimignano | Trebbiano |
| Grifi | Vin Santo | Vernaccia |
| Montecarlo | Vinattieri | |
| Montesodi | Vino Nobile di Montepulciano | |
| Morellino di Scansano | | |
| Moscadello di Montalcino | GRAPE ENTRIES | |
| Palazzo Altesi | Cabernet Sauvignon | |
| | Chardonnay | |

See also *Chianti*, page 38.

ISOLE e OLENA
1985
CEPPARELLO

## VALDADIGE DOC
TRENTINO-ALTO ADIGE, VENETO

🍷 Schiava, Lambrusco, Merlot and others

🍷 Pinot Bianco, Pinot Grigio, Riesling Italico and others

You will see what a hotch-potch of a DOC Valdadige is when I tell you that there are no less than four 'other' grape varieties that can go into the red version and six that might form part of the white. When you realize that the production area extends in a huge broad swathe along the Adige river, through Alto Adige, Trentino and northern Veneto, almost to Verona, you may begin to wonder what sort of a wine Valdadige is meant to be. Simple. It is the sort of catch-all mish-mash of a blend that is the staple of straightforward, young quaffing stuff. Accept it as such and from decent enough producers like C.S. di Mezzacorona, Gaierhof or Santa Margherita you won't be too disappointed. Expect more and even single-variety versions that have pretensions to higher things are likely to produce disillusionment. In Alto Adige the German-speakers call it Etschtaler.

## VALLE D'AOSTA

*Wine entry:* Valle d'Aosta

It is all too easy to forget about Valle d'Aosta, Italy's smallest region (3260 square kilometres/1260 square miles), tucked away in the north-west corner and sparsely populated (just 114,000 inhabitants). Even if you motor down to Italy through the St Bernard pass from Switzerland, or under Mont Blanc from France, there is not much there to convince you that you have changed countries. Names like St Rhémy, Étroubles, Gignod, or Courmayeur, Avise, Villeneuve, don't exactly have an Italian ring to them, neither do the snow-capped, craggy Alpine views remind you in any way of the Mediterranean you are heading towards. French is even the first language of this autonomous region.

The Dora Baltea river is the region's only sliver of non-mountainous terrain and is the life blood of Valle d'Aosta's viticulture. Its flow keeps the air moving and chases clouds away; the gorge traps summer heat and enables the grapes to ripen. 'Heroic viticulture' they call it and you need just one look at the precipitous slopes on either side of the river, with the vines clinging for all they are worth to sturdy pergolas on tiny terraces to see the heroism required to tend them. But heroism is a dying trait with just 900 hectares (2225 acres) of vineyard planted today against over 3000 hectares (7400 acres) at the beginning of the nineteenth century. There is a wide array of vines planted, including some indigenous and some only occasionally seen elsewhere in Italy. It would be a great pity to let it all disappear because of a lack of heroism in the Franco-Italian soul or the profitable lure of the tourist industry.

## VALLE D'AOSTA DOC
VALLE D'AOSTA

🍷 Gamay, Nebbiolo, Petit Rouge, Pinot Nero, Vien de Nus

🍷 Nebbiolo, Petit Rouge

🍷 Blanc de Morgex, Moscato, Müller-Thurgau, Pinot Grigio, Pinot Nero

As numerous areas along the Dora Baltea river (such as Chambave and Nus) developed established or rising reputations, the entire valley, down-river of Courmayeur, became Valle d'Aosta DOC for red, white and rosé wines, and a whole string of sub-denominations comprising old and potential DOCs, and wine styles, was created. From west to east these are Blanc de Morgex et de La Salle (white, from Blanc de Morgex grapes); Enfer d'Arvier, Torrette (both red, from Petit Rouge); Nus (white and *passito* from Pinot Grigio, but this local sub-variety often called Malvoisie!); Nus Rosso (red, from Vien de Nus); Chambave (white and *passito* from Moscato); Chambave Rosso (red, from Petit Rouge); Arnad-Montjovet and Donnaz (both red, from Nebbiolo). There are also varietal sub-denominations, for Gamay (red), Müller-Thurgau (white) and Pinot Nero (both red and, if the grape juice is quickly removed from the dark skins, white). To make it even more confusing, labels may be in either Italian or French and some styles only exist in minute quantities. There is just one advantage to such a polyglot grouping. If you are not too keen on one of the Valle d'Aosta wines, try another. At least you know it will be different.

There is a remarkably good viticulture and wine-making school, the Institut Agricole Regional, whose wines are exemplary. Others worth a try are from the Donnaz, Enfier and Crotta de Vegnerons de Chambave co-operatives, Alberto Vevey (Blanc de Morgex et de La Salle), Grosjean Delfino (Torrette, Pinot Nero), Malga di Marisa Daynè (Torrette, Müller-Thurgau), Bonin Cesarino (Arnad-Montjovet, Müller-Thurgau). Drink the whites young, the reds from 1988, '86, '85.

## VALPOLICELLA DOC
VENETO

♟ Corvina, Rondinella, Molinara and others

Hands up anyone who hasn't heard of Valpolicella. Quite. Hands up who regards Valpolicella as one of Italy's top wines. I thought so. It really is a sad state of affairs when such a fine wine – for it was, and can be, I assure you – becomes so debased. And it's not just the image of Valpolicella that has been debased, it's the wine itself. Originally grapes for Valpolicella were grown on the hillsides of a series of parallel valleys north-west of Verona near Lake Garda. The wine was much in demand; so much so that as time went by plantings spread eastwards on to less hilly and even unashamedly flat countryside. Even so demand continued apace and the temptation became ever stronger to squeeze as much production as possible from the grapes. By the time DOC arrived in 1968, an over-large area was dubbed Valpolicella, permitted a far too generous maximum yield, and a not particularly special zone in the centre given the sub-denomination Valpantena. The *real* Valpolicella – the original, but much smaller, westerly hill zone – was given the Classico tag. (But the greed of the producers remained unsatisfied and in 1988 they put in a claim for an increase in the maximum yield. At that point a small band of Classico growers, who cared desperately about the quality of Valpolicella and its image, initiated a concerted campaign to prevent the increase and – amazingly – won.) So it is clear that if you want to drink proper Valpolicella you must buy Valpolicella Classico.

Most Valpolicella is sold at two or three years old. Often it is already tired by then as it is too insubstantial to age properly. The exception is *ripasso*, the most traditional style of Valpolicella. After fermenting, the wine is racked into a vat containing the lees of the previous year's Recioto, a concentrated *passito* wine. It picks up richness, weight and structure and its bitter cherries flavour gets augmented by chocolate – altogether a much more serious proposition. Fair enough. But the EC does not permit the term *ripasso* to appear on labels. So you have no way of knowing which wines are and are not in this style! Between ourselves, though, Allegrini's, Le Ragose's, Quintarelli's and Serego Alighieri's wines are *ripasso*, as are Boscaini's Le Canne, Santi's Castello d'Illasi and Bolla's Jago. Masi's Campo Fiorin and Tedeschi's Capitel San Rocco are too, but are sold as *vino da tavola*.

A new style, exemplified by Masi's Fresco, is to make the wine for drinking before it is a year old. It is great: light and fresh, packed even more fully with all the typical bitter morello cherries flavour. For the normal style of Valpolicella, buy only Classico. Boscaini, Guerrieri-Rizzardi, Masi, Tedeschi, Tramanal and Zenato are among the few producers making wines way above average. Best years: 1988, '86, '85, '83, '81.

## VALTELLINA DOC
LOMBARDY

♟ Nebbiolo, Pinot Nero, Merlot and others

Valtellina is an Alpine wine, produced in a narrow strip along the steep-sided valley of the Adda river, which flows west across Lombardy, just south of the Swiss border. It is only the air movement caused by the river and the heat trap of the valley that enable the grapes to reach ripeness. When they do, and the winemaker knows his stuff, Valtellina is one of the most elegant and refined incarnations of Nebbiolo, locally

called Chiavennasca. The predominant flavour is violetty with some raspberry and walnuts, although Nebbiolo's characteristic tannin is still around. Valtellina Superiore is a cut above the normal version as it is almost all from Nebbiolo, and the maximum yield is reduced. It is also produced only in one or more of four sub-districts, all on the north side of the river and therefore with desirable south-facing vineyards: Sassella, Grumello, Inferno, and Valgella; just spit them out and see how useful they are to relieve tension. Sassella is reckoned to be the best, but a good producer such as Enologica Valtellinese, Negri, Pelizzatti or Rainoldi is a better bet than any particular sub-district's name. As they age the wines get less violetty, more truffly. Ten years, for good vintages, is the usual limit. Best years: 1988, '86, '85, '83, '82, '79, '78.

You may see Sfursat or Sforzato, on bottles. Sfursat wines are lightly *passito*, enough to get the alcohol up to a hefty 14·5 per cent although the wine stays dry. Some think Sfursat is the best type of Valtellina. I prefer elegance to clout.

## VECCHIO SAMPERI
SICILY

♀ Grillo, Inzolia, Catarratto

Thank goodness Marco De Bartoli had the initiative to start making Vecchio Samperi and the tenacity to continue making it against seemingly insurmountable odds, including opposition from ex-colleagues and even family. Had he not, Marsala would have no credibility whatsoever as a potentially high class wine. As it is, he has not only shown the splendours of which this wine is capable, but laid the blame for its decline to industrialized rubbish firmly at the door of the British. Vecchio Samperi is *un*fortified, just as all Marsala was before the British came along towards the end of the eighteenth century and started its trade, erroneously believing it needed fortifying with added spirit to preserve it during its voyage. Vecchio Samperi is not mucked around with in any other way either and made according to the purest traditional concepts. The wine is bone dry; it has a predominance of Grillo, the one grape that produces the necessary high alcohol without losing flavour (and which others have uprooted in favour of high-yielding, high-earning nonentities like Catarratto); and it is aged for many years in wooden barrels, successively blended with small quantities of much older wines in the time-honoured *solera* system, also used for sherry.

It is magnificent: deep amber, dry, intense, mellow, with chestnuts, brazil nuts, a little strong dry caramel and a touch of orange peel. Whether you plump for the 10-year, 20-year or 30-year-old version it will be a revelation. It is great either before or after a meal, or with cheese, nuts or even dark, continental chocolate. There is a younger version too, called Joséphine Doré, as elegant a dry aperitif as you could imagine.

## VELLETRI DOC
LAZIO

♥ Cesanese, Sangiovese, Montepulciano

♀ Malvasia, Trebbiano

Velletri is the southernmost of the semi-circle of vineyard zones straddling the large ridge of hills just outside Rome. As the furthest away from the Eternal City, it is slightly disadvantaged in its local market. This is a pity for Romans and good for us as the whites, with their creaminess and almond tang, are fresher, more delicate and altogether more attractive than most Frascati and other wines from nearer to Rome. Velletri has therefore become the house wine in numerous Italian restaurants in Britain. There is some easy-drinking Velletri red, too.

How come Velletri's wines are so much better than those of its neighbours? Because Lazio's only wine research institute is situated in the zone, and where better for conducting experiments on improving vines, grapes and wine than in your own backyard? Drink the whites young, the reds youngish. Best producer: Consorzio Produttori Vini Velletri (Villa Ginnetti).

## VENEGAZZÙ
### Vino da tavola
VENETO

🍷 Cabernet Sauvignon, Merlot, Malbec

🍸 Chardonnay, Pinot Grigio

Venegazzù, first produced in the 1950s, was one of the first super-*vini da tavola* to get itself noticed. There was a straight Cabernet Sauvignon, but it was the black label (special quality) Cabernet blend, Venegazzù della Casa that caught people's attention. Firm, peppery and black-curranty, it often is a touch *frizzante* which you may like – I don't particularly. Made north of Treviso, by the Conti Loredan Gasparini, originally for the sheer buzz of doing something different, it still stands out among the competition in eastern Veneto but, quite honestly, the Tuscan Cabernet big guns have completely over-shadowed it. Best years: 1988, '86, '85. There is also a large production of more ordinary wine, mainly Cabernet and fizzy Prosecco (white) for the local, north Italian, market.

## VERDICCHIO

Verdicchio may not produce wines that are packed full of flavour, but they certainly aren't neutral. The first time I tasted a whole range of wines from the Marche, without seeing any labels, every time I came to one I didn't like I discovered it was from Verdicchio. Since then the wines have changed a bit and I have changed a lot and I will now happily crack open a bottle of Verdicchio with the best of them.

Verdicchio is at home in the Marche. It has been there since the fourteenth century and hasn't spread further afield. Its name derives from *verde* (green) as the grapes, even when ripe, remain strongly greenish in colour. The wine, too, has a greenish tinge to its pale straw colour. Verdicchio produces one of the most refreshing of white wines with high natural acidity which keeps it crisp. It also makes Verdicchio one of the most suitable of grapes for sparkling wine, shown every time a new Verdicchio Spumante appears. The grape is also amenable to unconventional treatments such as late-picking or maturation of the wine in large oak casks. Its yield may not be reliable but it is hardy. With all these benefits perhaps it is not surprising that Verdicchio has stood its ground against the invasion of high-yielding Trebbiano across central Italy.

## ·VERDICCHIO DEI CASTELLI DI JESI DOC
MARCHE

🍸 Verdicchio, Trebbiano Toscano, Malvasia

VERDICCHIO DEI CASTELLI DI JESI
CLASSICO
1987
*CaSal di Serra*
·Umani·Ronchi·
℮ 75cl  12.5% vol

So the producers of the area of Jesi's Castles (Castelli di Jesi) wanted to carve out an image for themselves. So they chose a special green amphora-shaped bottle that, with the workings of the Italian mind, became known as 'La Lollobrigida'. Does that mean we can't take the wine seriously? Apparently it does. Despite the strenuous efforts of numerous estates to upgrade this light, clean, crisp wine from a technically faultless but uninteresting metallic-edged white, it still gets treated as a holiday quaffer, to be knocked back not tasted. But just try Verdicchio from Monte Schiavo's Colle del Sole and Il Pallio *crus*, Garofoli's *cru* Macrina, Umani Ronchi's *cru* Casal di Serra, the wines of Fratelli Bucci and the classic wines of Zaccagnini. Even Fazi-Battaglia, the best known of all for scroll-bedecked, curvaceous bottles with only super-clean wine inside, has a *cru* Le Moie that is worthy of more than a cursory glug. There are others too. These wines have a dry nuttiness with a rich-sharp, salty edge that the old wines lacked. All are ace with fish and seafood. Apart from Villa Bucci (the 1983 and '85 are still superb), drink young. More and more estates are bringing out sparkling wines, too, which reflect just how well suited the grape and the area behind the coastal towns of Ancona and Senigallia are to fizz. Good examples come from C.S. di Cupramontana, Garofoli and Zaccagnini.

This tranquil zone of rolling hills is well placed to be up with the front runners as Italy demonstrates its reformed, high-quality face to the world in the 1990s. Don't underestimate it.

# VENETO

There is no shortage of wine in the Veneto. Whether you feel like spending your days luxuriating in peaceful rumination by Lake Garda; imagining life as a Montague or a Capulet in Romeo and Juliet's home town of Verona; ambling from one imposing Palladian villa to the next in Vicenza; or lapping up the unique beauty of Venice, you will never be far from a glassful of the local wine. The province of Verona alone produces more than enough to satisfy the entire region. Some of the best-known and most widely available names come from there: Soave, Valpolicella and Bardolino. But a passing acquaintance with those three plus a random dip into the wines of the more easterly Piave and Lison-Pramaggiore zones or the more central Colli Berici and Colli Euganei, and you could be excused for thinking that the good folk of the Veneto are far more concerned about how much wine they are making than how good it is. Though perfectly adequate, much Veneto wine doesn't exactly get the taste buds ringing with delight. Too many of the vineyards are on its extensive plains and too many vines are allowed over-abundant yields, resulting in wines with not enough flavour.

The Veneto, however, doesn't lack potential once wine-making is in the hands of quality-conscious producers. They make the most of growing vines on the hill and prune vines ruthlessly to keep yields down (and thus quality up). Soave Classico and Valpolicella Classico (the Classico wines come only from the better hill sites), each with a number of estates committed to quality, are cases in point as is Breganze, with its eclectic range of wines. Less often seen are the wines of Colli Berici and Colli Euganei, similar zones making a number of single-varietal styles (Cabernet, Merlot, Pinot Bianco, Tocai and so on), whose hilly terrain, particularly in Colli Euganei, promises much better results than all but a few producers achieve.

The Veneto wine of Lake Garda is either young, cherry-fresh red Bardolino or white Bianco di Custoza. The hilly, southern part of the Bardolino zone overlaps with Bianco di Custoza's northern part. This has two advantages. Bianco di Custoza usually comes from

▲ The hills of Valpolicella Classico contain miles of dry stone walls and pergola-trained vines.

only the slopes best suited for white wine, and Bardolino only from slopes better for red; and producers are used to making white wines, hence they make an ace rosé Bardolino Chiaretto.

There is no doubt about the wine to drink in Venice. Although nearby Piave has eight wines from different grape varieties to choose from, most notably red Raboso, and although Lison-Pramaggiore, further east and almost in Friuli has even more, Venice is the place for Prosecco. Lorryfuls of bottles of this light, fruity fizzy stuff, from the grape of the same name, trundle down from north of Treviso to keep both Venetians and tourists happily lubricated and for fun fizz none could be better.

114

gorgo

**1987**

**bardolino chiaretto**

denominazione d'origine controllata
imbottigliato all'origine dalla
azienda agricola Gorgo
di Roberto Bricolo
Custoza          Italia

Bottiglia № 61503  A

750 ML ℮                    11.5% vol.

Controllo del Consorzio
Vino Bardolino
Incarico di vigilanza d.M. 5/9/83

| WINE ENTRIES |
|:---:|
| Bardolino |
| Bardolino Chiaretto |
| Bianco di Custoza |
| Breganze |
| Campo Fiorin |
| Capitel San Rocco |
| Colli Berici |
| Gambellara |
| Lessini Durello |
| Lison-Pramaggiore |
| Piave |
| Prosecco di Conegliano-Valdobbiadene |
| Recioto della Valpolicella |
| Recioto della Valpolicella Amarone |
| Recioto di Soave |
| Soave |
| Trevenezie |
| Valdadige |
| Valpolicella |
| Venegazzù |

| GRAPE ENTRIES |
|:---:|
| Cabernet Franc |
| Cabernet Sauvignon |
| Garganega |
| Merlot |
| Pinot Bianco |
| Pinot Grigio |
| Prosecco |
| Refosco |
| Riesling Italico |
| Sauvignon |
| Tocai |
| Trebbiano |

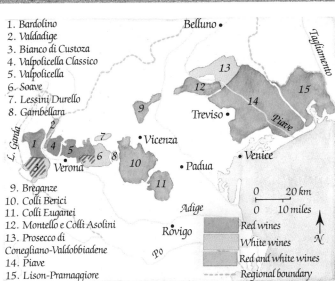

1. Bardolino
2. Valdadige
3. Bianco di Custoza
4. Valpolicella Classico
5. Valpolicella
6. Soave
7. Lessini Durello
8. Gambellara
9. Breganze
10. Colli Berici
11. Colli Euganei
12. Montello e Colli Asolini
13. Prosecco di Conegliano-Valdobbiadene
14. Piave
15. Lison-Pramaggiore

Red wines
White wines
Red and white wines
Regional boundary

0      20 km
0      10 miles

## VERDICCHIO DI MATELICA DOC
MARCHE

♀ Verdicchio, Trebbiano Toscano, Malvasia

The Matelica zone is smaller than Castelli di Jesi, and further south, further inland and higher. Its wines are like a veiled girl, renowned for her beauty. Everyone tells you someone else has seen her face and confirms she is very beautiful but no-one has seen her themselves. Verdicchio di Matelica is not quite as esoteric but its reputation for being superior to the Castelli di Jesi version came mainly from second-hand reports. It certainly used to be better but now that the Jesi wines have improved so much results are more even. In general, though, Verdicchio di Matelica has more weight, a little more roundness to its sweet-sour, salty, nuttiness and possibly greater ageing potential but drinking young is safest. Fratelli Bisci and La Monacesca are the leading producers. There is also a sparkling version.

## VERDUZZO

The Verduzzo grape makes some pretty lively dry whites but its real claim to fame is its sweet wines. A native of Friuli and best suited to the far east of Colli Orientali, it has spread westwards as far as the eastern Veneto and Lison-Pramaggiore and Piave. The further west it goes, the drier and more bitingly fresh it becomes. But it is more exciting when sweet. Sweet Verduzzo is richly honeyed – runny honey, floral – with a meadow full of flowers and, the touch that makes it work so well, it keeps its backbone of acidity. You *can* age it, I prefer it youngish and fresh – at two to four years old (but avoid 1987). From east Friuli is best. Ronchi di Cialla, Ronchi di Fornaz and, in particular, Giovanni Dri are the leading producers.

Dri's vines are in a particular spot in Colli Orientali called Ramandolo, which produces the best Verduzzo of all. He asked for Ramandolo to be a special DOC sub-denomination. The powers that be agreed, but the usual political wrangling resulted in a larger area of several communes around Ramandolo being entitled to the name too. Dri is miffed. He's entitled to be.

## VERMENTINO

Why Vermentino should be found in Sardinia, mainly its north, Liguria and nowhere else seems odd until you realize that the centre of its operations is in Corsica, which lies between the two. In both Sardinia and Liguria it makes light, crisp, appley, easy-drinking wines; more delicate in Liguria, less acidic in Sardinia. But before dismissing Vermentino as no more than Mediterranean Muscadet, it is worth mulling over just how much of its simple, refreshing snappiness is due to modern technological wine-making. Quite a lot, it appears. When the picking in Sardinia is a little late and the fermentation temperature control a little less rigid, Vermentino loses acidity sure enough. But if yields are restrained and all is done with care, it more than compensates with richness and flavour. Similarly, in Liguria, the wines sometimes have more perfume and personality than you'd expect. There may be more to Vermentino than meets the eye.

Vermentino is DOC in Liguria as Riviera Ligure di Ponente and in northern Sardinia as Vermentino di Gallura. This latter has a Superiore version at 13·5 per cent alcohol or more, which suggests the traditional style of Sardinian Vermentino: big, rich, alcoholic and flabby.

## VERNACCIA

Vernaccia means something along the lines of 'belonging to here' which goes some way to explaining why there are at least three grape varieties in Italy called Vernaccia (four if you reckon Alto Adige's Vernatsch or Schiava to be a variation on the theme), none bearing any relation to any of the others. Vernaccia number one is an ancient white variety from Tuscany, grown mainly around the hill town of San Gimignano. Its wines are white, dry and anything from lean to rich. Vernaccia number two is also white and from the central west of Sardinia, just north of Oristano. Strong, dry or fortified (either dry or sweet), its wines are sherry-like. Vernaccia number three is red and the wines it makes are sparkling; dry, *amabile* or sweet! It comes from central-southern Marche, around Serrapetrona. You'd be hard pushed to get a more disparate set of homonymous vines than that. All three are DOC.

Vernaccia di Serra Meccaglia, from Molise, is made with Vernaccia number one and, just to confuse matters properly, Vernaccia di Cannara (from Umbria) is not made from Vernaccia (any of them) at all. If you just mention 'Vernaccia', however, nine times out of ten it will be assumed you are referring to the San Gimignano one, which is by far the best known and most frequently seen.

## VERNACCIA DI ORISTANO DOC
SARDINIA

♀ Vernaccia di Oristano

This is Sardinia's most esteemed wine. It is certainly out of the ordinary. Made from abundantly ripened grapes, grown on a well-drained area just north of Oristano, on the west coast, the wine has at least 15 per cent alcohol and is dry. It is aged in wood for a minimum of two years (four for Riserva) – sometimes as many as 20. During this time there are successive blendings with small quantities of older wines in a *solera* system rather like that used for sherry and, theoretically, for the best Marsalas. Just like sherry (but not Marsala) a special yeast called *flor* appears which imparts its character to the wine. Not surprisingly, Vernaccia di Oristano ends up much like sherry, but a fine quality, dry, aged, oloroso sherry. There is also a *liquoroso* (fortified) version. This is even stronger, may be either dry or sweet but rarely has the class of the unfortified type. Long ageing does nothing but good for these wines. Far and away the best producer is Contini. The Produttori Riuniti and Josto Puddu are good too.

## VERNACCIA DI SAN GIMIGNANO DOC
TUSCANY

♀ Vernaccia di San Gimignano

San Gimignano, the 'town of towers' lying south-west of Florence, is on the itinerary of nearly every tourist in Tuscany. Who could resist visiting a medieval hilltop town, still plentifully supplied with tall, narrow towers (though fewer than there once were) built by its paranoaic, belligerent residents, each of whom built his tower higher than his neighbours' so that he would be able to attack them but be protected from attack himself? With so many visitors tramping up and down the steep streets, it wouldn't have been at all surprising if Vernaccia di San Gimignano had degenerated to a tourist gimmick of no intrinsic quality. A hearty pat on the back, then, to San Gimignano's wine producers, very few of whom have fallen into this profitable but short-sighted trap. Otherwise the wine would not have been the first to have been awarded DOC in the mid-1960s. Or would it?

Traditionally the wines of San Gimignano were golden in colour, rich, broad and often oxidized. The modern wave brought in pale, tight, lean, crisp and restrained wines with the characterful Vernaccia grape held so tightly in check that it had a real struggle to stamp its personality on the wine. Now some estates are back-tracking a little and, helped by modern know-how, slackening the reins. What results is a salty, creamy, nutty, tangy wine, with, in the hands of masters like Teruzzi & Puthod, a buttery richness that is almost reminiscent of good Chardonnay and which lasts a good three years or so. They make an oak-aged version, too, (Terre di Tufo) that enhances the illusion. Other good new-old producers include Falchini and San Quirico. Best years: 1988, '86. Spumante and fortified versions theoretically also exist.

## VIN SANTO
TUSCANY, UMBRIA, TRENTINO-
ALTO ADIGE

♀ Malvasia, Trebbiano, Grechetto,
Nosiola

The 'Holy Wine' is called Vino Santo in Trentino, where the grapes were traditionally left to dry until Holy Week, just before Easter; Vin Santo elsewhere. Unlike most *passito* wines, the grapes for Vin Santo are usually dried hanging in bunches in airy barns; only occasionally flat, on straw mats. Then they are crushed and put into very small barrels (50 litres is most traditional), called *caratelli* together with the *madre*, a little wine left from the previous year, which itself contains a tiny quantity of the previous year's, and so on. The juice stays sealed in the *caratelli* long past the considerable time it takes to ferment; three to six years is not unusual. The white juice deepens to gold. Then out it comes and, if all has gone well, amber nectar results.

But, and it is a big but, there is little consistency in Vin Santo from grower to grower. It is such an artisanal process that everyone's ideas on how to make it differ. For example, it may be dry, sweet or anything in between. More vitally, it may, indeed, be nectar or a corner-cutting con. I'd always take the gamble and try though.

The best, most wonderful, Vin Santo is from Avignonesi who make it with Grechetto, instead of the Malvasia/Trebbiano more usual in Tuscany, and keep it six years in *caratelli*. It tastes of apricots, nut kernels, honey, almonds, praline, dried figs, dried mushrooms and real, cracking caramel. Remarkable! Other Tuscan goodies are from Isole e Olena and Tenuta di Capezzana and, if you prefer Vin Santo dry (I don't), Giovanni Cappelli. Umbria's star is from Adanti (made from Grechetto) and Trentino's (from Nosiola) comes from Pisoni. Buy some *cantuccini*, hard, sweet, biscuits with almonds in, dunk them in the Vin Santo, chomp, slurp, and you will be in heaven.

▶ During the long, slow fermentation and maturation process in small *caratelli*, Vin Santo takes on a heavenly golden hue. It needs sipping in small amounts, getting the full benefits of its sweet, nutty aromas.

## VINATTIERI
Vino da tavola
TUSCANY, ALTO ADIGE

♟ Sangiovese

♀ Chardonnay

This rather superior super-Tuscan (the red at least) was created by a fusion of great minds, prominent among them super-winemaker Maurizio Castelli. Not satisfied with just any old Sangiovese grapes they decided to blend some Sangioveto clone from Chianti Classico with some Brunello clone from Montalcino. Castelli is enthusiastic about *barrique*-ageing, so the wine gets its necessary sojourn there before being turfed out into the big wide world. Initially the flavour is heavily oak-influenced but with every year of ageing, the wine becomes more complex and original. 1986, '85, '83 and '82 (the first vintage) are all impressive. It's certainly a wine to watch. There is now also a

Cabernet/Sangiovese blend called Rosso Secondo.

Vinattieri Bianco is made in Alto Adige. This gives Castelli the chance to make the sort of crisp, perfumed white with up to five years' ageing potential he likes, but which he could never achieve with grapes grown in Tuscany. Best years: 1988, '87 and '85.

## VINO NOBILE DI MONTEPULCIANO DOCG
TUSCANY

♟ Sangiovese, Canaiolo, Malvasia and others

Let's start with the bad news and get it out of the way. Vino Nobile is, at its worst, a sub-standard Chianti with a fancy name. When it first became DOCG, this was far too often the case. 'A disgrace,' said commentators far and wide when it made its debut at tastings in 1983. After all this was the first showing of Italy's first DOCG. It seemed Italy had fallen flat on its face at the first hurdle.

Now for the good news. Less than 10 years further on and this story seems like ancient history, so much have things changed in Montepulciano. Producers have realized one by one that the only way forward is for their wines to be as 'noble' as their name suggests; Vino Nobile won't sell on unfulfilled image alone. And at its best Vino Nobile is a deep, dense, spicy wine, with cinnamon, plums and tea flavours; with all the power and richness of Brunello and all the complexity of good Chianti. So it jolly well should be, given its good hilltop site, with excellent slopes and exposures for the vines, its situation well south of Chianti Classico, just east of Montalcino; and Prugnolo ('Plummy'), the local clone of Sangiovese, with its intensity and plentiful fruit. A measure of the improvement in Vino Nobile is the creation of a Rosso di Montepulciano denomination for lesser-aged wines or for those not considered good enough to go into the Vino Nobile. A few years ago producers wouldn't have dreamed of bothering to make such a selection.

Leading Vino Nobile estates are Avignonesi with its wines of great refinement, Boscarelli and Poliziano. Not far behind are Carletti della Giovanpaola, Contucci, Fassati, Fattoria del Cerro, Fognano, Poggio alla Sala, Valdipiatta. Best years: 1988, '85 and '82 are splendid; 1987, '86, '83, '81 good.

## VINTAGE TUNINA
Vino da tavola
FRIULI-VENEZIA GIULIA

♟ Sauvignon, Chardonnay, Ribolla Gialla and others

All sorts of magic can result when you blend different grapes together, and did when Silvio Jermann, one of the most gifted of Friuli's producers, created Vintage Tunina in 1975. The grapes are picked when well ripe; their yields are held right, right down; the precise blend of them varies from year to year, although Sauvignon and Chardonnay dominate. And there is no barrique-ageing to cloud the wine's pure flavours. Magic indeed! At two years old it is a fascinating dry white wine, at three quite weird and wondrous. Neither big and powerful, nor light and evanescent, there are hazelnuts and pineapple, woodsmoke and apples, cream and salt . . . plus many other flavours too numerous to describe – a brilliant, rounded wine unlike anything else. Best years: 1988, '87 and '86.

## ZAGAROLO DOC
LAZIO

♟ Malvasia, Trebbiano, Bellone, Bonvino

All the zones of the Castelli Romani hills, south-east of Rome, including Zagarolo, make Frascati-like wines: light, soft, almondy and creamy, and all became DOC in the late 1960s and early 1970s. Zagarolo, though, having got its DOC seems to have had problems knowing what to do with it: no DOC wine appeared until 1983, ten years later. By 1987 production was still only 717 hectolitres – a mere drop in the Frascati ocean. Perhaps they wanted their Presidential Decree just to hang on the wall while they carried on supplying basic young glugging wines, most dry, a little amabile, to the Romans in the time-honoured fashion.

# Bottles, Corks and Labels

SHAPE Curved bottle with low, sloping 'shoulders' for sparkling wine. The heavy lip is used for securing the wire muzzle.

SHAPE Many producers in north-eastern Italy use the tall, slender Germanic style of bottle.

An association of quality-conscious producers whose wines have to pass strict tests to receive the VIDE award.

COLOUR Dark green glass helps protect the contents from light. It is thicker and stronger for sparkling wine to withstand the greater pressure inside the bottle.

COLOUR Colli di Catone started the idea of using frosted bottles for the best quality Frascati wine.

SHAPE Frascati bottles are squat but this producer deliberately uses asymmetrical 'shoulders' as well.

Name of producer.

Name of the producer, one of the best in Frascati.

Wine name.

The 'mushroom' cork is always used for good sparkling wines. A metal cap covers the top of the cork to prevent the wire muzzle cutting into it.

*Dolce* means sweet. Asti Spumante is nearly always sweet.

Wine name. Asti Spumante is Italy's best known sparkling wine.

VQPRD is the Italian translation of the EC term for quality wine. Pinot Bianco is the grape used to make the wine.

Superiore means the wine has a slightly higher alcoholic content than straight Frascati.

You can rarely learn something about an Italian wine simply by looking at the bottle – few regions have traditional shapes and colours although groups of producers may sometimes adopt a special shape. Most of the best wines, both red and white, come in shouldered bottles made from dark glass. But you can learn a great deal by understanding the label, which carries a range of essential information, some of it required by law, and some at the discretion of the winemaker. There may also be a back label with additional information.

SHAPE Good-quality Chianti has abandoned the wicker flask in favour of the classic Bordeaux-shape bottle, called *bordolese* in Italy.

COLOUR The glass can be any colour according to the producer's preference but green or brown are the usual colours.

Vintage.

Riserva means the wines have had longer ageing. Only the best wines are usually selected for Riserva bottlings.

Wine name. Chianti Classico is one of the best Chianti zones.

Classification. In 1984 Chianti was upgraded from DOC to DOCG, the higher classification.

Cork stamped with estate name.

Alcoholic strength shown as a percentage of the total volume.

COLOUR Dark brown or green glass is best for keeping out light.

SHAPE The Albeisa bottle, similar to the classic Burgundy bottle with low, sloping 'shoulders', was selected by some Alba producers to make their wines look distinctive.

Monprivato is an individual Barolo vineyard in the commune of Castiglione Falletto.

Bottle contents. 75cl (750ml) is now the standard bottle size in the EC. The 'e' is an EC guarantee of volume.

Individual bottle number.

Wine name. Barolo is one of Italy's great red wines and comes from south Piedmont in north-west Italy.

Name of producer.

121

# STORING
# AND
# SERVING WINES

STORING Much as it might be fun – and impress the neighbours – to have a cool, cavernous wine cellar, with serried ranks of illustrious and ancient bottles gathering dust, and to which you can just pop down for a bottle of the '52 for dinner, you don't actually need a cellar to store wine. In fact, much of the time you don't actually need to store wine at all. Many wines can go from shop to glass in half an hour without suffering one bit. And with white wines in particular, often the younger and fresher they are the better. But it is much more convenient to keep some wine at home, ready for whenever you need it and there are plenty of wines which will be much better if you hang on to them before demolishing them. Sometimes a few months can make all the difference. Others will go on improving for a decade or more.

If you are going to keep wine for only a few weeks you can store it how you like and keep it more or less anywhere except the freezer (you'll get a nasty mess of slushy wine and broken glass) or the greenhouse (unless you want mulled wine). For longer periods you ought to keep the bottles lying flat, so that the wine stays in contact with the cork and stops it drying out. A dry cork shrinks, lets in the air and the wine oxidizes and goes off. The more even the temperature the better, although wines are far

more resilient than some folk would lead you to believe. It is a good idea to keep them in their cardboard boxes as these act as insulators and reduce temperature fluctuations. It is also better to store wines cool, around 10–12°C (50–54°F). But if they are kept warmer they will simply mature faster and vice versa.

The only other problem is finding the space. Cupboard under the stairs? Attic? Garage? Under the bed? There is bound to be somewhere if you think hard enough. It is worth it!

SERVING You don't have to pretend to be a sommelier to serve wine well. All you need to do is pour it slowly and gently into nice, big, curved, clean, clear glasses, filling them no more than two-thirds full so you can get your nose in and get a good whiff of the aromas. As for temperature, everyone advises you to serve white wines cool and red wines at room temperature. But how cool is cool? And when is a room at room temperature? A good average for reds is 15–17°C (59–62°F). But hefty, full-bodied wines can be warmer and fruity, lightweight reds cooler, and may be delicious lightly chilled. Whites are probably best at 10–12°C (50–54°F), the lighter, the sweeter or the fizzier the wine, the cooler it can be. But how *you* like it is right, whatever the thermometer says.

You can chill white wine quickly in the freezer. Everyone has done it even if they don't admit to it. But if the cooling is done more gradually in the fridge or, best of all, in a bucket of ice and water, the results are much better. You can't heat up a bottle of red quickly. You either get hot glass and cold wine, or baked,

stewy wine. The quickest, safest way is to pour it into a warm (not hot) glass and cup your hands round it for a few minutes.

There is a lot of talk about opening red wine early to let it 'breathe', but remember that just taking the cork out doesn't do much good. Just how much air can percolate through that small hole? And how far can it penetrate into the wine? The sensible way is to give wine proper air contact by pouring it into a jug, decanter or into glasses. Just a few minutes later it will be ready.

The only wines you need to decant are old ones which have a sediment. Stand the bottle upright for a good few hours first so the sediment sinks to the bottom, then uncork it without jolting too much and slowly and steadily pour the wine into a container. Once you see the sediment reaching the neck of the bottle stop. A torch held under the bottle shoulder helps. If you haven't a proper decanter any container will do. If you prefer you can rinse out the bottle and pour the wine back into it.

TASTING To make the most of a wine's taste your nose has to do some of the work. For a lot of flavour actually comes from smell – as anybody who tries to enjoy food when suffering from a head cold will know. Have a glance at the wine first – the colour should be attractive, the wine clear, not hazy, then give a good sniff. You'll be astounded how wonderful some wines smell. Next take a reasonable mouthful and keep it in your mouth for a little, making sure it comes into contact with all your tastebuds for maximum impact. The aromas will waft into your nose and mix with the taste sensations

from your mouth, giving you what you recognize as flavour. Fabulous!

FOOD AND WINE Whoever started to make rigid rules about what goes with what has a lot to answer for. You can – and should – drink whatever you like with whatever you like. You will be surprised how often different wines and foods match well. Italians rarely drink wine on its own, it is *made* to be drunk with food, which is a promising start. Wine styles and food styles evolved together.

Still, if you have to choose a wine to go with a dish, or food to go with that special bottle, guidelines can come in handy. Most Italian whites go brilliantly with fish and seafood, especially crisper, lighter ones such as Bianco di Custoza, Lugana, Arneis, Pinot Bianco and some from Sicily. Slightly fuller whites, such as Greco di Tufo, Vernaccia di San Gimignano, Frascati and rosés will be in their element with a wide range of meat dishes too – in Rome you'll find Frascati being drunk right through the meal. Lighter reds (Bardolino, young Chianti, Freisa for example) are at their best with lighter-weight dishes and fuller ones with weightier fare. A Riserva Chianti Classico or super-Tuscan with a steak, a Dolcetto with lamb, a Barolo or Barbaresco with game can be fabulous gustatory experiences. With pasta? Practically anything, choose your wine by the sauce. And don't forget you can spice up any dessert with a sweet Moscato, Malvasia or *passito*. One last tip, if the dish is characteristic of a region of Italy, the wines from the same area should match it well; that's been their job for hundreds of years.

# VINTAGES

Classifying a vintage (the year of harvest) into good, bad or indifferent is never straightforward for any country's wines. There are always those who make good wines in bad vintages and vice versa. There are also years when there is wide variation within one district, as in Chianti in 1987 when rain fell unevenly during the harvest. What is a 'good' vintage anyway? It is usually taken to mean, at least for reds, a year that produced well-balanced, sturdily structured wines which age longer than average and are superb when they are eventually mature. But they are usually pretty tough-going when young. And what about delicious fruit-packed years like 1983 for Nebbiolo in Piedmont and '86 for Chianti? Are these years to be condemned to a merely average score because they provide terrific pleasure five years on instead of ten?

In Italy, deciding a vintage's potential, whether for drinking sooner or later, is compli-cated further. The new wines from non-traditional grapes, the super-Tuscans and super-*vini da tavola* are just that – new. Although we may hazard a pretty-educated guess at how they are going to develop, we have no real experience to fall back on – anything, theoretically, could happen. Even with more traditional styles, wine-making techniques have been coming on so fast that ageing could throw up some surprises.

In the south there is an additional problem. Although vintages vary (don't let anybody kid you that in hotter climates all vintages are the same – there are just fewer really poor ones) there are as yet few vineyards with sufficiently severely restricted yields and few winemakers with the necessary experience and skills to allow these differences to become apparent. Specific vintages for these wines have not been recommended in the text.

| PIEDMONT | 88 | 87 | 86 | 85 | 84 | 83 | 82 | 81 | 80 |
|---|---|---|---|---|---|---|---|---|---|
| Barolo | 7△ | 6△ | 7△ | 10△ | 7★ | 6▽ | 10● | 5▽ | 7★ |
| Barbaresco | 8△ | 7△ | 8△ | 10△ | 6★ | 6▽ | 10● | 5▽ | 6★ |
| **TUSCANY** | 88 | 87 | 86 | 85 | 84 | 83 | 82 | 81 | 80 |
| Chianti Classico | 10△ | 6● | 7● | 10△ | 4▽ | 9★ | 8★ | 7★ | 6▽ |
| Carmignano | 10△ | 7● | 6● | 10△ | 5★ | 9★ | 8★ | 7★ | 7▽ |
| Brunello di Montalcino | 10△ | 7△ | 7△ | 10△ | 5★ | 9● | 9△ | 7● | 7★ |
| Vino Nobile di Montepulciano | 10△ | 7△ | 7△ | 10△ | 5★ | 8● | 9● | 6★ | 7▽ |
| **VENETO** | 88 | 87 | 86 | 85 | 84 | 83 | 82 | 81 | 80 |
| Recioto della Valpolicella Amarone, Ripasso Valpolicella | 10△ | 4△ | 8△ | 9△ | 5★ | 9● | 6★ | 10● | 7★ |

HOW TO READ THE CHART  △ = not ready  ● = just ready  ★ = at peak  ▽ = past its best

Scores for the major, northern, traditional red wines are given above. The numerals represent an overall rating for each year, bearing in mind that such measures can only ever be broad generalizations. There will be many variations with individual wines and producers. Whites are usually for drinking young (the exceptions are noted in the wine's entry in the A–Z).

# GLOSSARY

ABBOCCATO Medium dry.

ACIDITY Naturally present in grapes. Gives red wines 'grip' and ageing potential, white wines a refreshing 'tang'.

AGEING Essential process for fine wines and many everyday reds. May take place in vat, barrel or bottle and may last months or years.

ALBERELLO Vine-training system. Individual vines trained low like small bushes. Gives low yields, lots of alcohol.

AMABILE Medium or medium sweet.

BARRIQUE 225-litre barrel of new (or nearly new) French oak for ageing wine.

CANTINA SOCIALE (CS) Co-operative winery.

CERASUOLO Cherry-coloured. Often light red or deep pink.

CHARMAT Sparkling wine-making method. Second fermentation, to create the bubbles, takes place in closed tanks (*autoclavi*).

CHIARETTO Light-coloured rosé.

CLASSICO Heartland of a zone from where its best wines come.

CRU Wine from grapes of a single vineyard, usually of high quality. Term is in common use but not officially permitted.

DOC Denominazione di Origine Controllata. Wines of controlled origin, grape types and style.

DOCG Denominazione di Origine Controllata e Garantita. Wines from areas meant to be one notch above DOC zones.

DOLCE Sweet.

FINING Stabilizing wine by adding coagulants to wine which settle, drawing down impurities with them.

FRIZZANTE Lightly sparkling.

LEES Coarse sediment, such as dead yeasts, deposited by newly-made wine and left behind after racking.

LIQUOROSO Fortified. Wines strengthened by addition of grape alcohol.

MALOLACTIC FERMENTATION Transformation, spontaneous or induced, of harsh appley malic acid naturally present in wine to softer lactic acid. Usually occurs after alcoholic fermentation.

NATURALE Natural. Used for non-sparkling or slightly sparkling Mascato wines with lowish alcohol.

NOVELLO New wine. Wine for drinking very young, from November in year of vintage.

OXIDIZED Dull, fruitless wines caused by bacterial decay after over-exposure to air.

PASSITO Dried or semi-dried grapes, or strong, sweet wine made from them.

PERGOLA Vine-training system. Individual vines trained high, then at right-angles to ground. Used on narrow terraces in north Italy.

RACKING Transferring wine to a different container to clarify it by leaving sediment behind.

RIPASSO Valpolicella refermented on the lees of Amarone della Valpolicella to give extra richness.

RISERVA Wines aged for longer than normal. If DOC(G) minimum ageing period specified, which varies according to the type of the wine. Usually best wines are selected for Riserva.

SECCO Dry.

SOLERA Ageing method. Small quantities of young wine are used to top up casks of older wine. Ensures consistency of flavour over many years. Occasionally used in Sicily and Sardinia.

SPALLIERA Vine-training system. Canes are low trained on wires. Good for quality.

SPUMANTE Sparkling.

SUPERIORE Wine with higher alcohol, maybe more ageing too.

SUPER-TUSCAN English term for non-DOC wine of high quality from Tuscany.

SUPER-VINO DA TAVOLA English term for non-DOC wine of high quality.

TANNIN Bitter, mouth-drying element in red wine. Derived from grape skins, stems or new oak barrels. Softens with ageing. Essential for long-ageing wines.

TENDONE Vine-training system. Vines trained high. Gives quantity more than quality.

VARIETAL Single-grape variety or wine made from it.

VECCHIO Old.

VINO DA TAVOLA or VdT Table wine. Quality may be basic or exceptional.

VINO TIPICO New category for *vino da tavola* with some regional characteristics.

VIN SANTO Type of *passito* wine from Tuscany and Umbria. Called Vino Santo in Trentino.

# INDEX

A page reference in *italics* indicates main entry.

# ACKNOWLEDGEMENTS

**Photographs** supplied by Till Leeser/Bilderberg *3*, Mick Rock/Cephas *7*, Mick Rock/Cephas *9*, Mick Rock/Cephas *10*, Charlie Waite/Landscape Only *14*, Amberg/IFA Bilderteam *19*, Mick Rock/Cephas *23*, Mick Rock/Cephas *25*, Mick Rock/Cephas *29*, Mick Rock/Cephas *31*, Patrick Eagar *33*, Klaus Thiele/Bavaria Verlag Bildagentur *35*, K. Kerth/Zefa *38–9*, Mick Rock/Cephas *43*, Maureen Ashley *46–7*, Mick Rock/Cephas *50*, Mick Rock/Cephas *55*, Mick Rock/Cephas *58*, Mick Rock/Cephas *63*, Mick Rock/Cephas *64*, Löhr/Laenderpress *67*, Mick Rock/Cephas *68*, Mick Rock/Cephas *71*, Mick Rock/Cephas *75*, Mick Rock/Cephas *76*, Mick Rock/Cephas *79*, Mick Rock/Cephas *83*, Mick Rock/Cephas *87*, Mick Rock/Cephas *89*, Mick Rock/Cephas *93*, G. Hahn/IFA Bilderteam *98–9*, Patrick Eagar *101*, Mick Rock/Cephas *104*, Hubatka/Bildagentur Mauritius *108–109*, Mick Rock/Cephas *114–115*, Renate V. Forster/Bilderberg *118*.

**Editor** Fiona Holman; **Art Editor** Alison Donovan; **Editorial Assistant** Mary Pickles; **Indexer** Naomi Good; **Maps** Stan North; **Illustrations** Peter Byatt, Robina Greene.